Rethinking School Violence

Also by Sue Saltmarsh

THE DISCIPLINE OF GENTLEMEN
Masculinity, Markets and Private School Violence

Also by Kerry H. Robinson

INNOCENCE, KNOWLEDGE AND THE CONSTRUCTION OF CHILDHOOD
The Contradictory Relationship between Sexuality and Censorship
in Children's Contemporary Lives

QUEER AND SUBJUGATED KNOWLEDGES
Generating Subversive Imaginaries (*co-edited with C. Davies*)

DIVERSITY AND DIFFERENCE IN EARLY CHILDHOOD
Issues for Theory and Practice (*co-written with C. Jones-Diaz*)

FROM HERE TO DIVERSITY
The Social Impact of Lesbian and Gay Issues in Education in Australia and
New Zealand (*co-edited with T. Ferfolja and J. Irwin*)

Also by Cristyn Davies

QUEER AND SUBJUGATED KNOWLEDGES
Generating Subversive Imaginaries (*co-edited with K. H. Robinson*)

Rethinking School Violence

Theory, Gender, Context

Edited by

Sue Saltmarsh
Australian Catholic University, Australia

Kerry H. Robinson
University of Western Sydney, Australia

and

Cristyn Davies
The University of Sydney, Australia

First published 2012 by
PALGRAVE MACMILLAN

Palgrave Macmillan in the UK is an imprint of Macmillan Publishers Limited,
registered in England, company number 785998, of Houndmills, Basingstoke,
Hampshire RG21 6XS.

Palgrave Macmillan in the US is a division of St Martin's Press LLC,
175 Fifth Avenue, New York, NY 10010.

Palgrave Macmillan is the global academic imprint of the above companies
and has companies and representatives throughout the world.

Palgrave® and Macmillan® are registered trademarks in the United States,
the United Kingdom, Europe and other countries.

ISBN 978–0–230–57669–8

This book is printed on paper suitable for recycling and made from fully
managed and sustained forest sources. Logging, pulping and manufacturing
processes are expected to conform to the environmental regulations of the
country of origin.

A catalogue record for this book is available from the British Library.

Library of Congress Cataloging-in-Publication Data
Rethinking school violence : theory, gender, context / edited by Sue
    Saltmarsh, Kerry Robinson, Cristyn Davies.
        p.   cm.
    Includes bibliographical references.
    ISBN 978–0–230–57669–8
    1. School violence. I. Saltmarsh, Sue, 1963–
    II. Robinson, Kerry.   III. Davies, Cristyn, 1976–
    LB3013.3.R48 2012
    371.7'82—dc23   2012011176

10   9   8   7   6   5   4   3   2   1
21   20   19   18   17   16   15   14   13   12

Printed and bound in the United States of America

To all those pre-service teachers I have worked with over the past 17 years who have gone into schools with the priority of making a difference in young people's lives and making their schooling a more supportive, inclusive and positive experience – Kerry H. Robinson

For Lotus, Eloise and Estelle, in the hope that books like this one will create better, more equitable education – Cristyn Davies

For Jessica, Marissa, Aydin, Ayla, Annabelle and Jamie, who deserve safe schools and equitable futures – Sue Saltmarsh

Contents

Part III   Language, Representation and Practice

Figures

Acknowledgements

Many people have contributed to the successful completion of this project, and we gratefully acknowledge all those whose wisdom and guidance have played a part in seeing this book through to completion. It perhaps goes without saying that we are deeply appreciative of the love and support of our respective partners, families and friends – we thank them for, each in their own way, sustaining and encouraging us in (and despite!) our scholarly preoccupations and pursuits. We also wish to thank the many colleagues who have contributed to the completion of this project. Although it is not possible to name them all, we sincerely hope that our appreciation for kindnesses large and small has been, and will continue to be, evident to them. Particular thanks are due to the following: Olivia Middleton and Andrew James at Palgrave Macmillan, whose patience and advice during this project were greatly appreciated; Dr. Jenny Barr, who patiently assisted with proofreading and copyediting the final manuscript; the Faculty of Education at Charles Sturt University, Australia, which funded an invaluable writing retreat for the editorial team at a crucial point in the project; the Faculty of Education at the Australian Catholic University, Australia, which generously provided funding for project completion; Professor Deborah Youdell, who agreed to the use of data from the Plains High project analysed in Sue Saltmarsh's chapter, and whose work continues to be an inspiration; the many colleagues who generously contributed time and expertise in the form of anonymous peer reviews of the chapters in the book; and participants in research studies from around the world that are represented in this book.

Contributors

Deevia Bhana is an associate professor in the Faculty of Education at the University of KwaZulu-Natal, South Africa. She has published widely on issues of gender in schools and has a particular interest in gender and childhood.

Rachel Buchanan is a Lecturer in Education at the University of Newcastle, Australia. She teaches in the areas of educational philosophy and the sociology of education, and has published in the areas of educational philosophy as well as pedagogy and politics. Her research interests include philosophy, politics and the sociology of education, which she is using to explore the various dimensions of technology in education.

Moira Carmody is a Professor in Sociology in the School of Social Sciences and Psychology at the University of Western Sydney, Australia. She is an interdisciplinary scholar of education in the areas of gender, sexuality and sexual ethics. Professor Carmody is a national expert on sexual assault prevention education. Her current research is on working with young people around ethical sexual relationships.

Ronnie Casella is a Professor of Educational Foundations and Secondary Education at Central Connecticut State University in the United States and Visiting Researcher at The University of the Witwatersrand in South Africa. He is the author of several books, including *'Being Down': Challenging Violence in Urban Schools* (2001), *At Zero Tolerance: Punishment, Prevention, and School Violence* (2003) and *Selling Us the Fortress: The Promotion of Techno-Security Equipment for Schools* (2006), which examines relationships between the security industry and school districts.

Amy Chapman is a lecturer in Education Studies at the Australian Catholic University, Strathfield, Australia. Her research on the philosophical relationship between well-being and education and on issues in the construction of Self and Other have resulted in a deep interest in relational epistemologies in schooling. Recent publications include *The*

Paradigm Shift in Health (2009) and 'Can How We Come to Know the World Disconnect Us from the World We Come to Know?' (2011) (in *Tolerance, Education, Curriculum*).

Cristyn Davies is a Research Associate at the University of Sydney, Australia, where she is also completing her doctorate. She is an experienced researcher, writer, editor and tertiary educator. She has authored, co-authored and edited academic publications across a broad range of disciplinary areas, including Childhood and Youth Studies, Gender and Sexuality Studies as well as Cultural Studies and Education. Cristyn's scholarship, situated in the latter discipline, is focused around gendered and sexual subjectivity and knowledge within educational contexts.

Vijay Hamlall is a secondary school teacher and PhD candidate at the University of KwaZulu-Natal, South Africa. He is currently studying the ways in which conflict is negotiated in school settings.

Sara Knox is an associate professor in the Writing and Society Research Group and the School of Humanities and Languages at the University of Western Sydney, Australia. She is the author of *Murder: A Tale of Modern American Life* (1998) and a number of other works on representation and violence. Her most recent publication is a study of the moral geography of violence in the work of Hilary Mantel (*Australian Feminist Studies*, 25 (65), 2010). Her novel *The Orphan Gunner* (2007) won the 2009 Asher Literary Prize and was shortlisted for the Commonwealth Writers' Prize and the Age Book of the Year.

David McInnes is a senior lecturer in English, Text and Writing in the School of Humanities and Languages at the University of Western Sydney, Australia. His research areas include gay men's sexual cultures and HIV health promotion, gender non-conformity for boys and young men in school contexts as well as the spoken discourse of undergraduate pedagogy.

Martin Mills is a Professor of Education at the University of Queensland, Australia. His research interests include gender, pedagogy, school reform and social justice issues in education. Recent books include *Boys and Schooling: Beyond Structural Reform* (2009), with Bob Lingard and Wayne Martino; *Troubling Gender in Education* (2009), with Jo-Anne Dillabough and Julie McLeod; and *Teaching Boys* (2007), with Amanda Keddie.

Robert Morrell works in the Research Office at the University of Cape Town, South Africa. He has edited and written a number of books on masculinities in Africa. His works include *Changing Men in Southern Africa* (2001), *African Masculinities* (with Lahoucine Ouzgane, 2005) and *Baba: Men and Fatherhood in South Africa* (with Linda Richter, 2006). He is author of *From Boys to Gentlemen: Settler Masculinity in Colonial Natal, 1880–1920* (2001) and *Towards Gender Equality. South African Schools during the HIV/AIDS Epidemic* (with Debbie Epstein, Elaine Unterhalter, Deevia Bhana and Relebohile Moletsane, 2009). His most recent (edited) book is *Books and Babies: Pregnancy and Young Parents in Schools* (with Deevia Bhana and Tamara Shefer, 2012).

Kerry H. Robinson is an Associate Professor in Sociology in the School of Social Sciences and Psychology at the University of Western Sydney, Australia. She has published widely on her research interests, which include constructions of gendered and sexual identities, including how these are negotiated in educational contexts; gendered and sexual violence; anti-homophobia education; and constructions of childhood and sexuality.

Sue Saltmarsh is an Associate Professor of Educational Studies at the Australian Catholic University in Strathfield, Australia. Her ethnographic and discourse analytic work in the field of school violence considers the ways in which educational discourse, institutional cultures and pedagogic practices are complicit in the production of violent incidents. Her book *The Discipline of Gentlemen: Masculinity, Markets and Private School Violence* is a forthcoming title.

Introduction: The Case for Rethinking School Violence

Kerry H. Robinson, Sue Saltmarsh and Cristyn Davies

School violence is a complex issue that raises important questions about social and educational relationships and about the nature of schooling itself. Explanations of possible causes abound, as researchers, educationalists and communities alike look for answers to a problem that persists – and at times erupts with deadly consequences – in what are ordinarily considered to be safe and supportive places for children and young people. Numerous definitions of violence have attempted to describe, delineate and categorise terms such as 'bullying' and 'violence', yet these are subject to ongoing debate and generally reflect the philosophical and ideological underpinnings of particular disciplinary fields. Contributors to this book locate their work within a broad socio-cultural research tradition, informed by fields as diverse as sociology, anthropology, education, criminology and literary, media and cultural studies.

Rather than working with a single overarching definition of 'school violence', the investigations offered in this edited collection endeavour to establish and broaden perspectives that might, as anthropologist Veena Das puts it, 'enlarge the field of our vision' (2007, p. 4). We are interested, in other words, in exploring how questions of school violence might be rethought when the field of vision is broadened to include the intersections between the formation of subjectivities, the taken-for-granted norms of schooling practice and the cultural practices of everyday life. For Das, and indeed for contributors to this book, the question 'is not that of part-whole relations but of establishing the horizon within which we may place the constituent objects of a description in their relation to each other and in relation to the eye with which they are seen' (2007, p. 4). Violence in its multiple linguistic, visual, psychic, affective and embodied forms, therefore, is placed here in relation

1

to a range of historically located and discursively produced features of schooling and broader social and policy domains that might ordinarily escape notice as contributing to or perpetuating cultures within which school-related violence occurs.

Two key thematic concerns are evident across the chapters in this book. The first of these pertains to the ways in which the complex and dynamic operations of power shape the relations between individuals, institutions and culture. Power is understood here in the Foucauldian sense, not as something 'held' by some and 'wielded' over others, but rather as circulating between and productive of subjectivities and social relations. In such a conceptualisation of power, the individual subject is always located in relation to others and always negotiating power relations between self and the broader social world. In order to understand violence within these terms, then,

> it becomes necessary to consider how subjectivity – the felt interior experience of the person that includes his or her positions in a field of relational power – is produced through the experience of violence and the manner in which global flows involving images, capital, and people become entangled with local logics in identity formation.
>
> (Das & Kleinman, p. 1)

This is not to suggest, of course, that violence be understood merely as an abstract theoretical construct or as a circulation of power between impersonal processes and norms. Rather it is to understand the self who experiences or enacts violence as always already situated within relations of power and to understand that whether it occurs as embodied acts between individuals, as embedded within systemic institutional policies and structures or as woven through the norms of recognition that circulate in the texts and images of the mediated global landscape, 'violence is, always, an exploitation of that primary tie, that primary way in which we are, as bodies, outside ourselves and for one another' (Butler, 2004, p. 27).

A second recurring theme of interest to authors in this collection is the way that gendered norms and 'regimes of truth' (Foucault, 2002) are implicated in the ways that violence is understood, experienced and actualised by institutions, teachers and students alike. Gendered norms of masculinity, femininity, sexuality and so on are crucial to the formation and discursive intelligibility of the social subject. And while, as Judith Butler argues, such norms may operate in an impersonal way, 'we nevertheless come into contact with these norms through proximate and living exchanges, in the modes by which we are addressed and asked to take up the question of who we are and what our relation to the other ought to be' (Butler, 2005, p. 30). For many of the authors represented in this book, norms of gender – and in particular, the ways in which masculinity is performatively produced within the terms of verbal and physical hostility and aggression – provide an important lens through which school violence might be explored. Understanding the ways in which culturally situated meanings of heteronormative masculinity are played out in the relationships that boys and young men construct between self, other and schooling is crucially important to understanding why and how school violence occurs.

In the remainder of this introduction, we provide an overview of what we see as some of the pressing issues raised by extant school violence research, followed by a brief discussion of the book's structure and individual chapters.

Safe spaces/'dangerous places': Dualistic experiences of schooling

The global representation of schools as 'safe spaces'/'dangerous places' underpins the contradictory experiences of schooling for many teachers and students, posing critical questions associated with equity and social justice for school administrators and broader communities. The dominant view of schools has been, and continues to be, that they are generally safe and supportive places and that schooling is a context in which most parents feel confident in entrusting educational institutions with the care of their children. Schools have responsibility for children for extensive periods of time in the earlier part of their lives and also for many aspects of children's socialisation, including the development of academic and life skills that are considered a requirement for becoming a successful and productive adult citizen. Within this framework, educators take on an 'in loco parentis' duty of care, with the expectation of having children's best interests and well-being at the core of their teaching philosophies and practices. Many students successfully complete their schooling, taking away positive and rewarding experiences of their education.

However, the discursive constitution of schooling as a 'safe space' for children and educators continues to be disrupted and challenged, with extensive reporting in recent decades of a vast range of behaviours, incidents and practices in schools that can be encapsulated within the broad term of 'school violence'. Examples include shooting rampages, knifings, sexual harassment and abuse, homophobic and racist attacks and bullying, to name but a few. What this latter picture highlights is that schools can be equally 'dangerous places' for many students and teachers, undermining the quality and equality of their educational and teaching experiences. Media representations of school violence tend to pick up on the more sensational violent incidents such as shootings, student suicides resulting from bullying and harassment or the sexual abuse of students by teachers. Reports such as these influence how schools are understood within the broader community as dangerous places. These are critical examples of school violence, but what media sensationalism tends to overshadow is the everyday violence encountered in schools that becomes normalised within schooling cultures. Daily interactions between individuals in school communities create and maintain schools as dangerous places (O'Donoghue & Potts, 2007), and everyday classroom and playground experiences in which abusive conduct becomes commonplace have the effect of normalising violence.

Systemic violence operating in schools contributes to the construction of educational contexts as dangerous places. Systemic violence can be defined as any institutionalised policy, practice or procedure that negatively impacts on, or discriminates against, disadvantaged individuals or groups (Ross Epp & Watkinson, 1997). The impact of systemic violence can be psychological, physical, cultural, spiritual and economic in nature. However, as Ross Epp and Watkinson (1997) point out, systemic violence can impact on all students regardless of their backgrounds. The failure of schools to meet their responsibilities of a 'duty of care' constitutes systemic violence through omission (Harper, 2004). Often bullying behaviours that prevail in school grounds and classrooms also prevail in school staffrooms (see, e.g., Saltmarsh, this book). Corporal punishment and severe authoritarianism can perpetuate cultures of violence and oppression in schools (Harper, 2004; Morrell, Bhana & Hamlall, this book).

Another example of systemic violence is highlighted in an acceptance of violence in male team sports. Crotty (2007) argues that in Australian public schools in the late nineteenth and early twentieth centuries, a form of masculinity, which valorised aggression and violence, emerged in school sporting arenas. This masculinity became representative of a healthy manly vigour considered critical to the perpetuation of the nation and the British Empire, and Crotty argues that the growing acceptance of sporting violence has continued into contemporary times. Ironically, Crotty points out, it was this violence that was the target of research on violence prevention in Australian schools during the 1980s and 1990s. In addition, the acknowledgements of the failure of educational institutions, especially those affiliated with religious organisations, to recognise the physical and sexual abuse of students in their care by teachers in British, Irish, Australian and Canadian schools in the late nineteenth and early to mid-twentieth centuries provide a further example of systemic violence in schools (Coleman, 2007; Harper, 2004; Titley, 2007).

Curtis's (2007) Canadian research on violence in Ontario's elementary schools during the period 1846–1909 highlights this lack of acknowledgement of the systemic abuse of young people. Curtis argues that certain behaviours that were allowed to occur during this period would have been considered sexual assault in contemporary times. This avowal, Curtis argues, was due to the systemic removal of young people's legal and political credibility and power during the time, an increase in the systemic power of teachers and the unquestioning predominance of masculine authority in schools. Students' attempts to have such behaviours acknowledged as sexual maltreatment on the part of teachers were discursively dismissed as a consequence of students' lack of credibility. The ways in which schools handle these matters today can vary depending on a range of factors – the institutional history and culture of a school; dynamics between students, peers, teachers and other school officials; policies and procedures; and the ways in which policies and procedures are understood, interpreted and implemented by all members in the school community. The reputation of schools in the broader community can also influence the approach adopted by schools in addressing sexual and other forms of violence (Saltmarsh, 2007, 2008).

In many cases, the legacy of earlier traditions of violence and the abuse of power is still in evidence in today's schools. Masculinist school cultures that privilege physically aggressive sporting and other activities, or disciplinary traditions that shore up the entitlements and privileges of some at the expense of others, have a long history in educational institutions (Saltmarsh, 2008; Symes, 1998). Similar observations have been made about the role of disciplinary regimes of elite schools in producing forms of 'ruling class masculinity' (Poynting & Donaldson, 2005, Donaldson & Poynting, 2007) through which cultures of violence – particularly amongst socially privileged boys and men – are established and maintained across generations. School traditions that create gender and age hierarchies are similarly problematic, often tacitly inducting students into regimes of power and authority that are seen, in some schools, as a normal and necessary part of learning one's place in both school and society. Yet as research into sexually violent incidents in elite private boys' schooling has argued, 'disciplinary traditions and institutional ethos that legitimate and valorise hierarchies of personal and institutional worth are important contributing factors in the production of violence' (Saltmarsh, 2008, p. 114). An important understanding underpinning the work in this edited collection, then, is that context, history, tradition and everyday taken-for-granted practices all play a part in determining whether any particular educational setting can be thought of as a safe, dangerous or potentially dangerous place for students.

School violence: A global problem

School violence is prevalent across both developing and developed countries, with localised and cultural factors influencing the perception and manifestations of this violence in different contexts (UN, 2006). Despite the extensive body of international research on school violence in developed countries, research on violence against children conducted by the United Nations (2006) pointed out the extent and nature of school violence in developing countries, indicating the significance of gender in much of this violence. This report argued that school violence is a major barrier to equality of opportunity and outcomes in education, impacting on efforts to improve student enrolments, retention and achievements in developing countries. While gendered social relations and cultural practices contribute to the problem, existing legislative and policy frameworks must also be taken into account. For example, some countries, such as Pakistan, do not have laws that criminalise sexual harassment, so perceptions and approaches to this problem in schools differ from those in countries where sexual harassment has legal ramifications.

Greater legal attention to the problem does not, however, provide guarantees. Research on sexual harassment in schools undertaken by the American Association of University Women (AAUW, 2001) indicates that sexual harassment is a persistent problem in US schools. According to the AAUW report, 81 per cent of students of grades 8–11 experienced some form of sexual harassment by peers in their school lives (AAUW, 2001, cited in Petersen & Hyde, 2009, p. 1173). These findings are supported by a New York City study that found that 70 per cent of gay and lesbian students faced verbal, physical and sexual harassment at school (Goffe, 2003; see also Davies & McInnes, this book).

Importantly, these statistics have a human face, and the details of the pain and humiliation endured by victims of sexualised violence and harassment are a frequent reminder of the significance of the problem in individual lives. For example, in 2002 the British Columbia Human

Rights Tribunal in Canada ruled that a school board discriminated against a student by failing to protect him against homophobic violence in school. This experience echoes similar cases in Australia (see Harper, 2004; Lamont, 2007) in which some students subjected to repeated abuse, ranging from verbal attacks to being spat on, punched, having teeth knocked out or clothes set alight, have been awarded compensation for the suffering and ongoing psychological effects of abuse endured at school. Heterosexism and homophobia are pervasive systemic discourses in schools, perpetuated not only through students' everyday interactions but also through schooling curricula, pedagogy, policies and practices of both administrators and teachers. These discourses result in homophobic harassment and violence experienced by both students and teachers who are perceived to transgress normalised performances of masculinity and femininity (Davies, 2008; Davies & McInnes, this book; McInnes & Davies, 2008; Robinson, 2005a, 2005c).

School violence is also not restricted to secondary schooling or to tertiary educational environments, but global research has increasingly begun to demonstrate the prevalence of various forms of violence operating within early childhood, preschool and primary schooling contexts (Le Bon & Boddy, 2010; Robinson & Davies, 2008a, b).

New technologies and school violence

In recent years new technologies have become a major avenue through which violence, primarily in the form of online harassment, has been enacted, with serious and fatal consequences. Mobile phones, email and social networking systems, such as Facebook, My Space, websites, blogs and online chat rooms, have become a significant part of young people's daily lives. Yet these forms of communication provide an additional context in which the harassment of individuals or groups can occur. However, online forms of harassment offer additional possibilities for publicising the victimisation of others, which can be streamed to an infinite audience, intensifying the humiliation (Barak, 2005). A recent Canadian study (Cassidy et al., 2009), which surveyed 365 students in grades 6–9 (age 11–15 years) from three elementary and two secondary schools in a large metropolitan region of British Columbia, found that most students use the Internet on a daily basis and that their most common vehicle for cyber-bullying was via chat rooms or over email.

Online or cyber-bullying, as it is sometimes called, often starts at school and is continued on students' home computers. Within this context, harassers may remain anonymous, also intensifying the power relationships that underpin this behaviour, including the victim's fear of the unknown. Racist, sexist, homophobic statements can prevail and sexual photographs (real or altered) can be made public. Twenty-five per cent of students in the Canadian study cited above indicated that they would keep the bullying to themselves, with 9 per cent acknowledging that they received messages that made them afraid, and 4 per cent had suicidal thoughts (Cassidy et al., 2009, p. 399). There are similar findings in the Australian context, with a major study of cyber-bullying (Cross et al., 2009) finding that while cyber-bullying primarily takes place amongst high school students, 7–10 per cent of younger children are also affected. The recent case of Tyler Clementi, a Rutgers' freshman in the United States, demonstrates the potentially fatal consequences of this type of online harassment. Tyler committed suicide after being the victim of a homophobic incident in which his roommate secretly filmed him having sex with another male student in his room. The video was then broadcast on the Internet (Foderaro, *SMH*, October 1, 2010).

Research into cyber-violence indicates that both genders partake in this practice, but there are gendered differences in the way that males and females engage with this harassment (Barak, 2005). Sexual harassment, for example, is a major form of cyber-violence and tends to replicate the same power relations that occur in the real world around this behaviour, with boys being the main perpetrators (Shariff & Gouin, 2006). Canadian research (Cassidy et al., 2009) highlights that most cyber-bullying victims are marginalised youth that do not fit in with the dominant culture of the school, that is, those who are different – as a result of their dress codes, physical appearance, sexuality, ethnicity, poor academic or athletic ability, for example. However, this research also indicates that approximately one-third of all the students surveyed indicated that they had been cyber-harassed, pointing out that the 'average student' can also be the targets of this behaviour. Of particular significance in this research is that cyber-harassment was prevalent within friendship groups, highlighting the need for young people to examine the ways in which they interact with each other and the consequences of this behaviour. Those on the receiving end may view what is considered a joke by perpetrators very differently. However, this point is not just peculiar to cyber contexts, but is relevant to all contexts of school violence. Why students engage in cyber-harassment can vary, including the perception that it is fun, peer pressure or revenge for being harassed initially, but as with all other forms of violence, it is about exerting power over others.

Schooling and theories of violence

Currently, much of this violence is discursively constituted as the result of the pathological disturbances of a few individuals, rather than from complex socio-cultural, economic and political discourses underpinning individual or group behaviours and institutional practices and policies (Garbarino, 2001; Olweus, 1993). As a microcosm of broader societies, schooling constitutes and perpetuates many of the inequalities that underpin much social violence. How the various behaviours and practices that encompass school violence are culturally perceived and understood will impact on the strategies employed to prevent or counteract this violence. Sexual harassment and other forms of sexual violence against girls and women are widespread issues in schools across both developing and developed countries. However, as Leach (2006) points out, violence in schools in developing countries in particular, with only a few exceptions, is generally not framed in gendered and sexual terms. Violence in Asia and Latin America, for example, is rarely perceived to be rooted in unequal gender terms, and sexual harassment is seen as confined to universities (p. 25). In Latin America and the Caribbean, there has been a tendency to view school violence in terms of gang violence, often linked to drug and gun trafficking. Where violence in and around schools is fuelled by civil or armed conflict, its gendered dimension is often missed (e.g. Nepal and West Africa).

Larkin (2009) argues that the US Columbine shooting rampage redefined these extremist acts of school violence not just as revenge but also as a protest against harassment, bullying, intimidation, social isolation and public rituals of humiliation (see also Knox, this book). As pointed out previously in this introduction, schooling curricula, policies and practices play a critical role in constituting and perpetuating systemic violence in schools. Systemic violence, not just student interactions, contributes to the various forms of school violence that prevail globally. Larkin (2009) argues that one of the major causes of systemic violence is the discursive constitution of the 'norm' as white, heterosexual, middle class, English-speaking and male. This echoes the earlier works of Elizabeth Ellsworth (1994), who points out that the pervasive stereotypical discourses, exclusive curricula and classroom practices that reinforce sexist, racist, classist and heterosexist attitudes, to name but a few, perpetuated through this 'norm', impacts on all students.

Michel Foucault (1977) pointed out that mass formal schooling, like prisons, hospitals and factories, through its organisational practices and policies and curriculum, became an institution of social control, using continual surveillance to discipline and punish in order to instil social cohesion and create order and docility. Bureaucratic routines and authoritarianism, perpetuated through timetables, rules, regulations, disciplinary practices and hierarchies of power, operated to control and constitute the docile subject. National curricula and standardised testing that exist in many countries today contribute to this process identified by Foucault. His concept of the panopticon highlights how schools were constructed and organised in a manner that offered optimal opportunity for teachers and administrators to observe students' behaviour. Students became aware of being observed and curtailed their behaviours accordingly; these self-disciplinary practices made students easier to manage and control.

Current approaches to dealing with school violence

A common question that faces school administrators is how to successfully build safe school communities, where all members feel safe from bullying, violence and alienation. Attempts to deal with school violence have depended on the forms of violence experienced, but policies and practices have varied across schools and across different states and countries. In relation to extreme forms of violence involving shooting or the use of other weapons, schools have tended to adopt extremely punitive quick-fix measures that treat the problem at the individual behavioural level, at the expense of looking at the broader socio-cultural and political factors that underpin much of this behaviour (Casella, 2001a, 2001b, 2006; Knox, this book). Heightened parent and community concerns for their children's safety around such violence, particularly in the United States, quickly lead to severe surveillance measures, including metal detectors, increased security, zero tolerance and requesting students and teachers to report suspicious student behaviours (Morrison, 2007). However, as Morrison (2007) points out, there is no evidence that these measures reduce violence in schools. Rather, they tend to create a false sense of security and exacerbate the problem. Larkin argues:

> Although there have been grassroots attempts to reduce violence in schools, since Columbine, the federal government has made assault weapons easier to obtain and states have adopted more punitive juvenile justice sentencing guidelines. To a persecuted and angry student who wishes to attack his school and community, such social policies

are an invitation and a dare. To such a student, payback consists of killing convenient targets, making a statement, and dying in a blaze of glory.

(2009, p. 1323)

A zero-tolerance approach to violence has been incorporated in some schools, especially in the United States, United Kingdom and Canada. It aims to give a public message that the school is 'tough on crime', to counteract parent and community concerns, as well as fulfil accountability standards (Casella, 2001a, 2001b; Morrison, 2007). This strategy has been criticised as a band-aid approach that covers up the deeper social issues that underpin violence. School authorities do not question the underlying causes of the violence or the role of systemic violence in the schools, and this perpetuates violence (Ross Epp & Watkinson, 1997). Zero tolerance generally results in immediate expulsion for serious offences, including carrying weapons, serious bullying, sexual misconduct and drug dealing. In Canada the policy of zero tolerance is a provincial decision; in Ontario and Nova Scotia it is required, but is recommended in New Brunswick and Newfoundland. Some have argued that there is confusion over what zero tolerance means and that it has not been effective in schools (Casella, 2001a, 2006). In fact, Morrison (2007) argues that zero-tolerance policies have resulted in more minor incidents of misconduct receiving progressively harsher penalties; that expulsions have increased for disruption, attendance and non-compliance; that suspensions and exclusions are used inconsistently; that there is a minority over-representation in suspensions and exclusions; and that there is a high rate of repeat offending. Morrison argues, 'The evidence suggests that not only does zero tolerance make zero sense. But zero tolerance promotes intolerance, through discriminatory practices that licence discrimination' (2007, p. 58.)

In Australia, strategies to deal with homophobic violence in schools have tended to operate at the individual school level and at the discretion of school leaders and managers. Generally, this form of violence is dealt with on an individual case-by-case basis, considered to be similar to other forms of student misbehaviour in schools and primarily dealt with through disciplinary punishments. The homophobic discourses behind such behaviours are often not addressed (see Davies & McInnes, this book; Davies & Robinson, 2010; McInnes & Davies, 2008; Robinson, 2005a, 2005c; Robinson, this book). There have been attempts to curb this violence through educational resources and community campaigns, including the 2002 *Skool's Out* initiative. This campaign was aimed at encouraging effective responses to homophobic harassment and violence in and around schools, both public and private, in New South Wales, Australia. The focus was on safety and security in the school environment for all students, teachers, parents and community members (Kaye, 2004). A broader educational initiative implemented by the New South Wales Department of Education and Training aimed to address school violence more generally through an initiative called the Safe School projects. The success of both of these programmes has been limited, primarily because they do not adequately address broader socio-cultural and political discourses underpinning this violence that are entrenched at every level in society and in everyday interactions, and are perpetuated through systemic violence in schools (Davies, 2008; McInnes 2008; McInnes & Davies, 2008; Rasmussen, 2006).

In South Africa educators have tried to develop resources to curb the serious level of gender-based violence that occurs in and outside school environments in this country. Sexual harassment, jack-rolling, child sexual abuse, homophobic violence and bullying are all issues that teachers and students have to contend with on a daily basis. There has been significant recognition on the part of educators in this country of the socio-cultural factors contributing to perpetuation of these forms of violence. One such resource is *Opening Our Eyes: Addressing Gender-based Violence in South African Schools* (2001), which includes several teacher training modules addressing gender violence, homophobia and bullying, sexual harassment and policy development in schools and child sexual abuse and its implications for teachers.

The contribution of this book to shifting current debates about school violence

School violence, as has been outlined in this introduction, is a complex and troubling issue that affects students, teachers and communities worldwide. This book brings together a diverse group of international scholars researching school violence, and aims to disrupt and reconceptualise many of the taken-for-granted assumptions that currently underlie understandings of this phenomenon. It also aims to address many of the contradictions that exist around violent events that can hinder effective interventions. In contrast to extant collections concerning violence in schools, which are predominantly informed by discourses of individual pathologies, family dysfunction and preventative management strategies, this book proposes ways of *rethinking* school violence as a social and cultural, rather than psychological, phenomenon. As discussed in the opening section of the introduction, the first key contribution of this book concerns power relations and the ways that 'schooled subjectivities' (Youdell, 2006) are produced within unequal relations of power in many schooling contexts. The second key contribution offered by this book is a focus on gender and the ways that gendered norms of schooling all too often furnish the terrain upon which violent masculinities are able to be enacted and, in some cases, are privileged. The broad coverage of the book offers a response to an issue of pressing global concern – that of violence within educational institutions and its implications for violence that takes place within the broader contexts of interpersonal, social and political spheres.

Structure of the book

This book is divided into three parts. The chapters in Part I consider school violence as contextually produced; chapters in Part II raise major issues pertaining to the ways that gendered power relations are implicated in the production of school violence; and chapters in Part III focus on issues of language, representation and practice associated with violence in schools. In the first chapter in Part I, the author points out that school-related violence has been thought of primarily as a problem involving students who are in some way troubled and/or troublesome. As a consequence preventing and managing violence that takes place in schools and classrooms is generally focused on modifying the attitudes and regulating the behaviours of individual students. Sue Saltmarsh shifts the focus away from students who are involved in violent incidents, and instead turns the analytic gaze onto schooling itself and the part that it plays (even if inadvertently) in contributing to violent cultures and normative practices. Drawing on examples from school bullying and behaviour management policies, and utilising data from school ethnographies, Saltmarsh shows how an array of interconnecting threads woven through institutional cultures are implicated in the production of inherently violent social relations. She contends that discursive silences, often from those best placed to intervene or initiate change, raise questions about the limits of educational and professional knowledge. She argues that in order to bring about meaningful changes to student attitudes and behaviours, the first – and most important – step involves addressing those elements of school rules, ethos and management that are complicit in the production of violent schooling cultures.

The second chapter, by Ronnie Casella, examines the development of school security in the United States and South Africa. Experts often espouse one of two positions: the view that security equipment is a successful tool for maintaining safety and the more critical view that such equipment is an instrument of state surveillance and social control. By drawing on fieldwork in the United States and South Africa, Casella develops a new way of viewing the uses of security equipment in schools, arguing that school security has more to do with privatisation and consumerism than with safety or social control. School security represents the effects of neoliberalism on schools. In essence, another public concern – the safety of schools – becomes a commodity, which is provided by security businesses. Businesses convince consumers that security must be bought and provided to schools by professionals who have the advanced technologies and expert knowledge to keep a school safe. Individuals in South Africa and the United States 'buy into' this trend; they use their consumer power to buy security equipment and in doing so they reinforce social distances between those who own security and those who cannot afford the equipment. In countries like the United States and South Africa, Casella argues that security reinforces old social divisions based on race and social class.

Chapter 3, by Amy Chapman and Rachel Buchanan, considers the question of cyber-bullying in relation to social and cultural practices that are an everyday feature of young people's technology use. Like other authors in the book, Chapman and Buchanan are wary of the ways in which normative educational discourse positions young people as either victims or bullies. They point out that much research on cyber-bullying tends to overlook broader contextual factors, focusing instead on the individual. Using examples from online postings, they argue that online hostility and aggression are associated with gendered social norms that circulate in the realm of the everyday. They therefore call for stronger engagement with theoretical frameworks whose interest in context and culture offers productive ways forward for understanding the online attitudes and conduct of young people.

Chapter 4, the first in Part II, focuses on sexual harassment in schools in an Australian context. Kerry Robinson focuses on the socio-cultural practice of 'sexual harassment' and how it is performed and negotiated in schools by young people. The complexities that surround this behaviour are explored in relation to the contexts within which it is situated. Contextual factors critically inform the ways in which sexual harassment practices are read and negotiated by individuals, often resulting in major contradictions surrounding this behaviour. Within this context, Robinson stresses the need to reconsider sexual harassment in terms of its 'everydayness', which operates to silence and render sexual harassment invisible, normalising it in everyday gendered social relations. Critical to this normalising process of sexual harassment is its intersection with the performance of gendered identities. For example, sexual harassment is a powerful enactment of hegemonic masculinity, and concerns around popularity, for both girls and boys, make the negotiation of this behaviour unpredictable and contradictory. Robinson also briefly examines the intersections between sexual harassment and homophobic and heterosexist harassment. However, Davies and McInnes examine homophobic violence in depth later in this book (see Chapter 7). According to Robinson, the contradictions associated with sexual harassment have often been used to blame the victim for what is perceived as collusion or lack of appropriate responses. For example, why do girls see some boys' behaviour as sexual harassment and not similar behaviour by particular other boys? Robinson's focus on sexual harassment is framed within a broader discussion of perceptions of sexual harassment, querying who actually experiences and practices sexual harassment and considering the ways that it is represented in the media and popular culture.

Martin Mills in Chapter 5 examines boys and violence in schools. Whenever a particularly violent crime is committed, newspaper reports often make mention of the family background, ethnicity and class of the perpetrator(s). However, Mills argues, it is seldom that any attention is given to considerations of gender. That the perpetrator is a man is seldom remarked upon, the unwritten assumption being that instigators of violence are naturally male (evidence of this assumption is starkly apparent in media reports when the perpetrator is female). This assumption is to some extent justified; the majority of violent acts are carried out by men and boys. However, this is a not a 'natural' state of affairs but one which is grounded in essentialist constructions of gender and which serves the wider interest of the 'patriarchal gender order'. Since the 1970s feminists have been working to expose the political effects of men's 'ownership' of violence and to demonstrate that the world would be a safer place for women and girls and men and boys if those discourses that naturalised men's violence were disrupted. This has meant naming the gendered construction of violence. As is evident from news reports relating to most instances of violence, there is still quite some way to go in this regard. However, in many countries at the moment schools offer potential as sites for where such namings and disruptions can take place. Mills's chapter argues that rather than rejecting feminist concerns about schooling as irrelevant and harmful to boys' education, educational authorities need to use the spaces created by the boys' debate to embrace insights into boys' education offered by feminism. These insights will contribute positively to boys' educational outcomes and serve to make the boys' gender evident, especially in relation to violent behaviour.

Chapter 6 addresses students' gendered perspectives of violence in South African schools. The authors, Robert Morrell, Deevia Bhana and Vijay Hamlall, argue that the endemic nature of school violence in the South African education system is a major barrier to gender equity. The authors point out that while opinion is divided on the causes of widespread violence in South African schools, there is widespread acknowledgement that there is an urgent need to make schools safe. Many students in the South African context encounter extreme violence during their school careers – sometimes this violence stems from forces outside of school, sometimes it comes from teachers and sometimes from other students. Drawing on ethnographic research conducted by Hamlall, the authors highlight the gendered nature of school violence. Their interviews with teachers and students show how students' narrative accounts of their experiences of violence draw on discourses of masculinity to explain violent incidents and to legitimate their own violent conduct. Their narratives of violence reflect childhood and community experiences of violence, which in turn reflect the profound social inequalities that are a legacy of colonial and apartheid South Africa. The authors stress the agency of learners and analyse how both teachers and students either contribute to or undermine a climate of violence in schools.

In Chapter 7, the first in Part III, Davies and McInnes explore the ways in which homophobic violence is understood and recognised, particularly within schooling cultures. The authors examine the discourses through which same-sex attraction is constructed and the impact of these discourses in addressing the ongoing problem of homophobic violence in schools. This kind of violence frequently goes unrecognised by educators, or is met with disciplinary responses that leave little room for the perpetrators of such harassment and violence to reflect on their own subject position within relations of power. Davies and McInnes employ the pedagogy, *circuits of recognition,* as a framework to foreground the way in which social subjects are constituted interdependently. A moment of homophobic abuse serves as a moment of recognition. The perpetrator of homophobic violence is involved in 'othering' the abused through the use of hate speech, in a concerted effort to make the recipients of this abuse recognisable as a marginalised queer person/sexuality. The perpetrator of homophobic violence attempts to shore up his/her own identity as heteronormative. In such instances of linguistic violence, the perpetrator of the violence is attempting to determine the terms of recognition, generally by citing dominant discourses of heterosexuality, and the individuals being hailed by this linguistic violence are temporarily interpellated through discourses that can and frequently do cause injury. In such instances, a perpetrator is shoring up his/her heteronormative place in the grid of intelligible social positionings while casting the abused as more vulnerable and less valued. Davies and McInnes examine two cases of homophobic violence in the media before discussing some useful *circuit breakers* – that is, methods and practices that intervene in homophobic violence within schooling contexts.

In Chapter 8, Sara Knox takes up questions of representation of school-related violence in the media, focusing on school shootings and the tensions of identity and identification around which they centre. In a detailed analysis of examples from the United States and Europe, Knox explores how teens who went on rampages in school, shooting classmates and teachers, worked 'to style their killings (prior to, during, or after the act) to the representation of such killings in film, popular culture and literature' (Knox, this book). She observes that while school shootings relate specifically to the local, their 'media-mediation' is global. Knox argues that media logics inform the styles of killing used by these young people, such that the content of school shooting rampages can be seen as 'exportable', hence likely to appear in other such incidents. School shootings are intricately connected with heteronormative codes of masculinity, including forms of hyper-masculinity, in both the enactments of violence and their representation. There is, for Knox, a complex layering of styles in these acts and the ways that those who commit them depict themselves, their intentions and deeds in narrative accounts, manifestos, sound clips and visual images posted online. Knox's chapter calls to our attention the significance of representation to developing nuanced understandings of the enactment of violence.

Moira Carmody, in Chapter 9, provides an overview of a successful sexual ethics and violence prevention programme that she has developed for her work with young people. Educating young people about sexual assault and other forms of intimate partner violence is a challenging area for school educators. This is despite the fact that young people self-report high levels of violence in early dating relationships. Historically this area has tended to be ignored in most personal development curricula, and when it has been acknowledged, external anti-violence experts have been brought in. More recently in schools in the Australian state of New South Wales, additional curricula have been developed which attempt to educate young people about sexual consent and 'healthy relationships'. Carmody explores these developments and argues that they often unwittingly foster a discourse of danger and fear associated with adolescent sexuality. They also place significant responsibility on young women to manage the potential risks from young men and reinforce traditional discourses of heteronormativity, thus excluding young people attracted to others of the same sex. An alternative approach based on sexual ethics will be discussed based on empirical research on young rural and urban women and men of diverse sexualities about what they want from their sexuality education programmes. A sexual ethics approach challenges the risk discourses associated with both sexuality and violence prevention education. Instead it offers a framework for young people to explore knowledge and skills of ethical decision-making that balances both pleasure and danger in intimate relationships.

The concluding chapter provides a summary overview of key themes discussed in the book, and also considers implications for policy and practice pertaining to each of the chapters. The aim is to provoke productive dialogues amongst readers, educators and policy makers about ways in which the theoretical and practical questions raised by authors might make their way into decision-making and professional practice.

Part I
School Violence in Context

1
'The kid most likely': Naming, Brutality and Silence within and beyond School Settings

Sue Saltmarsh

Violence in educational settings is a complex issue and the topic of a considerable body of international research literature (see, e.g., Casella, 2001a, b; Elliott et al., 1998; Mills, 2001). This volume of research asks authors and readers to *rethink* what is known and believed about school violence, and in this chapter I draw on three narratives in order to query the brutality of discourses within which children are labelled and silenced. The chapter is concerned with systemic violence (Watkinson & Ross Epp, 1997) and its discursive effects, calling into question: labelling practices that name children as particular 'types' of social subject; silencing practices that denigrate, disregard and dismiss those most vulnerable in unequal relations of power; as well as those discursive silences that tacitly enable the reproduction of violence. Through the figure of 'the kid most likely' – in other words, children who are constituted as those most likely to experience educational failure, to commit criminal offences, to pose risks to themselves and others – the chapter considers how discursive practices of naming and silence powerfully reproduce and normalise symbolic and material violence within unequal relations of power.

In a collection of essays originally published in 1974, Michel de Certeau points out how violence is inscribed in technical procedures and scientific knowledges aimed at eliminating and appropriating other existences in the project of producing discursive and cultural 'unities'. He calls our attention to 'what ceases to speak and to be spoken' through the practices of othering, of colonising, of categorising and of naming. In educational settings, such practices may occur in myriad ways. At times they may take the form of overt instances of discrimination, harassment, vilification, exclusion and violence. Yet they may also be woven throughout many everyday assumptions and taken-for-granted approaches that make up normative discourse about what is necessary and appropriate within contemporary educational practice. For Certeau, the discursive effects of practices that marginalise, silence and exclude call into question the foundational claims from whence such practices derive their rationales. He writes, 'All the progress of our knowledge can be measured by the silence that it creates' (Certeau, 1997, p. 139). I undertake this discussion, then, in the current context of national and global politics – in which young people are increasingly subjected to heightened levels of suspicion and surveillance; ideological manipulation through policy manoeuvres such as values education, high-stakes testing and national curriculum; and marginalisation and oppression through the dehumanising agendas of neoliberal rationalities of governance. Certeau's insight pertaining to the violence of such endeavours informs my own approach to researching and theorising the ways in which social institutions operationalise and reinscribe the cultural production of violence. In this chapter, I want to argue that practices of naming and silence operate *together* to effect violent norms and violent social relations that all too often go unmarked in those official discourses that most powerfully impact on the lives of young people.

The figure of 'the kid most likely' is constructed across multiple sites within problematising discourses that represent young people 'as either deficient (and hence in need of education); delinquent (and hence in need of control); or dysfunctional (and hence in need of therapy)' (Griffin, 1993 as cited in Stainton Rogers & Stainton Rogers, 1998, p. 183). Young people thus conceptualised furnish the discursive backdrop to 'the kid most likely', a figure constituted as a knowable and recognisable social subject through a broad range of expert discourses, professional practices, policy initiatives, popular images and narratives and moral panics. A genealogical tracing of the discursive emergence of those young people who are categorised as most likely to be 'at risk' and to pose a risk to themselves, to others and to the moral, economic and social order more broadly is beyond the scope of this chapter. It is worth noting, however, that such tracings are the subject of a considerable literature concerned with highlighting their discursive effects on the lived experience of young people. As Susanne Davies points out, while philosophies associated with eugenics and social Darwinism may no longer be openly espoused as providing explanations for human character, behaviour and worth, their long discursive history has left indelible marks on everyday thought and practice within social institutions, playing 'an important role in rendering those least well-positioned in society vulnerable to professional and state intervention, abuse and exploitation' (Davies, 2005, p. 13). Indeed discourses of youth 'at risk' play an important role in naturalising notions of essential dispositions and qualities, and of centres and margins, that powerfully shape the lived experience of those least powerful. As Linda Graham and Roger Slee observe:

> Naturalisation effaces. In naturalising a particular mode of existence, we construct a universalised space free from interrogation, a ghostly centre which eludes critical analysis and thus recognition of the power relations embodied within notions of normalcy which exert influence over other ways of being.... When we identify categories of children, whether we refer to children at risk or children with a disability or children whose first language is not English, we not only make difference *visible* but work to maintain power imbalances and structural inequity by reifying *unnamed* attributes that carry social, political and cultural currency.
>
> (Graham & Slee, 2005, p. 16)

The point I want to make here, then, is that 'the kid most likely', while a heterogeneous construction with a multiplicity of formulations, is nonetheless insidiously inscribed on the bodies and lives of numerous children and young people upon whom the consequences and effects of brutalities and biases against 'the kid most likely' are continually brought to bear.

It is these brutalities and biases that provide the provocation for this chapter, and in the sections that follow I share three very different stories that together raise important questions about the complicity of pedagogic knowledges, professional practices and policy contexts in the cultural production of violence against 'the kid most likely'. My analysis is informed by Certeau's suggestion that 'If, by violence, we mean a growing distortion between what a discourse says and what a society does with it, then this very discourse functions as a manifestation of violence. It becomes itself a language of violence' (Certeau, 1997, p. 30). Certeau's is a critique of hypocrisy, of the violence that is produced in those disjunctions between what is said, known, accepted, believed, allowed to pass without censure or comment and what is actually *done*. In the context of the following examples, then, the questions I want to raise pertain to how certain practices of naming and silence illuminate those disjunctions, and raise questions about how violence is produced and maintained as a cultural formation.

The worry

Jonathan Talbot[1] is a worry. 'He looks so innocent', one of his teachers remarks, 'but he's a real worry'.[2] During my weekly research visits to Westland Preschool, I observe much in Jonathan's behaviour that is unsettling – in his interactions with peers, he frequently grabs, pushes, kicks, punches, bites and uses books, toys, boxes, chairs and other objects at hand as weapons that inflict pain and (potentially serious) injury, onto other children. His behaviour often presents a risk to the safety of himself and others, and his teachers openly express concern that unless something changes – soon – he is likely to eventually be excluded from formal schooling, to become 'another statistic' (Field Notes, Westland Preschool, 2006) with a risky and uncertain future. Despite his teachers' almost continuous monitoring of his whereabouts and activities, Jonathan is persistently found at the centre of turmoil. In relating Jonathan's story here, I acknowledge the difficulties that such circumstances create in the everyday life of Westland Preschool, and the subsequent demands on the time, physical stamina and emotional energy of its teaching staff.

Yet it is cultural knowledges and practices, rather than Jonathan's behaviour, that is the object of my research in early childhood settings, and I am therefore mindful of exploring how the discourses encountered and produced in everyday life shape the social relations and subjectivities of young people in educational contexts such as Westland Preschool. To that end, I observe with interest the ways in which violence intersects with and pervades discourses of learning, of teaching, of parenting, of childhood, of being a social subject with a legitimate past, a viable present and a possible future. Week after week, I note how discursive *ir*ruptions take place, observing how Jonathan and the other children and teachers at the preschool engage in complex performances of the symbolic and embodied violence that pervades what Judith Butler refers to as the 'domain of sociality'.

Of particular interest are the ways that Jonathan's de-legitimated subject positioning is articulated by his teachers and exploited by the other children at Westland Preschool. During every one of my visits to the preschool, I observe that turmoil is repeatedly instigated not only by Jonathan but also by the other children, who have developed a sophisticated repertoire of techniques for surreptitiously provoking, labelling and excluding him. The resulting outbursts persistently invoke responses from teachers that reinscribe Jonathan's status as 'the kid most likely' within a medicalised and pathologised grid of intelligibility. 'With Jonathan', one exasperated teacher informs me, 'you could almost go down the list and tick every box for ADHD, Oppositional Defiance Disorder, you name it' (Field Notes, Westland Preschool, October 2006). While professional educators have a well-defined vocabulary for naming – what Nikolas Rose refers to as the 'proliferation of an "expert" discourse' within which 'a whole raft of professionals ... have come to operate a quasi-psychological ethics' (Rose, 1999, p. 264) – the children at Westland Preschool demonstrate their own recognition of behavioural discourses, categorising Jonathan's behaviour in ways that document his transgressions and constitute him as a particular type of undesirable social subject. They routinely initiate conversations with me using Jonathan as a starting point:

> 'Jonathan hit me ... '
> 'Jonathan got in trouble ... '
> 'Jonathan's always naughty ... '
> 'Jonathan's a naughty boy ... '

What they don't say – but what I have observed on numerous occasions – is that Jonathan is often deliberately excluded from their play, ignored, pushed, shoved, hit and deliberately provoked. For the most part, such provocations take place outside the view or hearing of teachers, and in many cases the children watch closely to ensure that their harassment of Jonathan is not witnessed by their teachers. His tendency to lash out with physical retribution, though, means that those who initiate struggles with him are likely to end up in tears. Over several weeks, I observe a familiar pattern emerging: one or more children actively incite a negative response from Jonathan by hitting or shoving him, snatching a toy away from him, or overtly excluding him from play; when he lashes out, the screams of those who have provoked the retaliation are heard by teaching staff, who intervene immediately and carry Jonathan kicking and screaming from the offending scene; he is then scolded loudly and placed on a chair to sit alone; the wounded party is consoled and then accompanied and supported by a teacher in confronting him with the declarative, 'I don't like it when you do that, Jonathan.' The volume and veracity with which the injured child is explicitly instructed to repeat 'I don't like it' is often proportional to tears of the injured child. The teachers' reading of Jonathan's offence and its severity is such that teachers' raised voices and clenched teeth figure routinely in these instances of 'assertiveness training' and 'conflict resolution' into which the other children are being inducted.

Such scenes are played out numerous times each day, as Jonathan's *general* visibility as the performative playground bully is compounded by his '*compulsory* visibility' (Foucault, 1977, p. 187, emphasis added) as the naughty child who is repeatedly publicly reprimanded, isolated and humiliated by teachers and students alike. I am not intending to imply wilful abuse or dereliction of the teachers' duty of care, and am indeed mindful of the complexities they face in managing such a complex social environment. I also acknowledge that there are occasions on which they attempt to reason with Jonathan and attend to his needs, and I recognise, too, the necessity of preventing injurious behaviour in educational contexts where teachers have a duty of care to ensure children's safety and well-being. However, the circumstances within which Jonathan's story takes place provide a powerful example of the kinds of tacit injustices that make institutions complicit in the cultural production of violence.

There is an unjust brutality, for example, in the persistent naming of Jonathan and his behaviour as aberrant, while the complicity of others is masked by their tearful performances as innocent victims. Institutional complicity is underscored by explicit pedagogic techniques that effectively invest the other children's *unnamed* transgressions with institutional authority, giving rise to a disciplinary system that 'enjoys a kind of judicial privilege with its own laws, its specific offences, its particular forms of judgement' (Foucault, 1977, pp. 177–178). In this disciplinary system, Jonathan's legitimacy as a learner with the potential to recognise the feelings of others, to improve on his behaviour and to develop more meaningful forms of social interaction is effectively revoked by essentialising discourses that cast his behaviour as biologically fixed and determined. For example, one morning in the preschool playground one of the teachers asks if I have seen Jonathan, and I reply that he is playing in the sandpit with two other boys, pretending to have a party that involves lots of cake. The teacher replies by saying that:

> Jonathan's learned nothing this year, you know. Absolutely nothing. He can't even do a simple puzzle. And with the behaviour, most of the kids who come here, well they might hit or fight or something, but they learn pretty quick not to. But not him. It doesn't

matter how much he gets in trouble, it never makes any difference. So something in there's not connecting... I don't know what's happened today though – maybe his parents have put him on some sort of medication without telling us.

(Field Notes, Westland Preschool, October 2006)

Even on those occasions when Jonathan *can* be seen playing peacefully with other children – sharing, taking turns, cooperating – his behaviour is unable to be understood or recognised within the terms of social learning, of empathy for others or of developing greater self-control. Instead, even *desired* behaviours are silenced, stripped of legitimacy and attributed to interventions made possible through medical knowledges, rather than to the kind of agentive capacity that is routinely attributed to the other children. Jonathan's naming as a pathologised social subject thus contributes to his silencing as a learning subject.

Importantly to the purposes of this chapter, the dialogic relation between naming and silence is a crucial dimension of the imposition of disciplinary judgement on the 'kid most likely', and I share the following example as a way of exploring its potency.

On a recent noisy and chaotic morning at the preschool, the children engage enthusiastically in a period of 'free play' – some are dressing up in the home corner, clanking around the room in glittering high heels, arguing over dollies and their paraphernalia; a group of boys plays, as they regularly do, a game involving plastic dinosaurs and doll houses, staging hostile takeovers of the doll house chairs and its plastic television. They conduct fierce and noisy battles between the dinosaurs, who loudly devour one another in order to gain control of the imaginary ' "mote control" '. Other children play with wooden puzzles and blocks that have been laid out on tables, and several boys chase each other around the room imitating the raucous noise of the Bathurst races they have watched on television at the weekend.

Jonathan sits on the floor with a group of children who are playing with a bowl of plastic fruit and ice cream cones, while a teacher sits nearby monitoring their play. One of the other children takes over the bowl of plastic food and refuses to let the others continue to play with it. The teacher tries to gently cajole her into sharing with the other children. Jonathan tries, unsuccessfully, to grab a piece of the plastic food, and a struggle over the bowl ensues. The teacher intervenes, picking up a now kicking and screaming Jonathan and placing him on a chair at the opposite side of the noisy room.

The general clamour that has filled the room up until this point is powerfully disrupted when Jonathan's foot randomly connects with a wooden screen that lands with a thunderous crash on the hard linoleum tiles on the floor. There is an immediate hush of surprised, complete, awful silence – every child freezes, every teacher halts, and every eye in the room is drawn first to the site of the toppled screen and then to the small child responsible for the mighty sound. For several seconds no one moves or speaks as all stare silently at Jonathan, who nervously wiggles his leg, glancing back at them in turn. Eventually one of the teachers takes a step forward and says loudly and harshly, with an unmistakeable tone of disgust, 'Jonathan Talbot!' For several more seconds all stare silently, before first some and then others return to their play with now lowered voices.

(Field Notes, Westland Preschool, 2006)

I want to map my reading of this scene onto those prior discursive moments – those of bullying, injury, exclusion, domination, pathologising and naming to which Jonathan is routinely subjected – in order to suggest that the violence of these normative practices is insidiously woven into the space of silence brought about by the crashing wooden screen on the preschool floor. This is no neutral silence, but rather it is a silence that interrogates, insinuates, articulates prior events and anticipates others yet to come.

The teacher's angry and disapproving declaration of Jonathan's name speaks a past, present and future marked by transgressions for which *he* will be held fully accountable – not the contributing factors occasioned by others, not the policies and pedagogies of the educational institution, not the 'psy' inspired discourses that 'make it possible for each individual to relate to themselves and the course of their life in particular ways' (Rose, 1999, p. 270). Indeed, even as it reproduces the violence of prior events, the moment of discursive silence marks the *complicity* of social knowledges and practices which precede and exceed the individual. Nowhere, except in the silence of glances, a child's awkward squirming on a chair, the glare of an angry teacher, and of a room full of children and adults with nothing to say, is that complicity marked.

In the judgement silence pronounces on the complicity of others, of institutions, of accepted knowledges and pedagogic practices, there is of course a productive possibility – a moment in which the question of how things might be done and thought otherwise is made possible. Yet the authoritative, angry and punitive speaking of a single name seemingly forecloses such a potential gain, replacing the discursive query with a decisive answer that effects that most damaging of all violences – erasure. The question I want to raise and to hold open, then, is not the question of 'who is to blame' or of 'what should be done'. I am not endeavouring to uncover the 'truth' of Jonathan's behaviour, nor to attempt, in this space, any ultimate resolution. Rather, I am compelled to call into question how discursive power and its effects are operationalised and invisibilised through what is spoken *and* what is not in naming the 'kid most likely'.

The degenerate

He is visible and vocal, openly commanding attention through the brusk physicality of his presence in classrooms, sporting groups and playgrounds. He routinely struts across the schoolyard, making comments about students he dislikes and voicing his opinion at every opportunity. As a PE teacher at Plains High School, there is no shortage of opportunities for Mr. Pratt to exert influence on those around him. Elsewhere (Saltmarsh & Youdell, 2004), Deborah Youdell and I have written about our ethnographic research at Plains High School, with particular reference to the ways in which Mr. Pratt's language, attitudes and behaviours towards some individuals and groups in this western Sydney high school function to constitute 'marginalized student identities and disempowered subject positions' (Saltmarsh & Youdell, 2004, p. 10), reproducing practices of educational triage that effectively ration students' educational opportunities (Gillborn & Youdell, 2000). In our earlier work from the Plains High study, we note how Mr. Pratt's derogatory comments are instrumental in marginalising a sport class whose students are seen as failing to satisfactorily negotiate the masculinist discourses valourised within the school. We also note how other teachers remain silent during Mr. Pratt's denigration of students, and we argue that:

> ... the unquestioned acceptance of negative constitutions of the students by staff has a normative function, serving both to normalize the practices of assigning students to marginalized discursive positions, as well as to normalize and reinforce the predominance of teachers' views within the discursive hierarchy.
>
> (Saltmarsh & Youdell, 2004, p. 9)

Here I want to follow on from that work, bringing to bear once again Certeau's contention, cited at the beginning of this chapter, that 'All the progress of our knowledge can be measured by the silence that it creates' (Certeau, 1997, p. 139). In particular, I want to ask how the voice of one and the silence of others work together to establish a scene of violence and complicity that powerfully interrogates pedagogic knowledges and policy claims premised on notions of inclusion, safety and respect. Drawing on field notes recorded in the same study, during a lunch period spent in the Sport Teachers' Staff Room, I recall with considerable discomfort a scene in which Mr. Pratt establishes his discursive dominance amongst those in the staff room, before brutally targeting a student who appears at the door. In this scene, I have been invited by one of the other teachers to eat my lunch in the sport teachers' staff room, and the following discussion takes place:

Mr. Pratt (speaking to me): So what university are you from?
SS: Macquarie
Mr. Pratt (Now sitting with his back turned toward me): I don't rate Macquarie. My wife goes there. I don't rate it.
Mr. Carlo (One of the other male sport teachers): I went to Macquarie Uni once. I started a science degree there.
Mr. Pratt (looking at Mr. Carlo, and saying in a goading, patronising, mock-feminine voice): Ooooo, Mr.Carlo! A scientist!? Oooooo...Where's your little *bow tie*?
Mr. Pratt then begins flipping through some papers on his desk. He reads through one letter, and says in a disgusted tone: Well...some of these parents...like Joe Thompson's parents...*parents*... consider themselves to be *above* the Education Department!
He wheels his chair around to face me, and says angrily: Tell you what. In your notes, you oughta put, *Teachers* get treated badly because *parents* are *SPASTIC!* No, you probably can't put *spastic* in a report. How about *MENTALLY DEFICIENT.* Parents are mentally deficient.[3]

Multiple practices of naming and discrediting, speaking and silencing take place here, as Mr. Pratt assumes the place of one who is entitled to speak a language of derision and to foreclose even tentative attempts by others to recover the potential embarrassment of having a guest (me) openly insulted. Mr. Carlo's entry into the conversational space – as one who, if not prepared to mount an open challenge to Mr. Pratt's attack, might nonetheless be able to preserve a semblance of courtesy through the contribution of an additional perspective – is quickly undone. Even Mr. Carlo's mention of the traditionally masculine domain of sciences is subverted and used against him, while the other teachers sitting in the room remain completely silent. The diatribe against parents that ensues extends the reach of Mr. Pratt's power to encompass not only the professional space of the staff room but also the personal space of lives, responsibilities and familial ties beyond the school. His invocation of the Education Department establishes his location within 'institutions of power', within which institutional strategies operate to maintain 'a proper place' from which to speak (Certeau, 2002), while simultaneously de-legitimating the professional status and personal worth of those others in the room who might happen to be parents. Shortly thereafter, as the other members of staff continue to eat their sandwiches in silence, the following incident takes place:

Alan, a Year 9 boy, with whom Mr. Pratt often appears inexplicably annoyed when they encounter one another on the playground or in school corridors, comes to the door of the staff room. Mr. Pratt looks irritated, and with an exaggerated sigh tells Alan to leave, saying that he'll be out to talk to him in a minute. When Alan steps outside the room, the door remains open and I can see him waiting, close enough to be able to hear what is being said in the staff room. Mr. Pratt says rather loudly to Mr. Carlo, 'I'll tell you what. You know those 'Most Likely' Awards they give out at the end of school? Like 'Most Likely to Be Rich and Famous' or whatever. Well, that kid there, I'd give him the 'Most Likely To Become a Paedophile' Award. He just gives me the creeps. The way he looks at you, the way he comes up to ask you questions, the way he sidles up to the Year 7 boys. I'll tell you what, if he starts turning up here with lollies, we're *really* gonna have to worry.' He steps just outside the door to answer Alan's query. I have no doubt that Alan has almost certainly heard what has just been said about him.

(Field Notes, Plains High, 2001)

Mr. Pratt's behaviour here, as in many other instances that were observed throughout the duration of the Plains High study, is extreme, yet his comments and conduct nonetheless routinely go unchallenged by others with a duty of care for the students that he targets and denigrates. This scene is no accident or exception. Having established, at the expense of myself and others in the staff room, his entitlement to dominate absolutely in this and any other social domain of his choosing, his vilification of Alan goes unmarked and unchallenged. No one in the staff room makes eye contact, nor do they speak in defence of a student who has been constituted as 'the kid most likely' in terms that every publicly available educational discourse – of professionalism, of pedagogy, of social inclusion, of procedural fairness, of ethical practice, of duty of care – would consider inconceivable, impermissible, unspeakable. The severity of this arbitrary charge against the student lies not just in the immediacy of the accusation but also in its potency within broader discourses of social legitimacy. Indeed, according to Nikolas Rose:

> The limits of the permissible appear to be fixed only by two characteristics of our contemporary regime of freedom. There is conduct that is non-consensual, that is to say, where the freedom of another is violated: the epitome is the image of the paedophile. And there is conduct that is excessive, that manifests a lack of the exercise of will and free choice, whose epitome is the alcoholic or the heroin addict but which extends, as well, to the pathologies of 'liberation' exemplified by 'excesses' of the gay sex scene in the era before AIDS.
>
> (Rose, 1999, p. 266)

By constituting this student as the kid 'most likely to become a paedophile', *and* as one who poses a particular risk to younger boys, Mr. Pratt demonstrates the skill with which he is able to manipulate discourses of both violation and excess to establish his own position of absolute entitlement within an institution of power. His homophobic and misogynist derision directed at colleagues in the staff room is masterfully redeployed against a far less powerful target, in a public demonstration of the extent to which 'normal defines and oppresses what it designates as abnormal' (Dyer, 1997, p. 264). In this scene, where the speaking of violence is accompanied by the complicity of silence, Alan is simultaneously positioned as degenerate threat *and* as victim 'upon whom the theatre of identifying power is performed' (Certeau, 1986, p. 41).

While I am not intending to imply that such abuses of power are always so readily evident in other schools and other places, I *am* suggesting that incidents such as these establish the limits of pedagogic theories and educational policies to effect social change within their own epistemological terms. These limits are established precisely *because* they articulate the complicity of institutionally sanctioned hierarchies (between students and staff, and between staff differentially located by gender, race, sexuality and other identity categories), of professional behaviours (in which, e.g., colleagues do not openly criticise other members of staff in the presence of students), and of powerful discourses of homophobia, racism, misogyny and heterosexism around which naming and silence are choreographed.

The lost

His death was the subject of five separate inquiries, and there will be no more chances for Liam Ashley to learn the lesson that his family had hoped a couple of weeks in custody would teach him. Facing charges of breaching bail, illegal possession of a knife and a pipe, burglary, trespass, breach of curfew and driving whilst forbidden – crimes largely in relation to having broken into his parents' home and taken his mother's car for a drive without permission – 17-year-old Liam had reportedly exhausted his family's repertoire of responses to his difficult behaviour, and his parents hoped that a few nights in custody might act as a turning point. When he appeared before a New Zealand court on the 24th of August 2006, then, no bail was requested by the defence, and the court determined that Liam would spend the following two weeks in custody while on remand awaiting sentencing and the preparation of a probation report.

According to media reports, and later confirmed by the New Zealand Ombudsman's Report (Belgrave & Smith, 12 June 2007), Liam was taken from court and placed in the back of a prison van owned and operated by Chubb NZ, the company contracted by the NZ Corrections Department to conduct prison transfers, home detention and a range of other services. Liam had already complained, whilst he had been held in custody awaiting his hearing, of being picked on by other prisoners. Despite the magistrate seeking assurances that Liam would be kept separate from adult offenders while in custody, he was placed in a compartment of the transfer van with two adult prisoners, one of whom, George Charlie Baker, had a known history of violent offences. En route from the court to the Auckland Central Remand Prison, Liam was violently attacked by Baker who beat, strangled, stomped on him and broke his neck. Upon arrival at the prison Liam was pulled from the van unconscious and critically wounded. Although revived at the scene, he died in hospital the following day, and Baker was subsequently convicted of his murder and sentenced to a minimum 18-year prison sentence.

There are two crucial aspects of this story that I want to raise here as matters of critical concern with relation to naming and violence. The first of these is the complicity of neoliberal reform agendas in developed nations that have persistently subjected the provision of public services to market models. The corporate ethos adopted in the delivery of public services all too often diminishes the needs of those most vulnerable to costs that must be managed efficiently in order to deliver the greatest fiscal returns to the corporate sector and shareholders, and budget surpluses to government (Giroux, 2007). Within neoliberal market ideologies, people are 'primarily conceptualised as entirely self-interested competitive and independent individuals, in the end driven by asocial greed, while aspects of common goods and collective arrangements are left unconsidered and ultimately banished from the various social systems which constitute the individual's ecological environment' (Blakar, 2008, p. 33). Under such models, those who require public facilities – whether they be schools, hospitals, prisons, immigration detention centres – are easily constituted in the dehumanising terms of economic units to be taught, surveilled, treated, rehabilitated, monitored and processed. This view is supported by investigations into Liam's death, including the findings of the New Zealand Ombudsman's Report (Belgrave & Smith, 12 June 2007) that raised numerous questions about the contracting out of government services to private companies. However, when these questions were raised in the NZ Parliament in relation to Liam Ashley's death, the Minister for Corrections, Damien O'Connor, explicitly denied that the use of private contractors to provide services such as prison transfers was a cost-saving measure on the part of the Department for which he is responsible. Such a denial speaks to the hypocrisy with which decisions justified to electorates on the basis of their economic rationality are abjectly denied when the human toll of their brutal effects is occasionally laid bare in the form of broken lives and broken bodies. As Certeau observes:

> There is no law that is not inscribed on bodies...From birth to mourning after death, law 'takes hold of' bodies in order to make them its text. Through all sorts of initiations (in rituals, at school, etc.), it transforms them into tables of the law, into living tableaux of rules and customs, into actors in the drama organised by a social order.
>
> (Certeau, 2002, p. 139)

The materiality of law in this case powerfully inscribes the internal logics of neoliberal policy and its language of efficiency and profitability on the body of the prisoner-child who becomes the ledger upon which its substantive costs are tallied.

Importantly, though, there are other factors that merit consideration, and these link Liam's story with the other two considered in this chapter in significant ways. Amid the clamour of public inquiries, media speculation and political debate that took place in the aftermath of Liam's murder, his parents offered accounts to the media of an educational history marked by labelling, pathologising and social exclusion. In a statement released by Liam's family to the NZ press in the days following his death, for example, his father outlines the story of a child diagnosed with ADHD at the age of three. The Ashley's were requested to remove Liam from his first school after only a short time, due to what his father refers to as a 'lack of acceptance by mainstream education' (TV3 New Zealand, 2006). Liam had later been sent to board in a residential college until shortly before he turned 15, where he reportedly thrived. However, he missed his family and wanted to return home, so his parents enrolled him in a local college, with disastrous consequences. His father writes, 'Due to a lack of understanding and tolerance from the mainstream system, we were once again asked to remove Liam from the school' (TV3 New Zealand, 2006). These accounts of exclusions and disruptions speak to the institutional and discursive power invested in essentialising, medicalised explanations of behaviour that does not conform to normative expectations. As I argued in relation to the stories of Jonathan and Alan, while the processes of naming and of silence are complex and multifaceted, they nonetheless play a powerful role in young people's experiences of and beyond schooling. As Deborah Youdell points out:

> The 'who' a student is – in terms of gender, sexuality, social class, ability, disability, race, ethnicity and religion as well as popular and sub cultural belongings – is inextricably linked with the 'sort' of student and learner that s/he gets to be, and the educational inclusions s/he enjoys and/or the exclusions s/he faces.
>
> (Youdell, 2006, p. 2, original emphasis)

This is not to suggest a case for either causality or predictability, nor is it to imply that identifying contributing factors and circumstances might establish the 'truth' about what went wrong, what might have been foreseen or what could have been done otherwise. Rather, it is to argue that the naming and silencing to which Jonathan, Alan and Liam have each been subjected cannot be dissociated from the 'who' each might be able to be and become. The discourses by which Liam Ashley was named from the earliest period of his childhood as a particular 'type' of social subject appear to bear remarkable similarity to the discourses through which Jonathan Talbot is daily being spoken prior to his entry into formal schooling. Similarly, labels of deviance and criminality not unlike those used by Mr. Pratt to denigrate and humiliate Alan at Plains High are materialised with tragic consequences in the story of Liam Ashley.

Reflection

In each of these three stories, discursive practices of naming and silence have brutal consequences for the child who represents the figure of 'the kid most likely'. While their circumstances differ in many ways, each is arbitrarily labelled within school settings by medicalised discourses that position them within the terms of abnormality, deviance and risk. Each is impacted upon by discursive silences that effectively override accepted knowledges about pedagogic practice, professional responsibilities and institutional accountabilities. Such silences simultaneously call into question and establish the limits of these forms of social knowledge that are upheld as necessary for ensuring the well-being of children. In particular, these three narratives call for closer examinations of the complicity of professional discourses and institutional structures in the production of symbolic and material violence.

In each case, the constitutive force of naming and silencing is reinscribed by the complicity of witnesses who fail to speak or intervene in any meaningful way. At Westland Preschool, a small child's efforts to fend off the taunts and provocations of others are read as 'worrying' behaviour. Those who observe and respond to his outbursts fail to see the injustices to which he is subjected, thereby collectively reproducing them. In the Plains High staff room, those least powerful are arbitrarily spoken with a language of derision and contempt, while those best situated to intervene silently chew their sandwiches as though nothing of significance has happened. Meanwhile, in the back of a prison van where he should never have been placed, a young boy's life is ended in a culmination of labelling, silencing and institutional failures that marked his experience of schooling and later, the justice system.

These kinds of practices are implicated in producing privileged norms of recognition and conduct for which individual and collective responsibility must be shared. The violence produced in the difference between what is said and what is done in Western societies is pervasive, and in Certeau's terms none are exempt from the circumstances of its production.

I cannot exempt myself from this common situation by flashing my intellectual union card. Violence is not in the first place a matter for reflection, nor is it an object that can be put before the eyes of an observer. It is inscribed in the place from which I speak of it. Violence defines that place.

(Certeau, 1997, p. 29)

Acknowledging the complexities through which violence speaks and is spoken in the places where we stand as educators, as researchers and as family and community members is surely the crucial way forward. I would argue then for an insistent and collective speaking into those spaces of naming and silence – be they located in the micro-practices of schools and classrooms, or performed on the broader stage of national and global politics – that produce the kinds of conditions of impossibility that claim the learning, the optimism and the possible futures of far too many young people. As we endeavour to analyse discursive complicities not for the purposes of apportioning blame, but in order to 'obtain a means of discovering what has to be done' (Certeau, 1997, p. 30), perhaps we might open up new possibilities for 'the kid most likely' to make it through, to grow up, to join in, to answer back, to speak a new language in which the brutality of naming and silence has no place.

Notes

1. Names of all research participants and research sites have been anonymised.
2. Observational field notes were recorded in hand-written form by the author during site visits to Westland Preschool in 2006. Field note data were augmented with informal interviews with children, parents and staff, and formal interviews with preschool teachers.
3. Observational field notes were recorded in hand-written form by the author and lead researcher, Prof. Deborah Youdell, during site visits to Plains High School in 2001. Field note data were augmented with informal interviews with students and school staff, and formal interviews with teachers and members of the school executive. The author acknowledges with thanks Professor Youdell's permission to use data from the study in this analysis.

2
The Historical and Political Roots of School Violence in South Africa: Developing a Cross-National Theory

Ronnie Casella

School violence is a persistent international crisis, yet most analyses of the problem are very local in their focus. Many theories of school violence lack not only an international perspective but also political and historical contexts (Astor et al., 2006; Ohsako, 1997; Smith et al., 1999). This chapter argues two points. First, that theories stemming from work dating from the mid-twentieth century Europe, the United Kingdom and the United States are not always adequate in understanding school violence in a cross-national perspective in the early twenty-first century. Second, theories that account for historical and political contexts may be more valid in accounting for school violence in countries that are usually not at the forefront of theory development. In other words, though theories developed in the United Kingdom, Western Europe and the United States may have had validity in their own contexts, they do not necessarily transfer automatically to countries that have experienced vastly different histories and political situations.

This chapter, based on qualitative research in South Africa, aims to summarise the common theories of school violence, to indicate how they may not be pertinent when examining school violence in an international perspective (with specific reference to South Africa), and then to discusses one theory in particular – social disintegration theory – and how a broadening of this theory to take into account political and historical dimensions of countries' circumstances may help us to develop more pertinent cross-national theory. Finally, to highlight this point, the chapter examines three forms of school violence in South Africa related to gangs, corporal punishment and rape, and how these forms of violence emerge as significant when one undertakes a more historically and politically informed analysis.

This chapter aims to broaden the context of social disorganisation theory in accounting for school violence. The focus is on South Africa because it is a country with high rates of school violence and all the elements of social disorganisation (Jürgens et al., 2003; Seekings & Nattrass, 2005; Shaw, 2002). It is also a country with a unique history and political situation, which may impact school violence. The focus on South Africa is also meant to gain a better understanding of school violence as an international phenomenon. Astor et al. (2006) noted that a more international perspective may help us to better understand similarities among countries as well as differences that reflect unique cultural and national characteristics. Like other researchers, they recognise how 'nested contexts' (p. 107) can influence school violence, including contexts related to the school; neighbourhood; families; culture and economics. Along with economics, they also include the 'social, and political makeup of the country as a whole'. Their work broadens ideas about the context of school violence; they include, for example, the potential role of religion in aspects of school violence, something not seen in more localised analyses.

Theories of school violence

Most researchers of school violence view the problem in one of several ways: it is a problem originating from the school, from society or from the individual. Most theories are a variation of one of these three contexts or a combination of them. The following are some of the most-cited theories organised according to their context (individual, school, community). After describing them, they are discussed in terms of why they are not wholly appropriate in accounting for school violence in South Africa.

The individual context: Biological theory and rational choice theory

Of the theories that pinpoint individuals as the cause of violence, biological theory and rational choice theory are two of the most popular ones. *Rational choice theory* contends that all individuals are rational beings, and as such our decisions are based on a simple weighing of benefits and consequences (Akers, 1990; Cornish & Clarke, 1986). The theory states that individuals will naturally choose behaviours that benefit them and avoid behaviours that will have consequences. This theory has had some import in schools; it, for example, is the basis for zero-tolerance policies, which in essence aims to convince students that if they do not abide by laws and policies, the consequences will be dire (Noguera, 1995). It is also the basis of security initiatives, including the posting of police in schools and the use of security equipment: essentially, the aim here is to convince the *rational* person that it would be a better choice to abide by school policies since they will inevitably be caught if they do not (Casella, 2006).

Some have argued that violence has less to do with *choice* and more to do with biological factors. *Biological theory* states that some individuals are more predisposed to violence than others, and that they are born this way (Gould, 1981; Lombroso, 1876; Martineau, 1996). Here, violence is innate. If people can be predisposed to acquire from birth a range of diseases, why not the 'disease' of violence? In schools, this theory is often used to explain why boys 'act-out' more than girls. Also, the increased use of medications for children aimed to modify their behaviours attests to the success of this theory in shaping school practices.

Rational choice theory and biological theory both suffer from a limitation stemming from the fact that neither takes into account environmental factors. In the context of a transforming society like South Africa, environmental factors have a profound effect on individual actions, therefore it is not reasonable to assume that school violence stems from factors only related to individuals' choices or predispositions. For example, much school violence of the 1980s was specifically related to political violence, gangs and sometimes activism (Glaser, 1998a; Marks, 2001) – not choices and dispositions. Much violence stemmed from gangs, which as Glaser (2000) pointed out was in themselves a formation of several historical and political factors, including relocations, masculine identification, ethnic rivalries and competition for turf and women. This is not to say that rational choice theory and biological theory have no legitimacy, but rather, that they are insufficient in explaining school violence in South Africa, especially when we take into account the influence that its politics and history have had on nearly every aspect of life, especially schools and violence.

The school context: Strain theory and labelling theory

Strain theory is the belief that individuals who act violently have legitimate desires, but due to structural restraints, they turn to unlawfulness to fulfil those desires (Merton, 1957). As Hirschi (1969) explained, when a person desires success, this is a legitimate desire; but when that person is not able to obtain success through legitimate means, he or she may turn in desperation to illegitimate means. Poverty, for example, creates hardships within families that could lead otherwise peaceful children to act violently towards others; the problem here is not the intention or ambition of the perpetrator; the problem involves the structural impediments due to poverty that prevents individuals from acquiring through lawful means what their culture has designated as legitimate. While strain theory is usually put forward to account for juvenile delinquency in a general sense, researchers of schools have borrowed the theory to account for disruptive behaviours in school, positing that schools put up barriers that prevent individuals from acquiring what they see as legitimate and rightfully theirs. For example, strain theory can be used to explain hostility by a student in a lower-tracked class who is frustrated by his track designation and acts-out because he or she feels shortchanged (Casella, 2001a).

An explanation that focuses specifically on the context of schools is *labelling theory*. Adherents to this theory believe that students are labelled in particular ways by teachers and administrators and sometimes other students. Subsequently, students 'live out' their labels (Becker, 1963). Some refer to this as the self-fulfilling prophecy (Rist, 1970). A student may be considered by administrators to be a behavioural problem, be put in classes for students with behavioural problems, and act the way everybody else in the class acts, therefore 'living out' his or her label. The schools define what is 'normal' and those who do not fit in the definition are deemed abnormal, and therefore treated as such. These individuals may then resist in a hostile fashion, or even if they do not, they are still deemed aberrant due to their identities, not their actions.

In the context of South Africa, strain theory and labelling theory may have much validity, as they do in other countries. Some important research has determined that much school violence is associated with school factors, related to not only labelling and strain but also school disorganisation and what Devine (1996) called a 'culture of violence' (see also Hawkins et al., 1998; Leoschut & Burton, 2006). But in the context of South Africa, labelling theory and strain theory have some problems. Much violence in schools is perpetrated by people of privileged backgrounds, often middle-class and wealthy whites against poor blacks and coloureds. These middle-class and wealthy whites are not labelled (and if they are, they are given positive labels) and do not confront significant strains in life. So how do you account for this very prevalent form of school violence: violence perpetrated not *by* those but *against* those who are labelled and strained?

The community context: Social control theory, social learning theory and social disorganisation theory

For some, *social control theory* is a multi-layered manner of understanding violence, and in some research, especially that of Hirschi (1969), the theory has focused specifically on students. Individuals who adhere to this theory believe that violence is caused by an individual's lack of engagement with typical social controls. It has been argued that society has certain controls that promote peacefulness – these controls include both internal and external controls, such as self-esteem, morals and self-control (internal) as well as adult supervision, positive relationships with law-abiding peers and involvement in sports and other conventional activities (external). In each case, there is an unstated or indirect 'pull' that keeps individuals from engaging in delinquent behaviour. As Lawrence (2007) wrote, the question asked by social control theorists is not, 'Why do individuals become delinquents', but rather, 'Why do individuals *not* become delinquents?' What keeps them on track? Social control theory emphasises the power of parents, peers and school staff in applying these various controls needed to prevent delinquency.

Another theory, *social learning theory*, argues that individuals are taught to act violently. They are taught through their peers, families, popular culture and the media. This is the 'influence' argument: youths hang out with a group of kids who are a bad influence; or, youths play violent video games or watch violent movies that influence the ways they act. Because this theory focuses on cognitive processes, educators have eagerly adopted it. Bandura (1977) was one of the early developers of this theory, and others who have adopted his ideas have demonstrated sometimes in lab tests that children sometimes mimic what they see on television or the actions of unruly youths and parents. Bandura and Walter's (1959, p. 252) point was that individuals learn 'internal controls' from imitation and through a process of identification with, for example, parents: 'This process appears to be a result not so much of direct training by the parents, but rather of active learning by the child of attitudes and values which his [sic] parents need not have attempted to teach directly.'

Social disorganisation theory focuses on the environment in which individuals are raised and recognises ones surroundings as a central element to understanding delinquency. Gottfredson and Gottfredson (1985) re-evaluated data from the first comprehensive study of school violence, the Safe School Study (National Institute of Education, 1977) which didn't examine community context, and discovered that neighbour-hood disorganisation correlated with school disorganisation. In other words, where there is community breakdown, there is likely to be school-level breakdown. In their study of gun-related violence in and around ten schools in five cities, Sheley et al. (1992) found that the issues that caused the violence in the school originated from the community. This ecological view of violence can be traced to Shaw and McKay (1942) whose research indicated that economic conditions in communities have a profound effect on rates of delinquency; people not only become socialised to view violence as normal and acceptable, but anomie, a kind of social chaos and unrest, sets the tone for how people will act, influencing morals and standards of behaviour.

Social disorganisation theory is unique for its focus on the way macro-level factors may influence micro-level outcomes: how the composition of a community and population turn-over rates, for example, may affect individuals' behaviours. It is also unique in that it draws from other theories. In social disorganisation theory are aspects of strain theory, rational choice theory, social control theory, learning theory and perhaps others. For example, Laub and Lauritsen (1998, p. 132), in their discussion of the merits of social disorganisation theory, have argued that 'communities lacking strong local institutions such as well-functioning schools, strong churches, and successful businesses have a reduced capacity to exert informal social control over residents' behavior'. This is an idea borrowed from social control theory. Short (1997) argued that individuals from poor inner-cities often have nothing to lose, and therefore make choices – to act violently – that other people would not make. This appears to be a blending of social disorganisation theory with rational choice theory. The theory's connection to strain theory is obvious, as well: factors arising from disorganised communities can limit the life chances of young people, who may feel this 'strain', and then act lawlessly in their pursuit of legitimate goals.

Though promoters of social disorganisation theory (and other community-related theories) will tout their broad view of violence – that they look beyond the individual and the school – they still confine their analyses to communities and not nations. They also confine their analyses to the present day and do not take into consideration historical contexts. While they focus on the social and not just the individual, they lack political contexts that may be involved in the production of violent circumstances. In countries such as South Africa, where politics and the history of school violence have played such a large role in present circumstances, one would be shortsighted to end one's analysis with the present community.

An international perspective on school violence

Researchers have begun to examine school violence internationally and have recognised some difficulties (Astor et al., 2006; Ohsako, 1997; Smith, 2003). As mentioned earlier, the theories mentioned thus far tend to focus on urban areas; and when analyses are broadly conceived, they are applied sometimes to national analyses, but rarely if ever to international analyses. Akiba et al. (2002) have noted three theories of violence that have been developed to account for violence in an international context, but these theories do not focus on violence in schools, but rather violence in the general society. These theories include deprivation, age distribution and social integration. Deprivation refers to the theory that high rates of violence positively correlate with absolute and relative deprivation. In other words, a country with low GNP or GDP is more likely to experience high rates of violence. Age distribution refers to the theory that violence is associated with age, and in countries where there are a higher percentage of young people, rates of violence will be higher. Social integration is much like social disintegration theory, whereby high rates of divorce and other factors that prompt family disintegration positively correlate with high rates of violence. Though there is evidence to support these theories, and though each has been applied in international contexts, they do not account for school violence specifically, and moreover, they remain apolitical and ahistorical.

When interviewing individuals, I began with a basic question, 'Have you ever been a victim of violence in school, and if so, could you explain the situation, and in doing so, what caused the violent confrontation?' One 11th grader in a Soweto school summed up many of the pertinent issues when he explained:

> It's too many poor people living too close. Especially the townships, where I live in Meadowlands. The shebeens where people drink, drugs. People fight in school over money. You got a lot of boys on the street because they're not working, and you have people who just accept violence. When we have a strike in South Africa we don't just have a strike, we always have stabbings and beatings along with it.

The teachers go on strike and we have beatings, even students get beat for going to school, and teachers get beat because they come to work. You also have rapes, which has been going on forever, girls get raped at school. We got a disease, and there are many causes, but it isn't a disease that just infected us. It's like HIV – it started long ago.

This individual, and most others, pinpointed poverty; alcohol and drugs; family breakdown; unemployment; perhaps gangs ('boys on the street'); and the 'disease' of violence. These are the typical factors that many researchers identify to account for school violence. But he also made reference to the long history of violence, in terms of rape: 'which has been going on forever'. Also in terms of general violence: 'We got a disease, and there are many causes, but it isn't a disease that just [now] infected us.' He also made reference to strikes, in particular a teacher's strike that has caused violence in schools.

Other individuals alluded to historical and political contexts when discussing school violence, not just social and economic contexts, as is the norm in most theorising. One trend that makes rates of school violence high in South Africa is the prevalence of violence that does not ordinarily take place in schools in countries like the United States (Palmary et al., 2003). In interviews and observations, problems involving rape, corporal punishment and gangs were repeated problems, and though these are problems in other schools in other nations, they appear more extensive in South Africa. It is possible that the high rates of school violence are caused because the country has the usual problems (poverty, breakdown of families and so on) that result in the usual forms of school violence (assault, robbery and so on); but additionally, schools must contend with a higher degree of violent gangs, more instances of rape and greater use of corporal punishment (though it is outlawed). And it is these forms of school violence that may hint at the importance of a theory of violence related to the political and historical context of the country.

Gangs

In an interview with a principal of a school in Orlando, Soweto, the principal claimed, 'If I had the power to change one thing to help deter school violence it would be get rid of the gangs.' Other interviews (and some observations) also highlighted the prevalence of gangs in instigating school violence. As in Europe and the United States, gangs in South Africa are very much linked to territory (gang members are usually from the same neighbourhood or street); are ethnically homogeneous (gangs tend to be all or most of one ethnic group); and they tend to unite for reasons having to do with solidarity, protection, financial gain and to ward off boredom (Eliasov & Frank, 2000; Pinnock, 1997; Steinberg, 2004). But additionally, the gangs of today to some extent grew out of the gangs of the past that formed under the apartheid system of government, sometimes as units to battle apartheid forces.

There is much debate regarding the intent and origination of gangs in South Africa. This is because, firstly, there are many kinds of gangs from different regions of the country and a single explanation for why they were formed cannot account for this multiplicity. Second, it is not entirely clear whether or not gangs developed as anti-apartheid forces or for typical gang reasons. Glaser (1998a) was careful to point out that there was often tension between student groups who battled apartheid and gang members. He also noted that when students were associated with *tsotsis* (thugs) this tarnished the reputation of the anti-apartheid fighters who wanted to distinguish themselves from gang members. But Glaser (1998a) also pointed out that in time, especially in the 1980s, gang members became more politically driven. The term *comtsotsi* was used in the media and in conversations starting in the late 1980s to describe groups who were a mix of gang member and political activist. It is an amalgamation of 'comrade' and *tsotsi* (Seekings, 1996).

Steinberg (2004) also pointed out how apartheid strengthened gangs in that it gave them a common enemy. She described how in her interviews with gang members all referred to themselves as anti-apartheid fighters and some even longed for the apartheid days for it had given their gangs a purpose and greater cohesion. Even if we do not accept that gang members of today evolved from past political fighters, and are therefore a consequence of apartheid, we must recognise the fact that many gangs evolved from communities that were constructs of apartheid. Cape Coloured Gangs, for example, including the ones that Steinberg studied, formed out of the Cape Flats, which was an apartheid construct created by the Group Areas Act. Soweto gangs, likewise, formed as a consequence of their circumstances in being relocated to the makeshift townships that apartheid policies created.

In other words, the gangs often formed around territory, as other gangs have, but their territories were formed by the apartheid government. In the Cape Peninsula area, for example, townships and informal settlements grew. These included the townships of Khayelitsha and Gugulethu, which were predominately Xhosa. During apartheid, Xhosas were often required to live in Bantustans where there was little work, so they moved to the Cape Flats clandestinely, adding to the over-crowding and competition for jobs and resources. As early as 1977 the new townships around Cape Town contained 50 per cent more people than they were designed for (Shaw, 2002). Violence escalated dramatically in schools and neighbourhoods. Bombings, assassinations and necklace murders were committed by warring gangs and off-shoots of these gangs took advantage of the chaos for financial gain, creating a criminal world that today extorts, robs and kills in schools and communities.

Without this understanding, we would not know what sense to make of the student who explained in an interview:

> The problem with gangs is that they have lost their purpose, so now they just roll [assault] people for money and for the fun of it. They always did this, but they were also on the side of those who fought the police. So they were useful too. But now, they come into schools all the time and take our money, rape our girls. Maybe we should bring back apartheid, then they'd start fighting the police again and leave us alone.

Apartheid gave many gang members a common enemy and helped to make gangs strong; apartheid also set in place the circumstances and 'relocations' around which gangs formed. Many gangs of today are a product of these past gangs and political circumstances. Schärf and Vale (1996) also pointed out how the crumbling of apartheid helped to propel gang activity of a more complicated and syndicated form. As apartheid was drawing to an end in the early 1990s, many gang members realised that the opening of borders and greater internationalism would give them more opportunities to develop or expand illegal drug networks, money laundering, and other business or white-collar crimes. Even the end of apartheid had a role to play in the direction that gangs took in their creation of criminal syndicates. Considering how researchers have identified gangs as a persistent problem in schools, these aspects of gangs – their history and political links – should inform theory. It would seem an oversight to not take into consideration the role that apartheid has played in the formation of gangs that even today plague many South African schools.

Rape

Unlike the United States, Israel, Australia, Europe and New Zealand, where many theories and interventions on violence prevention are developed, rape is a persistent problem in schools in South Africa. Very little school violence prevention addresses rape specifically. South Africa not only has rates of rape that are among the highest in the world, but school rape is not uncommon and is sometimes committed by teachers and administrators (Jewkes et al., 2002). A survey by the Medical Research Council (2000) found that 37.7 per cent of rape cases of youths, where individuals divulged their perpetrators, involved teachers and school administrators as perpetrators. In interviews conducted by Human Rights Watch (2001), girls described being raped in classrooms, bathrooms, hallways and school offices. In my own interviews, school administrators also included the problem of girls being raped on the way to and from school. One school principal, a woman, had demanded that shoulder-height grass around the school be cut and that teachers be stationed outside the school to accompany girls to the school gate. The grass had been cut to avoid possible hiding places for rapists. In interviews with girls, it was common for them to explain how they manoeuvred through school partly in efforts to avoid sexual assault and rape. One explained:

> Whenever it's time to leave class to go to our next room, I always leave fast because I don't want to be left in the room with a teacher alone. We [my friends and I] will walk together and we never go out on the fields. I always go to the bathroom with another girl. My mother told me to do this. She said if I ever went to the bathroom alone she'd punish me.

Her description was similar to the types of precautions a girl in the United States might make while navigating particularly dangerous streets late at night, but not a school during daylight. This particular girl said that she had never been raped, but male teachers had invited her to their houses and to stay after school, and she had no doubt what they intended. Statistics bear this out as well: in a study of 11,735 woman 15–49 years old, 95 per cent had been raped before the age of 15 and 33 per cent were victims of rape by teachers in school (Jewkes et al., 2002). Fellow male students are also perpetrators, often 'jack-rolling' (gang-raping) girls on school grounds or just outside the school. In a classroom discussion, the majority of boys who expressed their opinion about rape said that if a girl agreed to go out with them, and if they spent money on them, they should subject themselves to sex whether they liked it or not.

There is no doubt that rape in school is prevalent in South Africa, that girls must prepare themselves against possible advances, and that many boys do not see this as a problem. In the comments of boys, there was sometimes a bravado associated with rape. Many saw rape as a simple matter of teaching girls to know their place – to show them 'who is boss'. The Human Rights Watch (2001) report bears this out as well; boys who were interviewed expressed feelings that rape was a way of controlling girls, undermining their leadership and making them understand that they were 'below' boys. Morrell (2002; Morrell, Bhana & Hamlall, this book) has argued that all school violence is gendered, and this is especially true in rape cases. Certainly, high incidents of rape in schools in South Africa reflect the high incidents of rape in society; but it is also a product of the school environment that in many ways condones violence, where even teachers and administrators are commonly perpetrators. But this crisis in education did not just erupt, but has a long history that involves the use of rape as a technique of war, the emasculation of black males caused by apartheid, and the reluctance of administrators and the country's ruling party to take a strong stance against rape.

The prevalence of rape in school is partly the result of historical and political circumstances in South Africa. As Segel and Labe (1990, p. 257) noted the 'emasculation of men by the joint forces of racism and capitalism is producing a sense of impotence and rage which is being expressed through violence against women'. Glaser (1998b) saw a similar dynamic in the origins of some gangs, whose activities included jack-rolling (gang-raping). He noted that the emergence of gangs had a lot to do with masculinity, whereby boys demonstrated their manliness through gang affiliation, and most subsequent gang activity involved sexual coercion of girls, a way of boosting ones manliness.

Researchers of rape are clear in their assessment that rape is an assertion of power, and in a society and political system where men were rendered powerless, as apartheid did, it is likely that they will attempt to assert their power and regain their manliness through subjugation of women. In time, this becomes an accepted practice, supporting a patriarchic culture, so that even today it is accepted among boys that subjugation of women is normal and even desirable (Vogelman, 1990). Maitse (1999, p. 56) stated that in the South African context, the idea that rape is a product of 'social deprivation is not rooted in historical reality'. Through war, apartheid and the concerted efforts to destroy proper schooling for blacks, schools have become hotbeds for sexual violence. They lack the structures and sometimes the adults to take serious efforts to curb rape; the boys in them have been socialised to think of rape as normal (as have many of the girls); and there is a history of rape used as a war strategy and means of subjugation that creates a culture of rape acceptance. It is likely that these elements of the country's history and political situation have contributed to the high levels of rapes in schools.

Corporal punishment

Corporal punishment is a problem in many countries, especially those in Africa where it is a widespread form of violence, but often not seen as a form of school violence. In the United States and Europe, as well, corporal punishment is practised. Though it was banned in South Africa in 1996, corporal punishment is still practised, especially in schools where the majority of students are black or coloured. Morrell (2001) noted that it is often considered a legitimate form of discipline partly because teachers do not feel that they have an alternative to corporal punishment; additionally, it is practised at home by parents who feel it is a logical form of punishment for their children. A 2003 survey of 952 parents confirms this finding; it was found that 57 per cent of the respondents with children used corporal punishment at home and 30 per cent had used it in the past month (Dawes et al., 2004). This is one of the biggest barriers to discontinuing corporal punishment in school: many parents are advocates of the practice.

Corporal punishment in South Africa is clearly connected to colonialism. It was common practice in colonial schools to whip and cane children for infractions of school rules and for performing poorly. In his study of colonialism and corporal punishment in Northern Nigeria, Pierce (2001) examined how corporal punishment was a way of dramatically subjecting 'natives' to colonial rule, in which the body becomes a site for marking one with the power of the state. This is not to say that is it a form of violence practised only by white adults against black children. In many schools in South Africa where teachers are black or coloured, it is also practised; also white students are sometimes punished corporally, though much less frequently than black and coloured students.

Though the practice has been outlawed it was used consistently in one school where research was conducted, and less consistently in two others. Incidents of corporal punishment were observed on several occasions; one teacher would purposely smack children on the knuckles with the wooden eraser to demonstrate in my presence how she was a good disciplinarian. In another case, a student was outside his classroom bleeding from the head, apparently after being hit with a cane by a teacher for stealing a hat. The security guard of one school walked around the perimeter of the school with a cane, which he'd use on children who would arrive late and tried climbing over the fence to get into school. Many of these students came from Soweto, and had to travel over an hour to Johannesburg and their lateness was often due to transportation problems.

There are many ways to make sense of corporal punishment. Some do not see it as a form of school violence, especially in the United States and Europe where it is becoming a less common means of discipline in school (though it is still practised, and in the United States still legal in nearly half the states). But a more international perspective on school violence would force us to recognise the seriousness of it. It is serious for several reasons: first, in some places it is widespread; second, it is state-sanctioned violence; and finally, it is sometimes brutal. What it means to be caned or whipped may include such severity that it leads to bruises, bleeding (as I observed), and even broken bones, cracked ribs, bald spots where hair is pulled out and other brutalities that cause hospitalisations (Holdstock, 1990). Corporal punishment is an extreme expression of authoritarian schooling developed during colonialism in order to suppress and infantilise black and coloured youths. But as mentioned before, it was also used in Afrikaner schools to discipline white children, so it would be a mistake to view it as a direct and sole result of colonialism. Other factors are also involved, such as religion, general disciplinary beliefs, traditionalism and outright aggressiveness by some adults. But how do we account for the extreme forms of corporal punishment, and its overwhelming popularity, specifically in Africa?

Certainly, colonialism plays a role, for it was during colonialism that it developed as the most common and accepted way of disciplining 'natives'. Harber (1996, p. 159) called it part of 'a legacy of the authoritarian type of school organization and curriculum institutionalized during colonialism in the first part of the 20th century which has come to be regarded as "normal" '. Certainly, corporal punishment is practised in countries that did not experience colonialism, but there are some data that show it is most prevalent in countries that have experienced colonialism or have a history of authoritarian rule (Rao & Pierce, 2001). Even when we examine corporal punishment in light of the fact that it is practised very often by blacks who have been beaten themselves as children, or grew up under apartheid – who were in essence victims of corporal punishment and oppression – we can understand these circumstances as well as related to history and politics, for numerous studies have shown that 'violence breeds violence' (Fry, 1993; Haugaard & Feerick,

1996). It is likely that those who have been beaten will beat others; teachers who as students were beaten will beat students. This too is an outcome of a history that has not only condoned violence but also socialises a society to view violence as a normal response to unacceptable behaviours.

Conclusion: A histo-political theory of school violence

As noted, there are many theories accounting for school violence. In the context of South Africa, it would seem that social disorganisation theory, along with strain theory and control theory, is relatively persuasive in accounting for high rates of violence in schools. It is possible that other theories have merit as well, but given the severe level of poverty in the country, the strains on families caused by poverty, HIV/AIDS, unemployment and other relentless social problems, and the general breakdown of many communities, it would seem that these three theories – that deal most specifically with the social context of school violence – would have pertinence. Indeed, there is plenty of evidence to suggest that school violence in South Africa is an extension of a troubled society, and no doubt, to some extent it is. But as countries in Africa, South America, the Middle East and elsewhere transition from war-torn countries to relative stability, as has been the case with South Africa, one must wonder if the old theories, that were after-all developed primarily by scholars in countries that had not experienced such transitions, are in fact valid. In other words, theories developed in the mid-twentieth century in the United States, Western Europe and the Untied Kingdom to account for violence in their own countries may not hold true in the twenty-first century in the context of post-colonial and war-torn countries, or, for that matter, any country with drastically different political and historical circumstances.

In their study of school violence in 37 countries, including South Africa, Akiba et al. (2002) analysed cross-national data that suggested that school violence is not directly related to the level of violence in society in general. This debunks much research that draws a clear connection between juvenile violence and school violence: where there are high rates of violence in society at large, one can expect high rates of violence in schools. They also found that school violence is related to absolute deprivation in a country (the overall poverty level of the country) and age distribution (where there are more young people, there are greater incidents of violence), but not necessarily to relative deprivation (economic inequality and stratification) or to social integration factors, involving divorce rates and racial, ethnic and linguistic het-erogeneity. They suggest that school violence is better accounted for by examining within-school factors: that, for example, improving the quality of education for all children may have a more positive effect than eradicating social problems in the greater society. Where they did notice a correlation between school violence and society at large, it had to do with GDP, which they saw as the only national variable that contributed to school violence, once characteristics of schools were controlled. It would seem that school violence is greater in developing countries.

Yet, how do we account for the fact that social indicators are not always a good measure of school violence, but that GDP often is, and that when cross-national analyses are undertaken, it appears that developing countries have higher rates of school violence? Based on my own reading of cross-national data, combined with the research presented here, it appears that a country's development, though related to school violence, is also related to its past political situation. While South Africa is probably more developed than most 'developing countries' it has many of the hallmarks of a developing country, many of which are related to its historical and political situation, specifically apartheid, which has left the country a legacy of violence which distinguishes it from more developed countries. For example, though problems of school violence are relatively severe in the United States, schools in the United States do not usually contend with rape, severe corporal punishment and gangs to the extent that South Africa does. A brief examination of the 37 countries where data demonstrated high percentages of school violence, we find in fact that the United States has moderately average rates of school violence (Akiba et al., 2002). Countries that have high rates of school violence included, for example, Hungry, Romania, Philippines, Cyprus, South Africa and Latvia, each of which have recently gone through, or are going through, a period of unrest and political transition. In comparison, those countries where students report fewer incidents of school violence included Denmark, Singapore, Switzerland, Norway, Belgium and Sweden – countries that have experienced in recent years much more political stability than those countries with higher rates of violence (with the exception of Singapore, perhaps).

One would have to test the validity of such a hypothesis: that in an international context, school violence, though related to social and school contexts, may foremost be related to historical and political contexts. To do this, more quantitative research needs to be done to determine actual rates of violence in schools so that accurate comparisons can be done. This is quite difficult for several reasons. As Astor et al. (2006) noted, different countries define school violence in different ways. For example, 'bullying' does not mean the same thing in all countries. In Hebrew the word for bullying implies physical violence by a larger individual; whereas in Japanese, the word for bullying has more to do with social isolation and shame (Astor et al., 2006; Yoneyama & Naito, 2003). For this reason, cross-national studies would do better to not study 'bullying', per se, but to instead study more specific behaviours: for example, 'How often have you been verbally ridiculed' is a better question than 'How often have you been bullied?'

International analyses are difficult because data are not always reliable. For example, the research in the cross-national study conducted by Akiba et al. (2002) relies on student and teacher reports, which may or may not be accurate. Also, teacher reports in their research deal specifically with disruptions in math and science classes, since the data came from TIMSS, which may not adequately represent teachers in other subject areas. These are shortcomings that represent the difficulty of both gathering and interpreting cross-national data.

Implications for practice

Only recently have researchers, in spite of the challenges, recognised the importance of a more international theory on school violence. Can we apply the old theories, most of which were developed in a national (or more limited) context, to newer international contexts? Do theories developed to explain violence in the United States and the United Kingdom apply to other countries as well? It is likely that in some countries issues of religion, civil war and government repression may play a role in school violence. With a more international theory, not only may we develop better ways of understanding traditional forms of violence, but we might find ourselves facing the unfortunate task of dealing with forms of school violence, such as rape and corporal punishment, that are virtually dismissed in traditional, more localised analyses. Certainly more quantitative research that checks for correlations between high rates of school violence and political volatility in countries is needed. Is it possible that some forms of political volatility and government repression actually keep a lid on school violence? Do countries with similar political histories have similar forms of school violence (i.e., rape), or do countries with similar political histories experience different forms and rates of school violence, and if so, why? Does this mean that a histo-political theory does not apply in cross-national contexts, or could it mean that other factors, such as religion, may also come into play, so that a more nuanced political theory that takes into account school, social and individual-level factors, in conjunction with a histo-political theory, is needed. If nothing else, a more international perspective forces researchers of school violence to grapple with these questions, not in order to dismiss other theories, but to add to them a more global context.

3
FYI… Virtual Space Has a Context: Towards an Alternative Frame for Understanding Cyberbullying

Amy Chapman and Rachel Buchanan

Whether we like it or not, computer-generated realities are networked into our everyday lives. From simple financial transactions and communicating via email to participation in social networking sites, writing personal blogs, video posting on YouTube and the formation of avatars to navigate online or as new identities for virtual worlds such as *Second Life*, digital communication and online participation is ubiquitous. The popularity and currency for young people of having an online presence suggests that there is something motivating them to shift their social space and relationships into the virtual. Whilst often these connections or networks offer opportunities for friendships to flourish, they also provide a platform for negative and distressing relationships, sometimes dominated by persistent and aggressive communication – or cyberbullying.

Despite a growth in research and practice dealing with cyberbullying, many questions are yet to be posed, let alone answered. Given the limited theoretical discourse regarding cyberbullying (Dooley et al., 2009), our aim in this chapter is to contribute to the conceptual and theoretical discussion of cyberbullying whilst we explore a number of social and cultural influences impacting upon young people's negotiation of virtual space. Drawing on diverse orientations, such as sociology, poststructuralism, postmodern feminist and technological theories, we move towards developing an alternate framework for conceptualising cyberbullying. We provide an examination of the available research on cyberbullying to demonstrate that this literature forms a normative discourse that positions young people as either bullies or victims in cyberspace and ignores the wider social context and emerging online socio-cultural practices. With the aim of identifying these dominant discourses currently at play in the cyberbullying discussion, this chapter will first provide a summary of research in the field, and second propose a potential alternative conceptual framework that could be employed to expand the investigation.

The bullied and bullies in the terrain of cyberspace

Young people are now enmeshed in a technological world. International studies suggest that adolescents are spending increasing amounts of time online (Boyd & Marwick, 2009). This is evident in Australia, where, as of 2007, 91 per cent of Australian families have Internet access (ACMA, 2010). For young Australians, online participation is the second most popular media activity after watching television (ACMA, 2010). This digital immersion puts them at risk of experiencing cyberbullying (Englander et al., 2009).

A relatively recent phenomenon, cyberbullying is not well understood. Although it has been the focus of increasing research in diverse areas such as sociology, education, law and psychology, the diversity of approaches evident in the study of cyberbullying has resulted in incoherence in the field (Schrock & Boyd, 2011; Tokunaga, 2010). The differing definitions of cyberbullying has resulted in an inconclusive understanding of rates of prevalence, the significance of gender, the ages of those affected and the relationship of cyberbullying to education.

Several researchers draw upon the definition offered by Bill Belsey, a Canadian activist working to reduce cyberbullying:

> The use of information and communication technologies such as email, cell phone and pager text messages, instant messaging, defamatory personal websites, and defamatory online personal polling Websites, to support deliberate, repeated, and hostile behaviour by an individual or group, that is intended to harm others.
>
> (cited by Campbell et al., 2008, p. 21)

The organisation founded by Belsey (www.stopcyberbullying.org) suggests that cyberbullying involves only young people – defined as children, pre-teens or teens – and argues that for an incident to be understood as cyberbullying minors have to be involved on both sides; the involvement of adults means that something else is occurring – cyber harassment or cyber stalking. For Belsey, except in the case of death threats, cyberbullying is not a one-time communication; repetition is a key facet of the definition offered by Belsey and subsequently drawn upon by other researchers (Campbell, 2005; Dooley et al., 2009).

Belsey's definition is not universally used, and this could shed light on the divergent incidence rates seen in the literature. Some researchers do not include 'repeated' in the definition of cyberbullying that they draw upon, and thus one-time communications can be understood as cyberbullying. Also, others do not limit cyberbullying to events that only include children and have thus researched adults' experiences of cyberbullying (Coyne et al., 2009; Englander et al., 2009). Willard offers the following definition, which focus on the medium as the defining feature of cyberbullying: 'Using the internet or cell phones to send hurtful messages or post information that's designed to damage the reputation or friendships of others' (in McLoughlin et al., 2009, p. 178). Such differing definitions have resulted in inconclusive data on the incidence of cyberbullying; in addition many surveys are based on self-reporting – which can be problematic on account of participants differing and inconsistent understandings of cyberbullying, and social desirability which may inhibit people from reporting bullying behaviours on their part (Menesini & Nocentini, 2009).

The research on cyberbullying and gender has thus far produced inconsistent findings (Tokunaga, 2010). Several studies report that gender is not a factor in cyberbullying (Hinduja & Patchin, 2008; Patchin & Hinduja, 2006; Ybarra et al., 2007). This conflicts with studies that have found that boys are more likely to engage in cyberbullying than girls (Li, 2007); conversely Kowalski and Limber (2007) report that girl cyberbullies outnumber boys. It has also been reported that females are disproportionally the victims (Li, 2007; Schrock & Boyd, 2011; Ybarra & Mitchell, 2008). Schrock and Boyd (2011) hypothesise that different patterns of online participation may affect the likelihood of being a cyberbully or a victim. For example, males are found to post more personal information online (placing them at higher risk of being cyberbullied), and females post more images; similarly males are more likely to have a public profile and females more likely to have private profiles.

Some initial explorations of gender, aggression and cyberbullying have suggested that females are more often both victims (Li, 2007; Schrock & Boyd, 2011) and aggressors (Kowlaski & Limber, 2007). Ponsford suggests that cyberbullying is used by female perpetrators as it fits the norms of female relational aggression which 'stems from the way in which society constructs meaning about what it means to be a girl, and how girls are taught to display aggression' (2007, p. 4). Wood (2007) argues that direct aggression is discouraged in girls and encouraged in boys – thus children learn to express aggression differently due to socially learned gender roles. Cyberbullying then is theorised as being an attractive medium for female relational aggression as the bullying is indirect, and fits in with the accepted norms of female behaviour (Ponsford, 2007).

Much research suggests that cyberbullying is an extension of school-yard bullying (Hinduja & Patchin, 2011; Wong-Lo & Bullock, 2011). Within mainstream conceptions of bullying, the discourse of the bully and victim is tantamount. The pathology of the bully or 'perpetrator' (Shariff, 2008) is often highlighted. It is claimed that bullies can exhibit the quality of leadership (Olweus, 2001). They enjoy successful social relations with peers and teachers (DiGiulio, 2001) and 'are generally drawn by the need for power and recognition in order to make up for a lack of confidence and self-assurance' (Shariff, 2008, p. 17). 'Targets' or 'victims', on the other hand, are characteristically marked for exclusion (Olweus, 2001). The social categories of ethnicity, religion, social class and gender often provide justifications for selecting victims. Scholarly reviews on bullying also point out that until recently research has mostly been conducted by those working in the domain of psychology who view bullying as a developmental issue amongst children (Smith & Brain, 2000).

Ringrose and Renold (2010) depart from such approaches by examining bullying as a normative discourse. Explicitly drawing attention to their proclaimed feminist poststructural position, Ringrose and Renold introduce the questions:

> What does it mean to be called a bully or victim at school given the wider public meanings of such categories?.... What does it mean when the concept of 'bullying', which largely ignores socio-cultural dimensions of power and identity, constitutes the dominant discursive framework through which schools can interpret and intervene...?
>
> (p. 574)

They assert that to be positioned as bully or victim was neither 'desirable nor powerful' (p. 582) for young people. We agree that discourses portraying youth both as needing to be protected whilst also being protected from themselves can hide the complex contextual dynamics behind cyberbullying practices and fail to examine how patterns of social categories, power and aggression make their way from the schoolyard and into cyberspace in ways that often confound the bully/victim dichotomy.

According to Gonick (2004) this bully/victim discourse has been particularly troubling for girls in that their aggressive expression has actually been positioned as being both pathologised and naturalised. Ringrose (2006) considers how feminism has been enfolded through the contradictory 'post-feminist' narrative of the 'mean girl' or 'relational aggressor'. Deconstructing girls supposed natural tendencies towards 'relational aggression', she argues that the 'mean girl' 'is firmly rooted in feminist cultural theories of feminine difference, through which a developmental psychology debate over girls "indirect" and "relational" aggression has been staged' (p. 406).

> This universalisation and normalization of girl meanness elides complex differences among girls and vastly different familial, community and educational contexts under which femininity, aggression and violence are to be constituted and regulated. The new universal mean girl works to mask how much of the concern and controversy over 'indirect' and 'relational' aggression surrounds 'saving the selves' of primarily white and middle-class girls.
>
> (Pipher, cited in Ringrose, 2006, p. 407)

We share the concern that 'the bully/victim binary offers few material or practical resources ... to articulate or address the social content of meanings of their conflict. It also has a very problematic discursive effect of engendering heightened defensiveness, anger and anxiety' (Ringrose & Renold, 2010, p. 587). Cyberbullying, like almost all acts of youth aggression, is the outcome of the complex interaction between individual, social, cultural and relational influences which are in need of further investigation.

It is then to an examination of the socio-cultural context of young people's digital participation that we now turn. Boyd and Marwick urge this change in focus:

> For many youth, technology is part of their everyday lives, and must be examined in that context. The key to addressing online safety is to take a few steps back and make sense of the lives of youth, the risks and dangers they face, and the personal social and cultural logic behind their practices.
>
> (Boyd & Marwick, 2009, p. 410)

We seek to offer a tentative exploration of the context in which cyberbullying occurs. The following discussion has been written with the intention of being speculative and invitational rather than definitive and conclusive with the aim being to examine the wider digital practices and participation of young people so we can begin to think about cyberbullying as a form of youth aggression that takes place within a socio-cultural context that can stimulate, promote, reinforce and rationalise aggression and bullying acts.

Towards a 'youth culture' POV: Alternative frames for thinking about cyberbullying

'Socialising' and 'entertainment' are considered to be the most widespread uses, particularly for the 14–17 and 18–24-year-old groups, of mobile phone and Internet use in the Australian community (ACMA, 2008). Such information communication technologies (ICTs), it has been argued, have transformed the ways in which many young people not only establish and maintain their social networks and relations but also the way young people present themselves and their identities (Cooper et al., 2000). Oksman and Turtianinen (2004), drawing on the work of sociologist Erving Goffman, propose that the current media landscapes created by teenagers actually constitutes new forms of interaction whether it be through the creation of a personal space, self-presentation or relations with others. This creation of a digital identity or a digital space where one can display one's personality has been characterised as being a performative strategy of masquerade, a playful process of appropriation (Kenway & Bullen, 2005; Mallan, 2009). The creation of online identities is a relatively new form of identity formation and as such the rules are still being developed. Although online participation is attractive 'flashy, fast, frenetic, fantastic and fun' (Kenway & Bullen, 2005, p. 35), 'such pleasures as consumer-media culture evokes comes with both benefits and costs' (p. 37).

By conceptualising cyberbullying as being located within these socio-cultural practices of online participation, we propose, in a similar view to Oksman and Turtianinen, alternate approaches to thinking about cyberbullying. We proffer such understandings as a way of beginning to 'think differently' about cyberbullying so as to more fully appreciate how some young people are rewriting their identities 'not [in] a global village, but a shifting landscape of individual and collective identities, one inhabited by individuals situated in specific historical and cultural contexts' (Hawisher & Selfe, 2000, p. 285).

A (cyber)room of one's own

An alternative place to start an examination of cyberbullying from a socio-cultural perspective would be to examine why young people spend so much time online and to examine what it is that they actually do. Ito (2008) argues, 'particularly since the advent of the television, and even more with the advent of the Internet, children's media have become a mechanism for kids to get "out" more, in virtual and imaginary spaces produced through media networks' (p. 201). In addition to this, Giroux (2006) asserts that there is very little available cultural space for young people. Media representations of youth usually portray teens as out of control, dangerous forces; youth are simultaneously demonised and idolised, leaving them in the paradoxical position of being highly regulated, protecting them from the outside world and the outside world from them. He asserts that public space has been captured by corporate forces leaving little non-commodified public culture for youth to access. The lives of teenagers are highly structured, between school and home commitments, and for many teens the attraction of the Internet is that it facilitates participation in 'unregulated publics while located in adult-regulated physical spaces such as homes and schools' (Boyd, 2007, p. 21).

Boyd (2007) notes that use of social networking sites function as ways for teens to construct their identities and type themselves into being; that is, they are creating and maintaining an 'informal identity that is acknowledge[d] by others in a shared cultural space' (Willis, 2003, p. 407). This is achieved through the creation of a profile on sites such as MySpace, Facebook; one's profiles allows for the display of things such a photo or avatar representing oneself, lists of things one likes (music, movies, etc.) and a list of friends. These profiles are increasingly important for young people, functioning not just as a public display of their relationships but as an online space in which they present themselves (Boyd, 2007; Mallan, 2009).

The idea of a 'digital bedroom' (Sefton-Green & Buckingham, 1998) assists in furthering this conceptualisation of young people's online participation. When young people are on the net browsing, chatting, playing or bullying, the site is often a computer in someone's bedroom (the most accessible unregulated space for young people in the regulated space of the household). Mitchell and Reid-Walsh (2002) suggest that both boys and girls of all ages participate in a type of 'domestic or bedroom culture' (p. 151) located in virtual space when they are on the Web. They note in their discussion of homepages created by young girls: 'the girls' mindset of playing on the computer as a popular culture activity in a private space' (p. 151) suggests that wherever the physical location of the computer in the home (be it in the bedroom or living room) young people conceive of virtual space as a type of 'bedroom culture'.

But a room that no one sees is worse than not having a space at all. In the context of the Internet:

> you are what you share...In the economy of ideas that the web is creating, you are what you share – who you are linked to, who you network with and which ideas, pictures, videos, links or comments you share.
>
> (Leadbeater, 2008, pp. xi, 6)

Understanding cyberculture as a form of bedroom display gives us an alternative understanding of the context of cyberbullying. Pegrum describes those who end up publicly ridiculed as 'early casualties in a massive, unplanned social experiment, where the rules for self-presentation and socialisation are evolving minute by minute' (2009, p. 57).

One recent solution to the problems created by such bedroom display has been documented in popular media as the practice of 'personal branding'. 'Parents must teach children as young as eight how to craft a "personal brand" ' (Narushima, 2011) to avoid the disastrous consequences of social media sites that threaten both to illuminate and to record the worst of adolescent behaviour. Cultivating an acceptable personal brand via social networking sites takes place when social network users are held to account and regulate their bedroom displays by the imagined gaze of a 'local justice of the peace, your future boyfriend, the man you're going to marry, the mother-in-law of the man you're going to marry and your future employer for the job of your dreams' (Williams, cited in Narushima).

The complexity of such a representation is undeniable: 'digital literacy is tricky. It's easy to write your narrative badly or organise your display clumsily and find yourself misunderstood or ostracised...and out of a relationship or a job' (Pegrum, 2009, p. 57). It is not just a matter of 'being' cyber, but 'doing' cyber. In other words, the performance of a cyber identity is necessary for the subject position to be not only recognised but also to be taken seriously. And such a performance necessitates an awareness of the representations that will enable such recognition. Spaces where you can display yourself such as Facebook, MySpace and Bebo carry an inherent danger, in that the rules are not clearly defined and people that represent themselves poorly might find themselves paying a high price.

Using Foucault (1979), for whom the exercise of disciplinary power could be thought about using to Jeremy Bentham's notion of the 'Panopticon' (Foucault, 1979, p. 200), this high price, it could be argued, is enacted via the mechanism of surveillance. By relying on techniques of coercion through a method of observation, the Panopticon was an apparatus by which those in power are the observers of those whom power is exercised upon. In terms of cyberbullying, in essence young people's digital space is subject to the apparatus, whereby 'TheirSpace' is always surveyed by a broader online community, thus enabling inmates, residents (or in this case, young people online) to be under the gaze of an official at all times (Foucault, 1979, pp.170–174). Thus in this conceptualisation, the cyber room may be a room of one's own, but it is a space subject to continual surveillance.

To friend or not to friend that is the question

In contemporary life, words, images and their users infiltrate our lives via email, Facebook and MySpace updates, and texts messages, sometimes to the point of saturation. Through such technologies, the sheer number and assortment of relationships in which we are participating, the frequency of contact, intensity and endurance and relations are changing.

Although described as digital town square, cyberspace would be better understood as a series of networked relationships, especially when considering young people's online participation. Young people are increasingly dependent upon digital participation for inclusion in their peers groups (APA, 2009; Boyd, 2007). Boyd's research makes it clear that for young people online participation is less about interaction with strangers but more about the 'public display of connection' between those one already knows. And for Willis, although young people's online participation is about the formation of an identity, simultaneously it is 'also about [the] putative, comparative, and hierarchical social placing of [that] identity' (Willis, 2003, p. 407).

For example, comments posted underneath a YouTube clip of a segment that aired on national network television regarding a bullying incident between two high school students that took place in Australia in early 2011 state:

> This guy is such a load of steaming pile of crap I can smell it! You are a bloody liar. Even if he did say that to you it doesn't mean you should go and hit him you idiot!

bet little skinny buck toothed bitch has a little weiner...he kinda looks inbred and mildly retarded...cracker aussie.

(http://www.youtube.com/watch?v=__IjcLVBBYc_)

Classed, raced, gendered and heteronormative discourses are clear in these comments, highlighting the way in which online participation amplifies the gendered, classist, racist and sexualised hierarchies that exist offline (Pegrum, 2009). Bailey points out an important subtlety for initial considerations of how existing marginalising discourses find their way into cyberspace: 'It is important to distinguish between the cyber-subject as a figure produced by current thought about cyberspace and the actual people who enter cyberspace every day' (2011, p. 339). In this way it is possible to consider a digital divide, not only in terms of access to ICTs (Buchanan & Chapman, 2010), but also as cybersubjects who are shaped through online representations that are intertwined with the production and reproduction of sexual and gendered identities, racial divisions and classed hierarchies.

Marginalisation based on embodied categories seem conflicting to those who assert that the dream of virtual space is all about the actual obsolescence of the body. This bodily elimination, whose aim has been to open up possibilities for creating new, self-ruling identities (Poster, 1997), free of the restrictions of socially imposed categories of sex, gender, race and class (Haraway, 2000), do not seem to be so liberatory in considerations of cyberbullying. That online communication has enabled the many forms of communication now available to us is undeniable, but it may also be salutary to remind ourselves that both our online and face-to-face communication runs the risk of being increasingly less intimate and depersonalised (Laura & Chapman, 2009).

This notion of 'the face' as central to our capacity to intimately relate to others has been developed by numerous philosophers, particularly Emmanuel Levinas and Judith Butler. Butler (2009), drawing on Levinas, claims 'violence is one "temptation" that a subject may feel in the encounter with the precarious life of the other that is communicated through the face. This is why the face is at once a temptation to kill and an interdiction against killing' (p. 172). The absence of the 'face' in online communication may actually depersonalise our interactions so much so that we conceive of different lives in ways where some lives seem to count while others barely feature at all. This raises key questions around the nature of embodiment in cyberspace and may hold ramifications for considering the socio-cultural context of young peoples' aggressive interactions in the virtual world.

Such dehumanising characteristics were illustrated in a recent incident reported in the popular media documenting how students from schools located in some of Sydney's affluent suburbs were involved in the broadcasting of sexual remarks online with social networking being used to rate school students on their sexual exploits (Stevenson & Moses, 2011). The article, printed on the front page of one of the largest circulating papers in the country, reported that the 'Rootrater' site had posted offensive slurs and abusive comments predominantly about young women. About one girl an anonymous poster had written:

> She goes all right but she had a really hairy bum whole [sic] and she squirts too much.
>
> (cited in Stevenson and Moses, 2011)

> Another poster wrote of a girl: Chunky thighs, huge arse… always available for a root for those who are hard up.
>
> (cited in Stevenson and Moses, 2011)

Despite its online nature, the gaze of female bodies is evident, and includes a demand for attractiveness with the context of being heterosexually desirable. This is much the same way that children's offline identity work and peer relationships are subject to pressures that replicate exiting marginalising discourses (Renold, 2000).

Thus, for us, an exploration of cyberculture cannot rest on an examination of individual practice – the examination must be widened to consider the emerging dimensions of spatiality and interpersonal relationships; these offer a starting point to investigate how the gendered, classed and racist aspects of the offline socio-cultural context become magnified in cyberspace.

The lure of the 'Virtual' arena

The idea that we are living in a new time – an 'Information Society' comprised of 'Virtual Space' – is a persuasive, if not seductive and sometimes frightening perspective. Envisaging the 'global virtual community' as a warm and fuzzy place where 'we can all be friends' misses much of the complexity of what may be really at stake. 'The global village narrative, it is becoming clear, simply will not work for much of the world in the next century – it is too reductive, too western, too colonial in its conception' (Hawisher & Selfe, 2000, p. 286). Such a context provides us with a thought-provoking point of departure for our consideration of cyberbullying and its socio-cultural context, as young people begin to grapple with the questions of what it means to be embodied beings in this technological world.

Whilst it is not our intention in this chapter to capture the complexity of such a position, we do hope to work towards identifying how notions of cyberbullying can be located within this wider context in order to generate alternative understandings of the problem. Our earlier examination of some of the socio-cultural practices associated with young people's online communication reveals that cyberbullying can be situated in the context of young people using online participation as a process of identity formation, supplementing the traditional means of identity formation that they have available to them with new digital means (Mallan, 2009) dominated by notions of spatiality and networks and troubled by the notion of embodiment. This growing cultural emphasis on technological change and digital knowledge is noted by Willis, who states:

> Youth are always among the first to experience the problems and possibilities of the successive waves of technical and economic modernisation that sweep through capitalist societies. Young people respond in disorganised and chaotic ways, but to the best of their abilities and with relevance to the actual possibilities of their lives as they see, live and embody them. These responses are actually embedded in the flows of cultural modernisation, but to adult eyes they may seem to be mysterious, troubling, and even shocking and antisocial. Schools are one of the principal sites for the dialectical playing out of these apparent disjunctions and contradictions, which misunderstood, underlie some of the most urgent education debates.
>
> (2003, p. 391)

His analysis illuminates the moral panic around young people's digital participation, and why cyberbullying is reported in sensational terms, with little regard for why young people are engaged online as opposed to elsewhere. Willis suggests that we should be paying more attention to youth culture, as it is increasing the way that young people identify themselves, as they become 'less defined by neighbourhood and class than they are by these new relations of commodity and electronic culture' (2003, p. 402).

Conclusion: Beyond the bully/victim dichotomy

Whilst it is in no way our purpose here to deny that cyberbullying is an act of aggression that has serious repercussions for both the victims and perpetrators of the acts, that it represents a serious issue for parents, educators and policy makers (Couvillon & Ilieva, 2011), our aim is to explore how the current positioning may have stifled us in thinking about many of the socio-cultural complexities contributing to the occurrence of cyberbullying. Our research on cyberbullying reveals that little is known about the topic outside of the pathologising bully/victim dichotomy. The lack of deeper theoretically informed knowledge on this topic brings to mind Apple's warning that lack of knowledge may be a form of control; for '[t]o know is to be subject to demands' (2010, p. 10). For all the reasons that cyberbullying is fraught – the larger audience, the permanence of the written word, the lack of inhibition that comes with anonymity – we need to explore what it is the Internet illuminates. We urge a closer examination of the wider cultural practices that are driving young people online. We seek a fuller appraisal of youth culture, one that takes account of the ways that young people have managed to create spaces, identities and relationship displays for themselves, all within a context that is still very much gendered, classed, raced and heteronormative. Illumination of online socio-cultural practices will hopefully shed greater light on the factors hidden by the bully/victim dichotomy.

Part II
Gender and School Violence

4
Sexual Harassment in Schools: Issues of Identity and Power – Negotiating the Complexities, Contexts and Contradictions of This Everyday Practice

Kerry H. Robinson

Introduction

Over the past three decades educational researchers in Australia, United States, United Kingdom and Canada, in particular, have provided an extensive overview of the practice of sexual harassment in high schools and its impact on the students and teachers who experience and/or witness this behaviour (Brown et al., 2007; Epstein, 1997; Gruber & Fineran, 2007; Halson, 1991; Herbert, 1992; Howard & England Kennedy, 2006; Jones, 1985; Keddie, 2007; Klein, 2006; Larkin, 1994; Leach & Sitaram, 2007; Mahony, 1985, 1989; Renold, 2002; Robinson, 1996, 2000, 2005c). Much of this research reinforces that sexual harassment is an integral part of schooling cultures, experienced on a daily basis, and is often dismissed or rendered invisible through its 'normalisation' within hegemonic discourses of gender and sexuality, especially heterosexuality. However, the 'everydayness' of this widespread practice in schooling and its foundations within socio-cultural relations of identity and power continue to be eclipsed by the dominant discourse of sexual harassment as stemming from the psychopathological behaviours of problematic individuals. Further, in more recent years sexual harassment in schools has tended to be viewed within the more general framework of bullying, which is also constituted within psychopathological discourses. Within this context, sexual harassment becomes both depoliticised and increasingly more invisible (Brown et al., 2007).

Based on empirical qualitative research undertaken with students and teachers in both co-educational and single sex boys' and girls' high schools in Australia, this chapter explores the multiple, complex and contradictory nature of sexual harassment. This research reinforces the view of sexual harassment in schools as a widespread socio-cultural phenomenon, but it goes further to suggest that this practice is integral to the constitution and regulation of identities. It also examines the ways in which sexual harassment is utilised to constitute and regulate schooling practices and organisational hierarchies of power, such as those associated with authority. To understand sexual harassment, a feminist poststructuralist and discursive theoretical approach is incorporated in this discussion (Doughty, 2006; Foss & Rogers, 1994; Robinson, 2005c; Wood, 1994), with a particular focus on the ideas and concepts of Michel Foucault. A discursive theoretical approach makes it possible to gain a greater awareness and understanding of the complexities, contexts and contradictory nature of sexual harassment. How individuals perceive and react to sexual harassment is based on negotiating the various discourses operating in the context in which the behaviour is enacted or encountered. According to Michel Foucault (1974) knowledge is constituted within the discourses operating in society, which are historically and culturally formulated. He defined discourse as 'practices that systematically form the objects of which they speak' (1974, p. 49). Ball defines discourse in the following manner:

> [Discourses are] about what can be said and thought, but also about who can speak, when, and with what authority. Discourses embody meaning and social relationships, they constitute both subjectivity and power.
>
> (1990, p. 2)

As Robinson and Jones Diaz (2006, p. 29) point out, 'according to Foucault (1974), discourses operate through language and constitute the different knowledge we have available to us about the world and those in it'. As there are different versions of events or different ways of viewing and understanding issues, events, practices, individuals, groups and so on, there will be different discourses that constitute our knowledge or 'truths' about them. Foucault argues that our subjectivity or self is constituted in the discourses that we take up as our own. He also points out that power operates through discourse and that individuals negotiate the power relations that exist through their location within particular discourses available to them. Individuals are not fixed subjects, but are fluid and often contradictory; they can shift across discourses as a result of negotiating the power relations that exist and in terms of the 'investments' (Hollway, 1984) they have in a particular situation. For example, there are multiple discourses that constitute understandings of sexual harassment; and the multiple readings of this behaviour will influence the way this behaviour is either taken up by perpetrators as a means of power, control, or affirmation of identity, as well as the ways in which the behaviour is experienced. Consequently, reactions to sexual harassment are frequently contradictory, based on negotiations around the identity of the harasser, the person's relationship to the harasser, the identity of the person experiencing the harassment and the perceived consequences of reacting to the behaviour in certain ways, including the impact on the person's popularity within peer groups.

It is through everyday language and practices, constituted in discourse, that social structures, identities and social realities are created, shaped and regulated. Sexual harassment is normalised, naturalised and legitimated through everyday discursive practices, especially those of powerful groups, which create and recreate power relations and constitute the subject – for example, what it means to be a girl or a woman, or a boy or a man, which are relational categories (Bingham, 1994). Sexual harassment is viewed as a technology of power operating to regulate and police the constitution of identities, social and institutional practices and relationships, and to maintain hierarchies of power. Gender performativity (Butler, 1990) is utilised in this discussion to highlight the significance of sexual harassment in the constitution and regulation of gendered identities. Butler defines performativity as 'the aspect of discourse that has the capacity to produce what it names' (1994, p. 33). Sexual harassment is also a means through which institutional practices and hierarchies of power are perpetuated and regulated within schooling. Additionally, sexual harassment is a technology of power that operates to constitute the authoritative figure as the hegemonic masculine subject – a process that has implications for everyday disciplinary encounters in schools for those who do not fit within this context (Robinson, 2000).

Sexual harassment is not only a powerful normative regulator of gender and gendered relations, but is also utilised as a means of reinforcing and policing hegemonic socio-cultural relations of power associated with other aspects of identity such as sexual orientation, class, ethnicity and race. The multiplicity of these subject positions from which power is experienced and understood influences perceptions and experiences of sexual harassment. As Foss and Rogers (1994, p. 165) point out, 'The specificity and multiplicity of any individual's social positions complicate the application of generalizations about sexual harassment'. Although sexual harassment is primarily directed at girls and women, some boys and men, who do not take up hegemonic masculine performances of gender or sexuality, can find themselves the targets of various kinds of sexually harassing behaviours. The intimate intersections of sexual harassment with homophobic and heterosexist based forms of harassment are widely experienced by queer students and teachers, or those who are perceived to be queer.

Despite several decades of devising and implementing strategies to deal with sexual harassment in schools, or educational institutions more generally, there has been little success in effectively counteracting this behaviour. This is not surprising when one considers that current school policies and practices around sexual harassment generally do not see this behaviour as a widespread socio-cultural practice that operates everyday to constitute and regulate identities and relations of power. The urgency of counteracting the discursive and material constitution of sexual harassment as an integral component and regulator of the performance of hegemonic masculinity was recently highlighted in an Australian newspaper report on cases of sexual violence perpetrated by five- and six-year-olds on other children in primary schools in the state of Queensland (Hansen, 2010). Until the complexities, contradictions and the contexts of sexual harassment are considered within a socio-cultural framework, strategies will continue to miss the point of this practice.

The research in context and defining sexual harassment

This discussion is based on Australian qualitative research undertaken by the author in six New South Wales (NSW) government co-educational high schools. The research included surveys, focus groups and in-depth interviews with students, aged 12–17, and with teachers and administrators. It also involved undertaking observations of classroom and schoolyard activities over a 3-week period. The range of schools involved provided a diverse population of students and teachers from a variety of ethnicities, socio-economic backgrounds and geographical locations, including rural, coastal, industrial, suburban and metropolitan areas. It is important to acknowledge here that the sexual harassment and intervention practices identified in this research were similar across all the schools, with minimal differences occurring. Consequently, the discussion in this chapter talks generally about all the schools involved in the research, unless otherwise specified. It is also critical to point out that the sexual harassment experienced by teachers in this research, especially female teachers, was a serious issue experienced from peers, managers and students. Some girls also acknowledged experiencing sexual harassment from their female peers, which they acknowledged as being more problematic, primarily as they saw it as a serious breach of trust, often coming from girls in their friendship groups. However, this chapter focuses on the most common sexual harassment experiences occurring in these co-educational schools – the sexual harassment between girls and boys, that occurring between boys, and the sexual harassment of female teachers by boys.

What actually constitutes sexual harassment has been a focus of much debate since its conception in the 1960s. Definitions can vary considerably across disciplines. In terms of education, definitions can vary from country to country, across province/states and across school systems. In this research the term sexual harassment includes gender-based harassment, which contributes to the stereotyping of males and females as particular types of sexual subjects. The 'everydayness' of the socio-cultural practice of sexual harassment and its relationship with young people's lives is one that is often rendered invisible in representations of this phenomenon. Sexual harassment is a problematic term in many ways and the images that are frequently portrayed of this behaviour often reinforce the predominance of this phenomenon as an adults' issue occurring primarily in workplaces and tertiary educational contexts. It is most often represented as an issue facing women in non-traditional forms of work, where they threaten the masculine status quo, as depicted in the film *North Country* (Caro, 2006), or the boss/secretary scenario in the film *Nine to Five* (Higgins, 1980), and in contexts where those in authority positions use their power to elicit sexual favours from those with less institutional power – as depicted in the recent high-profile Australian case involving Kristy Fraser-Kirk, an employee of the retail company David Jones, who tried to sue the company for $37 million as a result of allegedly being sexually harassed by the former CEO of the company, Mark McInnes (Lahey, 2010). A figure of $850,000 was finally settled out of court (Jamal, 2010). These examples epitomised what students in this research commonly considered sexual harassment to entail, with very few students seeing the term as relevant or applicable to their lives or experiences.

Though it is important to have a definition of sexual harassment due to the legal implications of this behaviour, it is critical to point out that definitions often provide narrow understandings of this behaviour, including the way that it is experienced, the contexts in which it happens and who does the harassing and why. Traditional definitions most often dismiss the political nature of the behaviour, constituting the subject as generic, fixed and stable. As pointed out in the introduction, individuals are shifting subjects, negotiating a variety of discourses from their differing subjectivities when perceiving and responding to sexual harassment. Definitions of sexual harassment need to be sensitive to the socio-cultural nature of this phenomenon, to the local and specific experiences of this behaviour, to the complexities and contradictions of responses, to the links to identity and to the intersections of identity as well as to the multiple power relations operating around this behaviour.

Sexual harassment as performance of hegemonic masculinity

Prior to and during the time of writing this chapter, several major stories emerged in the Australian media about the culture of sexual harassment and sexual violence prevalent within groups of Australian elite football players, in areas of the Australian military and police force, and within an elite university college in one of Australia's most prestigious universities (Allard, 2008; Braithwaite, 2006; Pollard, 2009). All these incidents reflected a culture of sexual harassment and violence that was constituted within hegemonic masculinity and that was directed primarily towards women. In relation to the incident in the elite university college, it was reported that a group of male students, who identified themselves as anti-consent, set up a 'pro-rape' page in the sports and recreation section of *Facebook* (Pollard, *SMH*, 9/11/09). This incident epitomised what was described by a former male College Master as reflective of 'a form of tribalism' perpetuated in residential colleges, 'which could be and is probably well described as sexist'. What was particularly poignant in one of the reports was a comment made by a woman who had been raped in her room on campus, who stated, 'Boys who are intelligent, rational and lovely to women in their own personal life will still step up and protect one of their own in order not to be excluded' (Pollard, *SMH*, 9 November 2009, p. 8). What was particularly concerning was how all these reported incidents, including the sentiments expressed in this woman's comments, echoed the existence of a similar culture associated with hegemonic masculinity and sexual harassment in schools (Robinson, 2005c). In addition to these incidents, there was one in the United States, which was also featured in the media at this time, highlighting another dimension to the culture of violence associated with hegemonic masculinity in educational settings. Tyler Clementi, a Rutgers' freshman, suicided after being the victim of a homophobic incident in which he was unknowingly filmed having sex with another male student in his room, which was then broadcasted on the Internet (Foderaro, *SMH*, October 1, 2010).

In initial understandings of sexual harassment, feminists pertinently pointed out that this behaviour was not about sex but about power, focusing virtually exclusively on male power over females. However, as I have argued previously (Robinson, 2005c), in contrast to these earlier works, sexual harassment is also significantly about male power within male groups. Hegemonic masculinity, and how successfully it is performed, is often measured by the dominance, aggression and intimidation shown towards the 'Other' – the gendered, sexualised, racialised 'other' for example. In terms of the gendered 'other', it is girls and women, or those boys and men who take up less dominant forms of masculinity. Sexual harassment is integral to the performance of hegemonic masculinity and its use is considered a legitimate and expected means through which boys and men express and reconfirm their position within male peer groups.

Butler (1990) points out that the 'realness' of doing gender lies in its recitation and in the ability to compel belief in the 'authenticity' of the performance in others. For young men the judgements of their male peers are critical to the measurement of how successful they are at doing their masculinity. Butler's notion of performativity is useful for understanding the ways boys and men who locate themselves in the discourse of hegemonic masculinity assert their gendered subjectivities. It is crucial to point out that the concept of gender 'performance' is always one that is enacted within strictly defined cultural boundaries. Consequently, the performance of hegemonic masculinity constructs and reconstructs the hegemonic masculine subject, perpetuating the dominant social scripts of what is considered 'appropriate masculinity' in that group. How and where hegemonic masculinity is played out, culturally and historically, is the means through which hegemonic masculinity gets established, instituted, circulated and confirmed (Butler, 1994).

Sexual harassment becomes a practice that constitutes and helps cement gendered cultural bonds between those boys and men who take up this form of masculinity as their own, creating a sense of individual and collective identity. Sexual harassment becomes part of the embodiment of the performance of hegemonic masculinity through

these everyday articulated acts and gestures, constituting boys' masculine identities in the process. For young men who locate themselves in
this discourse of masculinity, doing their gender is made meaningful
through their engagement in the sexual harassment of girls, or through
the gendered and sexualised harassment of other boys and men who
are considered not to be performing their gender and sexuality cor-
rectly. The perspective that sexual harassment is something that some
boys and men 'have to do' becomes very real for some who are aware
of the consequences of not getting their performance of masculinity
right amongst their peers, including being the subject of similar harassment and violent punishments. This process has serious implications
for young women who find themselves the target of sexual harassment
from male friends, as pointed out in the following comment by Cynthia,
a senior high school student:

> I went through a bad time when I was called things, touched, forced
> to kiss boys, talked into other sexual things against my will, had
> rumours spread about me, had offensive telephone calls, pretty much
> everything. I spoke to friends about everything because I don't like
> to keep things bottled up, but I regret not telling someone who could
> have done something about it. The thing that hurt the most was the
> person who did most of these things to me was a male friend I trusted
> and cared about.

This comment by Cynthia highlights the ways that male 'friendship',
as a relational space, is performatively produced by men and boys.
It is a space in which trust co-exists with its violation, with its shifting nature dependent on negotiating the relations of power associated
with hegemonic masculinity and getting one's performance correct in
front of their male peers. The intensity of this cultural male bonding
can eclipse any relationships boys might have with girls. This experience reinforces the secondary status of the feminine subject within these
male peer groups, making a mockery of their personal friendships with
boys, and represents a serious breakdown in trust, which may always be
precarious in such relationships.

The normalisation of sexual harassment
in heterosexual relations

Sexual harassment is not only a technology of power through which the
normative hegemonic masculine subject is constituted and regulated,

but it is also integral to the constitution of the normative heterosexual subject (Jones, 1985; Renold, 2002). The performance of normative hegemonic masculinity is played out in relation to the normative heterosexual feminine subject, and vice versa – a relationship epitomised within what Judith Butler (1990) terms the heterosexual matrix. Sexual harassment acts to discipline, normalise and produce the 'appropriate' female subject, to regulate gendered behaviours, and to maintain hegemonic relations of power between males and females read within the context of heterosexuality. Within this process, sexual harassment becomes naturalised and normalised through the everyday language and practices of the hegemonic masculine subject – 'boys will be boys' – and is viewed and experienced by many girls as a consequence of their gender; as one young woman pointed out, sexual harassment is 'just a part of being a girl'. This everyday process of gendering renders many areas of sexual harassment invisible in the schooling context. As James, a junior high school boy, commented, 'sure we say and do things to girls, but no more than normal!'

Sexual harassment is often discursively constituted as an expression of sexual interest within heterosexuality. For some young men it is perceived to be a legitimate way to demonstrate their sexual interest in a young woman. As Peter, a senior high school student explained, boys often use sexual harassment 'because guys sometimes have to do things to get girls' attention, it's in our nature and some girls like some of these activities'. In fact many teachers participating in this research perpetuated this discourse, perceiving sexual harassment as a reflection of young men exploring, albeit rather 'awkwardly' and 'childishly', but certainly 'normally', an emerging awareness of the opposite sex and a demonstration that they have an interest in girls. Significantly, young men's sexual harassment of girls and women is a critical means through which to reconfirm their heterosexuality and reassure their male peers that they are legitimate masculine subjects. The perception of many teachers that boys' engagement in sexual harassment is no more than just 'immature' attempts at romance and a 'part of growing up' results in many instances of this behaviour being dismissed. As one male teacher commented:

> When you've got kids going through puberty I would imagine it [sexual harassment] happens constantly. They are at a time when they are evaluating what is acceptable and unacceptable behaviour. As far as kids are concerned most of it could be put into the category of growing up. What could be labelled a sexual harassment is possibly misunderstood. There would be very little of it.

Consequently, teachers often advised girls that they should not really feel threatened by this behaviour, that they should feel flattered in some way, and generally be more patient with boys as they move through this natural but awkward phase.

This tension between sexual harassment and sexual interest becomes problematic for young women to negotiate leading to conflicting and contradictory feelings and responses to the behaviour. The following comments from young women highlight this tension:

> If I like that boy it doesn't worry me, but if I don't I get angry.
>> (Mary, a Junior high school student)

> You get guys who sit there and check out the girls, they watch and say things to each other and call out things. That makes you feel uncomfortable unless of course you like one of them, then you're glad that he's noticed you, even if it's embarrassing.
>> (Melissa, a Senior high school student)

> It depends on the person doing it. You might like them so you don't mind too much.
>> (Julia, a Junior high school student)

Within the dominant discourse of femininity, attracting and keeping a male is representative of the successful heterosexual feminine subject (Hollway, 1984; Renold, 2005). For many young women, resisting or challenging boys' sexually harassing behaviours can mean risking too much. Resistance can result in losing the boys' attention and interest, losing a potential relationship, and ultimately losing one's popularity amongst peers – both male and female. As Alexis, a middle high school student points out, some girls will tolerate a great deal of sexual harassment, even from their boyfriends, despite their feelings, in order to 'keep' them:

> I hate the way he treats me sometimes, particularly in front of his mates, but if I say anything he just gets cut, so I don't say anything. I'm scared I will lose him if I do.

Negotiating and responding to sexual harassment is a complex process, requiring individuals to assess a broad range of critical issues associated with the multiple power relations they are encountering. One's subjectivity across gender, class, sexuality, race and so on will significantly influence this process. For example, gender, ethnicity, and race can intersect in experiences of sexual harassment, with racism being an additional issue that needs to be considered by individuals in their responses (Fieldon et al., 2010). Responses to sexual harassment will be contextually based and will change according to the shifting discursive reading of this behaviour. Feminist poststructuralists have highlighted the shifting and contradictory nature of subjectivity, arguing that individuals negotiate the various discourses available to them in a particular context and that they base their decision-making on what 'investments' they see they have in the situation encountered (Hollway, 1984). Individuals will have greater 'investments' in certain discourses than others. For example, for many young women being popular and being perceived as attractive by boys is critical to their performance of femininity so they will 'tolerate' sexual harassment in certain contexts.

Young women highlight that sexual harassment does not always manifest itself in straightforward feelings, but rather it frequently results in mixed and often contradictory feelings – for example: anger, embarrassment and shame intersecting with feelings of being flattered with the attention received from young men. However, feelings and responses are often dependent upon an individual's perception of the severity of the harassment, fears of potentially escalating the harassment further, previous experiences of negotiating harassment, witnessing how others responded to similar behaviours and fears of being ostracised by peers. Responses, as pointed out above, can be further complicated by the identity of the harasser – whether individuals know the person, whether they like or dislike them, whether they are popular or unpopular amongst their peers, whether they are 'good looking' or not; even the person's racial and class identity can impact on how young women react.

Consequently, responses to sexual harassment will not always be the same, with individuals choosing varying options at different times, according to what they perceive might be the most successful strategy, or the most 'appropriate' response in that particular context. Others may not view these choices as appropriate responses. Young women's contradictory responses to sexual harassment are often the basis of some teachers' perceptions that young women encourage sexual harassment by boys. Young women's frustration and anger around this everyday sexual harassment can on occasions result in girls losing their tempers and lashing out at the boy(s). However, for many, ignoring the behaviour is frequently viewed to be the easiest and safest option, reflecting the advice often offered to girls by their teachers when they did complain. This advice tended to be more about changing young girls' behaviours, which was often perceived to be an easier option for teachers, than tackling the problem of sexual harassment and/or changing boys' behaviours.

Reactions and emotional responses to sexual harassment can be somewhat delayed, as the full extent of the impact of the behaviour may not be perceived at the time of the incident. Feelings are often internalised and put aside in an effort to avoid showing the harasser that the behaviour has affected them. This strategy is about retaining a sense of power and not wishing to give the harasser the satisfaction of a reaction they may have been seeking. As indicated by Melissa, the full impact of the harassment is often not felt or dealt with until long after the incident has occurred: 'The total of what they say doesn't really hit me until I'm by myself and their words come back to haunt me'.

Teachers also encountered the tensions around the contradictions of sexual harassment facing young women. One teacher, Penny, recounted the following experience:

> I exploded about an incident today where a group of boys were calling girls sexually derogatory names. The girls were just laughing it off, but I could see that it was upsetting them. The boys think it is normal, it is the language of today. According to my standards that was not appropriate behaviour. I guess it is the times. I'm just a bit out of touch these days. The girls ended up getting upset with me for intervening and making them look bad in the eyes of the boys.

This situation highlights the complexities of sexual harassment in young women's lives, as well as the problems it poses for teachers' interventions. What seems most critical to the young women in this instance is negotiating the behaviour without 'losing face' with the boys. Despite obviously feeling upset, the young women's investments were in trying to retain some sense of power through not losing either any popularity they may have had or any future 'chances' of a relationship with the boys, and not being unfavourably viewed by the boys in any way. Consequently, 'laughing off' the young men's derogatory comments was considered the most appropriate response in this instance. The teacher's intervention in this context was considered disempowering and problematic. However, it is important to point out that in a different context, these young women may have appreciated the teacher's intervention and support. Consequently, teachers, who perceived girls to be 'finicky' and 'untrustworthy', often positioned young women as the problem, impacting on their decisions to intervene or not in these behaviours. These young women were viewed as having problematic personalities and were blamed for encouraging boys' sexual harassment. This belief echoes a long-standing broader perspective often associated with women, where they are discursively constructed as 'at fault' or responsible for inappropriate male behaviour. Women who are raped, for example, are often discursively constructed as 'asking for it' through their behaviour and/or through the 'inappropriate' clothing that they were perceived to be wearing at the time (Brownmiller, 1976; Opinion Matters, 2010). It is critical that sexual harassment intervention strategies reconsider the complexities of this behaviour in young women's lives, as well as the crucial role that it plays in constituting and regulating gendered identities and heterosexuality.

Sexual harassment of GLBTQ students and teachers

The homophobic harassment of GLBTQ students and teachers in schools has been extensively reported in the literature internationally (AAUW, 2001; Hillier et al., 2005; Kosciw & Cullen, 2002; Town, 2002; Warwick et al., 2004). As Davies and McInnes deal with homophobia and heterosexism in schools in depth in this book, it is only touched on here. It is important to acknowledge the intersection between sexual harassment and homophobic and heteronormative discourses. The research, on which this discussion is based, reinforces the prevalence and severity of the harassment experienced by GLBTQ students and teachers in schools. Sexual harassment is a heteronormative technology of power that is utilised against GLBTQ students and teachers as a means of policing and regulating normative gendered and sexual identities. As Kenway et al. (1997, p. 103) aptly point out, 'when girls are harassed, it is very often because they are girls, when boys are harassed it is not because they are boys but [because] they are the wrong sort of boys'.

The precariousness of the safety and emotional well-being of many GLBTQ students in schools is reflected in this research, especially through the intense anger often directed at them, particularly by young men, whose performance of masculinity encompasses an aggression and 'hatred' towards the sexual 'Other'. It often only took a young man, who was known to be gay, or perceived to be, to go too near, or accidentally brush past certain boys, for the action to be considered a sexual 'come-on' or a sexual threat; this was generally met with what was perceived to be a legitimate barrage of abusive and violent behaviours. Charlie, a middle high school student, was quick to relay his anger about what he called 'fags' coming too close to him, when he commented, 'I felt like belting the crap out of him' – a comment that reflected the sentiments of many of his male peers. Homophobic violence affirms hegemonic masculinity and policing and controlling normative sexual boundaries is part of some young men's definitive peer-group cultural practices (Herek, 1993; Mac An Ghaill, 1994).

Gender and sexual harassment constituted within homophobia and heterosexism was an everyday occurrence in this research within and across young men's groups. Being called a 'poofter' or 'fag' was considered to be the ultimate slur by some young men, who viewed it as a personal public questioning of their masculinity to be aligned with those 'queers' they openly detested. Such name calling fostered acute anger and aggression as highlighted by David, a senior high school student, who was called a poofter by other young men: 'I had an urge to kill the harassers, or hurt, maim or severely injure them'. This openly aggressive and violent homophobic sentiment amongst young men shocked some teachers. The following comment by a woman teacher, Lisa, highlights this concern:

> We did a lesson on homosexuality and lesbianism and the students were very narrow in their thinking. It was almost to the stage of worry, like gay bashing was a good thing.

These overt violent sentiments are similar to the findings in a survey on sexual harassment conducted throughout secondary schools in the United States (AAUW, 2001). This American research stated that being called gay would be more upsetting to young men than actual physical abuse (AAUW, 2001, p. 23).

Christopher, a middle-years high school student from a co-educational school in the research on which this discussion is based, experienced a torrent of verbal and physical sexual harassment from other boys, and some girls, as a result of being 'too effeminate' and openly ambiguous about his sexuality. The boy confided in the researcher that he was gay, but pointed out that he would never tell anyone at school. Christopher's everyday schooling experiences included being the target of constant homophobic humour, sexual comments, taunts and innuendoes, as well as physical assaults (often of a sexualised nature). These practices are a critical component of performing hegemonic masculinity and consolidating heterosexuality (Kehily & Nayak, 1997). On one occasion, the researcher witnessed an incident involving Christopher and two other boys during a class being observed. As Christopher was leaning over a desk talking to a young woman about his work, two young men moved up behind him, one of whom pushed a large ruler aggressively into the back of his trousers and into his bottom, laughing and commenting, 'Get it up you, you filthy faggot'. Christopher, holding back tears, was obviously shocked, embarrassed, and physically hurt by the incident, as the two other boys shoved him and laughed. The class teacher, unaware of the full details of the event, sent all three boys, including Christopher, from the room where she attempted to clarify what had happened. After hearing all versions of the event, she focused on her disapproval of fighting in class and then they were all asked to return to the classroom. There was no further intervention in the incident by the classroom teacher. After the class, the researcher asked the teacher whether she would deal with the homophobia which had led to the incident amongst the boys at another stage, to which she replied, 'He [Christopher] brings it on himself in the way he behaves!'

Christopher's experience outlined above highlights how teachers' attitudes towards non-gender conforming students impacts on their intervention in this kind of harassment. Teachers' locations in homophobic discourses that often underpin a failure to intervene, or to intervene in an ineffective manner, also operate to police and regulate normative gender and sexual identities, as well as condone the homophobic harassment and violence. Teachers have a duty of care to all their students and a failure to intervene appropriately due to one's own biases can have dire effects on those experiencing the harassment. The effects of this harassment can be far-reaching, affecting young people's educational achievements and their health and well-being (Denborough, 1996; Irwin et al., 1997). The high incidence of youth suicide amongst GLBTQ young people demonstrates the severity of the alienation and homophobic violence and harassment they often experience (Denborough, 1996; Donagy, 1997; Mac An Ghaill, 1994). This is epitomised in the fatal violence encountered by Mathew Shepard in the United States, a 21-year-old student at the University of Wyoming, who was tortured and murdered near Laramie, Wyoming, in the United States, in October 1998. After being brutally beaten by two other men, Shepard was left tied to a fence for 18 hours in a remote rural area in a coma before he was found. His injuries were so severe that doctors could not operate on him and he never regained consciousness before he died five days later. This case highlights the willful blindness that is often associated with such acts of violence associated with performances of hegemonic masculinity, especially in cases where the victims are known or perceived to be gay. This violence is often legitimised through perpetrators claiming 'the gay panic defense'; that is, a temporary loss of control resulting from the belief that the victim was making sexual advances towards them – a plea that was initially claimed by those who killed Shepard.

Connections between sexual harassment and other sites of inequality

Sexual harassment not only intersects with gender and sexuality, as discussed above, but often intersects with other sites of identity and difference, such as, but not limited to race, ethnicity, social class, age and disability. Wen-Chu Chen (1997, p. 59) argues that:

> Racial inequality is as much a dimension of the sexual harassment experiences of Asian-American women as is gender inequality. White and non-Asian men, holding stereotyped notions of Asian-American women, may subject Asian-American women to more extreme sexist attitudes and behaviors, which the men would not expect from their white or non-Asian counterparts.

In schools in this research, many young women from ethnic minority backgrounds, including Australian Aboriginal girls, were subjected to sexual harassment that was constituted in racist and classist discourses. One teacher recounted an experience of intervening in a case of sexual harassment of a young woman by two boys in her school, where one boy simulated ejaculating over the girl by throwing the left-overs of his carton of milk on her. When the teacher chastised the boy, he commented that she 'deserved it' as the 'snobby bitch needed to be brought back to earth'. Several Asian-Australian young women acknowledged experiencing sexual harassment from some white male students, whose sexually explicit comments were framed in stereotypes about Asian women being compliant and eager to sexually please men with a range of exotic sexual acts (Robinson, 2005c). Some young men from Asian backgrounds commented that they also experienced sexual comments by other boys, in particular based on stereotypes around Asian men being 'effeminate'. A young Fijian man indicated experiencing harassment by both girls and boys about the potential size of his penis, based on racial stereotypes about black men's bodies.

Racial and ethnic discourses impacted on the way that some teachers viewed sexual harassment amongst students in this research. Boys from Middle-Eastern and Arabic backgrounds were often considered to be the most likely and frequent perpetrators of sexual harassment, as they were perceived to be from 'chauvinistic' cultures that had little respect for women (Robinson, 2000, 2005c). This perspective was not generally supported in this research, but rather what tended to be highlighted was that such stereotypes were so pervasive that they often eclipsed recognition of the sexual harassment perpetrated by white boys, or by boys from other ethnic minority groups. Several male teachers, working in schools with high proportions of boys from ethnic minorities, indicated that boys from certain minority cultural backgrounds were more likely to make sexual suggestions to girls who were from white Australian backgrounds, rather than to girls from their own cultural backgrounds. This perception was based on the view that these boys upheld the importance – something respected and expected – of 'virginity' and 'purity' in young women from their own cultures, as their potential future wives and mothers of their children. Additionally, it was believed that these boys considered many white Australian girls as 'easy' sexual targets in comparison to girls from other cultural backgrounds – a stereotype echoed in the comments of several young men from minority backgrounds.

The intersections of identity can significantly influence the ways in which young people interpret, experience and respond to sexual harassment (Fielden et al., 2010; Richardson & Taylor, 2009). The intersection of sexual harassment with other forms of identity such as race, sexuality, class and so on operates to intensify the power and impact of this behaviour. Not only is the practice of sexual harassment an integral part of the performance of hegemonic masculine subjects, it operates to consolidate the power of particular racial and ethnic groups over others, and to reassert middle-class values. Some young people may choose to remain silent about the sexual harassment they experience, fearing further harassment of a sexual, racist or homophobic nature if they make complaints. Institutionalised racism and homophobia in schools can result in reluctance to trust the system or school authorities (Goodall & Huggins, 1992; Kalantzis et al., 1990).

Fielden et al. (2010) argue that taking a generic approach to sexual harassment can be problematic – 'naïve', 'potentially dangerous' and 'inappropriate – in the context of the complexities associated with the interactions between race, ethnicity and sexual harassment. They point out that these interactions are also influenced by socio-cultural and religious variables. Linn et al. (1992, p. 110) also stress this point:

> For some women, cultural beliefs have taught them that in order to survive, you don't make trouble; don't speak up if you are harassed.

Indeed, for some women cultural beliefs have taught them that the act of speaking up is more shameful than the act of harassment. For other women, cultural beliefs have included a strong tradition of speaking up and affirming the powerfulness of women.

Interestingly, some young women's contradictory feelings and responses to the everyday sexual harassment by young men is probably influenced by their own racist values, as indicated by the following remark made by Jessie, a senior high school student from a white Australian background:

> Usually it's my friends mucking around. Other times when wogs do it, it makes me mad cause they can be really perverted.

The intersections of these aspects of identity with gender and sexuality, in the context of sexual harassment, and how they impact on the perpetrator's motivations or the 'victim's' experiences warrant a greater focus when educating about, and developing policies and strategies to deal with this behaviour.

Sexual harassment as a technology of power within the organisational structures of schools – the case of gender, discipline and authority

In this discussion of sexual harassment as a complex, contradictory and contextually based socio-cultural phenomenon, it is important to highlight how this practice can operate as a technology of power not just amongst student groups, but as an integral part of the reconfirming and policing of hegemonic discourses of gender, power and authority within schooling structures and practices in an organisation. This process is linked especially with the sexual harassment by male students (primarily) of women teachers and of some men who do not fit the dominant discourse of masculinity. Within this context, the sexual harassment is eclipsed by the perception that it is just 'kids mucking around' as a result of the teacher's 'lack of authority' and 'inability to control a class' – essential characteristics of the good teacher discourse – that is perceived to be the problem by some colleagues and senior school executives. The sexual harassment of teachers by students challenges the more conventional understandings of this behaviour involving power that is perpetrated by individuals in positions of authority over those with less authority and power – as generally constituted in the teacher and student relationship. It also does not fit into peer-to-peer sexual harassment, which is the most common form of this behaviour that occurred in the schools in this research. In the case of the sexual harassment of women teachers by boys, it is the power exercised in masculinity and its cultural relationship to the feminine subject – often constituted as the sex object of the male gaze – that particularly underpins this harassment. However, as pointed out previously, relations of power associated with sexual harassment are also integrally related to intersections with race, ethnicity, sexuality, age and so on.

The sexual harassment of women teachers by male students (or of some men who do not fit the characteristics constituted within hegemonic masculinity) is often linked to the dominant Western discourse of authority. Authority refers to 'a mutually recognisable normative relationship giving one the right to command or speak and the other to obey' (Friedman, 1973, p. 134). Someone 'in authority' is generally seen to be entitled to obedience, rather than having to persuade or coerce others into obeying (Jones, 1988). However, Jones (1988, p. 122) points out that in Western political philosophy, authority is commonly regarded as a type of social control, where 'sometimes the differentiation between authority and force is not clear'. The secondary school is a context in which this relationship becomes particularly obvious through the prevalence of powerful and autocratic discipline methods often implemented to reinforce teacher authority over students (Robinson, 1992, 2000).

The dominant discourse of Western authority encompasses hegemonic, white, masculine values and practices and excludes those frequently related to females, the feminine and those considered 'other' in this context (Collins, 1990; Connell, 1985, 1995b; hooks, 1990; Jones, 1988, 1993). Authority in secondary schooling, as in the broader community more generally, must be considered in relation to the ways in which representations of 'authoritativeness' have privileged certain groups within society. Historically, the dominant discourse of authority has contributed to women within the teaching profession frequently being viewed as poor disciplinarians, often lacking the necessary 'masculine attributes' to control older children, especially boys (Oram, 1988; Strober & Tyack, 1980). Apart from being gendered, others have highlighted the racialised and sexualised essence of the dominant discourse of Western authority, as well as its relationships with age and social class (Collins, 1990; Connell, 1985, 1995b; Cranny-Francis, 1995; Gittins, 1998; hooks, 1990). As Cranny-Francis (1995, p. 45) points out, 'the west is a powerful force in assuming itself to be the "centre" of "authority" and "correctness"'.

This discourse of the legitimate authoritarian subject and body is actively constituted and regulated within schooling structures, practices, rules and resources, and epitomised in the 'gender regime' existing in many schooling systems (Connell, 1985). Other issues, such as sexism, racism, heterosexism and ageism, further influence the intersections operating between gender and what is considered legitimate power and authority. All function simultaneously to influence students' and teachers' stereotyped perceptions, attitudes and behaviours towards gender, power and authority in everyday schooling. Additionally, the Western ideal hegemonic masculine body is culturally inscribed with characteristics representative of 'legitimate' power and authority – for example, deep and commanding loud voices; and being strong and tall in stature. Consequently, within this process, the feminine female subject, the non-hegemonic masculine male subject and often the non-white subject are constituted as lacking 'authentic' and 'legitimate' authority (Connell, 1985; Jones, 1988; Kimmel, 1994). This perception was prevalent amongst students and many teachers who participated in this research. The following comments by students typify those made by numerous students, both boys and girls:

> You don't give cheek to female teachers who look like tomboys because they're tougher and grouchy. The feminine ones you give a bit of cheek to.
>
> (High school boy)

> Women teachers give you more detentions because they can't handle it. They are softer, weaker and you can get away with more. They aren't as hard as men teachers.
>
> (High school boy)

The practice of sexual harassment becomes a means through which teacher authority is contested and power relations associated with identities simultaneously reasserted. However, the dominant discourse of authority is mobilised to successfully silence claims, and to justify and/or render invisible practices of sexual harassment (Robinson, 2000). In the process it reinstates the hegemonic position of this particular type of authority, and associated disciplinary practices, in schools. Additionally, it simultaneously operates to sustain and regulate racial, ethnic, gendered and heteronormative status quos in schools.

Those male teachers, who took up non-hegemonic performances of masculinity, often became simultaneously 'sexually suspect' and perceived as potentially gay. They often encountered sexual harassment that was constituted in homophobic and heterosexist discourses. Teachers who experience sexual harassment by their male students (or female students on occasions) in the classroom or in the school grounds often do not report this behaviour fearing the consequences of being perceived as 'bad teachers', with 'no authority', and of being unable to 'control a class'. This fear intensifies for teacher trainees, early career teachers and those going for promotion (Robinson, 1996). For some women teachers, the experience is internalised as their failure to adequately deal with boys' behaviours and their inability to maintain their culturally legitimised and expected position of power within the adult–child and teacher–student binary relationships.

The positioning of many female teaches, and some male teachers, in this perceived deficit authority discourse resulted in their generally being viewed as easy targets of sexual harassment and practical jokes, especially from boys, and their lessons were often seen as a 'good muck around' (Beynon, 1985; Connell, 1985). Many women teachers complained that certain boys were uncooperative and refused to take directions from them, a point echoed by a young man who highlighted the fact that most boys disliked being reprimanded in class by women teachers:

> Male students think that male teachers have more control over them because they are stronger. Male students take more notice and take it better when male teachers tell them how and what to do. They have less respect for female teachers.
>
> (Middle high school boy)

The perceived illegitimacy of some women's authority in students' eyes was reinforced through the daily practices of some of their male colleagues. For example, some male teachers considered it to be their right and duty to intervene in female teachers' classes when they perceived a disciplinary problem occurring, with the aim of establishing order (Beynon, 1987; Robinson, 1992).

Conclusion

This chapter has highlighted the critical importance of identifying sexual harassment for what it is, a complex, contextual and contradictory practice and a pervasive socio-cultural phenomenon that operates to constitute and maintain dominant relations of power across gender, ethnicity, sexuality, age and so on. Sexual harassment is an every-day occurrence in schools, but its existence and frequency is often rendered invisible and unproblematic, primarily through its links to young people's performances of gender, especially boys' performances of hegemonic masculinity, and to perceptions that the behaviour is 'a natural part of growing up'. However, sexual harassment in these schools is also a form of systemic violence, where institutional hierarchies of power and authority constituted in discourses of hegemonic masculinity, are regulated and policed through the utilisation of sexual harassment. In order to devise effective strategies to disrupt this behaviour, it is critical to address the local complexities, contexts and contradictory nature of these practices operating in schools.

Implications for schooling

The issues raised in this chapter have significant implications for schooling on several different levels, including policy development, the curriculum and the professional development of teachers and school administrators. Each is briefly addressed below:

(i) School policies need to perceive and address sexual harassment as a complex socio-cultural phenomenon that is integral to performances of gender and that intersects with other aspects of identity, such as sexuality, race, class, age and so on. Common practices of perceiving sexual harassment as instigated by problematic individuals with pathological problems, and subsuming this behaviour within the context of bullying, eclipse the complex discursive nature of this widespread practice. Approaches to sexual harassment need to consider its complexities and the contradictions associated with those who experience and perpetrate this behaviour. For example, it is important that policies demonstrate an understanding of the complexities of racialised sexual harassment or of heterosexist sexual harassment. Also, it is critical to highlight the way that sexual harassment becomes normalised in the everyday lives of young people.

(ii) Sexual harassment needs to be addressed in the school curriculum to increase young people's awareness and understandings of the political nature of this phenomenon and of the ways that it becomes normalised in their everyday lives. Until the stereotypes of sexual harassment are critically deconstructed with young people, this behaviour will continue to be viewed within the 'boss/secretary' binary, or the problematic individual, and considered irrelevant to young people's circumstances. Educating around sexual harassment also requires a focus on its intersections with homophobia and heterosexism, racism and classism, to name a few critical areas that influence how this behaviour is used as a technology of power.

(iii) Increasing awareness and understanding of sexual harassment needs to be a critical compulsory component of teachers' and school administrators' professional development. Teachers also need to consider how sexual harassment operates in young people's everyday lives, as well as how it operates as a technology of power in regulating and policing organisational hierarchies of power. It is also critical that teachers examine their own practices in order to consider how their own perceptions and values can perpetuate sexual harassment.

5
Schools, Violence, Masculinities and Privilege

Martin Mills

This chapter explores the practices of violence performed amongst boys in schools. Whilst most boys are not violent, violent practices performed by some boys serve as a means to privilege men and boys, in relation to women and girls, within the current gender order. Connell (1987, p. 98) has referred to the gender order as the historical set of relations between men and women that construct normalised definitions of masculinity and femininity. Violence is integral to maintaining the current gender order. The normalisation of boys' capacities for violence, especially against girls and women, and its contribution to a gender order that favours the interests of men and boys have been well documented by feminist literature (see, e.g., Bhana, 2006; Jones, 1985; Leach & Mitchell, 2006; Mahony, 1989; Robinson, 2005a, 2005b, 2005c). However, it is important to acknowledge that not all men and boys benefit equally from this state of affairs. Boys' violent practices, and the fear associated with them, also work to shore up the privileges of particular boys (and men). In this chapter there is an exploration of how violence is implicated within anti-schoolwork cultures in ways that can disadvantage working-class boys academically and of how violence within an elite school is used to maintain meritocratic justifications of privilege. However, the chapter also demonstrates the commonalities within these different communities relating to the ways in which homophobic discourses work to privilege heterosexist constructions of masculinity. The chapter concludes with a consideration of the ways in which violence is a presence in the various ways in which many boys 'survive' schooling.

The chapter draws on data collected through a number of different research projects conducted in Australia. These projects include an exploration of the implementation of gender and violence programmes in schools; an evaluation of anti-racist strategies adopted in schools; and a national study of boys' educational issues (see, e.g., Lingard et al., 2009; Mills, 2001; Milojevic et al., 2001). The schools from which data are taken include Irish Saints, a small Catholic primary school located in an urban low socioeconomic area; Mountainview, a small rural co-education government high school; Tamville, a large urban high school located in a mid-range socioeconomic area; St Adams, a large Catholic boys' school located in a low socioeconomic area; and English Queen's, an elite boys' private school. In each instance interview data were collected from students, teachers and administrators at the school, alongside classroom and playground observations. Common across these projects was an association between masculinity and violence. In this chapter there is a focus on the interview data collected from students in order to explore the dynamics operating between boys.

Within each of these schools there are, as Paechter (2007) would suggest, drawing on the work of Lave and Wenger (1991), 'communities of masculinity practice'. These communities intersect with other communities of gendered practice and shift and adapt to changing times. Thus, men and boys (and indeed girls and women) move in and out of such communities of masculinity practice both within schools and beyond. Within each of these communities various masculinities and femininities are not fixed and are constantly being negotiated, (re)constructed, policed and valorised (see, e.g., Keddie, 2005). Each community confers certain benefits on its members. However, membership of these communities is not automatic. As Bauman (2001) indicates in his work on communities, the notion of a community is not a harmless one; a community can only exist when there are outsiders who are deprived of community benefits. Thus, it often takes significant work to be accepted as part of a community. As Paechter (2007, p. 23) states:

> To be accepted as 'fully masculine' in a particular social grouping, one must therefore display certain characteristics and behaviours; without this, one is not seen fully as a member of a group. Hence, it is not simply a matter of claiming membership of a particular community of masculinity or femininity; one has to be accepted as a legitimate participant by those who are already members.

In by far the majority of instances, outsiders to the dominant communities of masculine practice operating within schools are girls and women. However, there are particular boys and men who are also denied access to such communities. The communities of masculine practice that exist within the schools from which the interview data are drawn for this chapter are very much shaped by local contexts as well as broader conceptions of idealised masculinities. This chapter explores some of the ways in which the borders of these communities are patrolled by boys, often through violence, to preserve the status of that community.

The chapter's concern is with boys' violence against other boys, what Connell (1995b) refers to as 'transactions amongst men'. It suggests that any attempts to address violence in schools need to acknowledge that such violence and the perceived threat of such violence work to maintain both the current gender order and existing hierarchies of masculinities based on, amongst other things, class, race and sexuality (see also Martino & Pallotta-Chiarolli, 2003, 2005). As Connell (1995b, p. 83) has noted, violence is 'important in gender politics amongst men'. That boys are the primary perpetrators of violence in and around schools is largely uncontested (see, e.g., Mills, 2001; White Watson, 2007). However, the focus on boys' violence is not to suggest that girls are never violent. It would be foolish to have romantic idealised versions of girls and to assume that they do not also engage in violent or aggressive practices (see, e.g., Bhana, 2008; Brown, 2005; Duncan, 2006). Girls can be violent towards each other (Bright, 2005). There are examples of this in most schools. They can also perform violence against boys (Duncan, 1999). However, incidents of girls' violence need to be read differently from those of boys' violence (Brown, 2005; Osler, 2006). For example, violence by girls often works in ways that support boys' practices (see, e.g., Duncan, 1999). The focus on boys' violence towards each other in this chapter is also not to deny the significant threat and practices of violence directed by boys towards girls. Such violence is critical in the maintenance of a gender order that favours the interests of men and boys. As Connell (1995b, p. 83) has noted in relation to the advantages accruing to men from the existing structure of gender relations: 'A structure of inequality on this scale, involving a massive dispossession of social resources, is hard to imagine without violence. It is, overwhelmingly, the dominant gender who hold and use the means of violence.'

However, whilst boys' violence, including the perceived potential for violence, towards girls underpins the current gender order, boys' violences against each other also work against the interests of girls at the same time as marginalising particular men and boys within schools, and beyond. Status within most masculine communities in schools does not solely accrue through demonstrating one's superiority in relation to girls but also by demonstrating superiority over other boys. Such latter demonstrations take place on sporting fields, the playgrounds and classrooms of most schools, both primary and secondary (Keddie, 2003, 2005, 2006; Mills, 2001). Within these arenas there are several forms of violence deployed by boys against other boys in schools and their causes and effects can be many. There are the violences that police the gender regimes in schools by punishing boys who align with girls; some which discipline those boys who appear to have rejected traditional values of masculinity; some that are employed to direct attention away from one's own potential to be a victim; and there are other forms of violences which are deployed to assert one's own superiority over other boys. In each of these cases what is at stake is the construction and defence of a normalised form of masculinity (Martino & Pallotta-Chiarolli, 2003) that underpins the community of masculinity practice operating within a school. This chapter explores the ways in which boys who engage enthusiastically in schoolwork in working-class schools can sometimes become the targets of violence within their communities. It then focuses on the kinds of violence deployed in more privileged schools. It identifies the role that homophobia plays across diverse economic locations in maintaining what Martino and Pallotta-Chiarolli (2003) refer to as 'gendernormative' behaviours. It finishes with the conclusion that many boys perform and condone violence in schools as a matter of survival.

Anti-schoolwork cultures

There has been a significant amount of literature documenting the ways in which some boys in some schools are anti-school and demonstrate antipathy towards those boys who engage enthusiastically with schoolwork (Epstein, 1998; Frosh et al., 2002). This is not a new phenomenon (see, e.g., Willis, 1977). This anti-school culture was evident in a number of the working-class schools visited as part of the projects from which the data are drawn here. For instance, a group of year 11 boys at St Adams, an all boys' secondary school located in an industrial regional city in Australia, outlined the kinds of boys who experienced bullying at their school: 'The little ones that you see wandering around with books in their hands and stuff, you know, the smarter ones usually'; and ' . . . a lot of guys that don't play sport are sort of . . . put down a bit. Like the guy that just goes in the library and just wants to read and stuff like that.' These boys indicated that most of this harassment is not physical as it usually 'only' involved other boys 'throwing food at them'.

This same anti-school discourse was apparent in the comments of a year seven boy at Irish Saints, a small working-class inner city primary school, who explained that for boys, 'doing well' at his school was not always a good idea:

> People (boys) who study hard here, they usually get bullied because they get top marks for everything. Like other people bully them and everything. They go, 'Oh, you're a brain, you're a brain'. Like, 'Why don't you just come with me, stop studying. It doesn't mean anything. It's only a test'. They say 'Oh, you're a brainy, you're a brain-i-ac' and everything and if there's like a brain and glasses, they call them 'Brainy head', or go 'four eyes, come here', and stuff like that.

Another year seven boy at this school, one who usually did well at his schoolwork, described the kinds of punishment that were meted out to him:

> When I was away these other two boys took stuff from my desk, like my scissors, my pencil case. And they fart on my dictionary. And they wrecked my calculator, got ripped apart. And I got another one and they smashed that.

Another year seven boy at this school who performed well at school-work talked about how he was continually being harassed and called 'fat' and a 'bookworm'. Hence, within these two working-class schools a particular form of masculinity is being marginalised. Such a masculinity is represented by boys who 'wander around with books in their hand' or 'get top marks'. These anti-schoolwork discourses are also accompanied by comments about the physicality of boys who are good at school, for example, they are referred to as 'little', 'four eyes' and 'fat'. Within such discourses boys who are positive about their schoolwork are especially vulnerable if they are perceived as not meeting the physical standards of normalised masculinity within the particular community of practice in which they are located.

In the same way that physical attributes associated with masculinity (or lack thereof) are foregrounded within the discourses of derision directed at boys who engage with schoolwork, so too can there be a racist tone to the attacks. Within Irish Saints, which has a very multicultural school population, a group of year seven girls spoke of their concern about a boy, Mark, a high achieving boy from Hong Kong who was regularly bullied by other boys and was often referred to as 'Ching Chong Man'.

Jackie: He works at a grade eight level. Hardly anyone likes him. Most people don't understand him – like when he talks he talks fast and quiet. He's nice. Yeah. He's friendly. He doesn't call you names. He doesn't swear.
Martin: And does he get picked on by some of the boys?
Julie: Like one says, 'I hate you, I hate you.'
Martin: And what do they hate about him?
Julie: They hate that he always gets good marks and they don't.

In a discussion with a group of grade seven boys, a group which contained Mark, the policing effects of racialised boundaries were made evident when Mark indicated that in both the classroom and the playground he was often derogatorily referred to as 'Chinaman' because he was good at school. The racism that Mark experienced because he performed well at schoolwork was further compounded by his location outside of the community of masculinity practice at the school because, in relation to sport, 'he's slow and not very good at it'.

The punishing of boys who like school can change as students move into the higher grades of high school. However, whilst less obvious, it is often still there. For instance, the group of year 11 boys from the boys' working-class school, St Adams, indicated that in the senior years it is much more likely that the punishing of boys who engage with schoolwork would involve 'exclusion'. They noted, for example, the following: 'You get someone who's into reading and stuff and they'll just, it's just like exclusions more often, they're pretty much told to go away and go and sit by themselves and read. Just sent away.' A grade 12 boy at this same school tried to explain why many boys at the school did not do well:

Well they've got mates, mates out of school, that failed school. They're scared that if they're going to pass a subject they're going to go to their mates and they're going to find out. Then they're going to be told to go away, and they think these mates are so cool, so really, really good and everything like this, that they have to fail every subject.

This latter comment indicates that boys do not just operate within one community of masculine practice and that they do have to consider those other communities to which they belong outside of school.

Within the communities of masculine practice operating within the working-class schools identified here, there are particular constructions of normalised masculinity that are grounded in expectations that boys are anti-school. This construction is also aligned with broader understandings of hegemonic masculinity (Connell, 1995b) which suggests that 'normal' boys are physically robust (e.g., are not overweight and don't wear glasses) and loud. It would be a mistake to assume that anti-schoolwork discourses are so powerful that all boys in such schools fail to engage with the schooling process. However, such an engagement is not always easy. Diane Reay's (2002) wonderful account of Shaun's story indicates some of the emotional stresses for one boy from a working-class background who tried to negotiate an engagement with schoolwork whilst not losing his reputation as a 'hard' boy in the playground. The anti-school cultures, and associated violence and harassment, in many working-class schools unfortunately work into a politics that privileges those from more affluent circumstances.

Privilege

The anti-school culture and violence that exist in some working-class schools contribute to stereotypical constructions of 'working-class' masculinities as dangerous. This was demonstrated in the comments of many of the boys at English Queen's elite private boys' school. For many of these boys violent bullying was something that happened in 'other' schools. For instance, one boy described his fear of having to go to the government school in his home town in the country:

> I dread going to the high school at (rural town) as opposed to coming here because just things, like it's easier to do well here because there's encouragement, like if you're smart, people don't pay you out, you know, they don't necessarily think you're really good for it, but they don't, you know, they let you be smart, they let you work hard.

In many ways the depiction of a government school in a rural community as being one where learning is not valued and where if you work hard others 'pay you out' is based upon assumptions of working-class masculinities as being more violent and more anti-intellectual than the masculinities present in this upper-class school.

However, expectations that elite boys' private schools are places free from violence is clearly misplaced, violence is a presence in many such schools (see, e.g., Saltmarsh, 2007; Stoudt, 2006). At English Queen's, evidence of bullying existed, although many of the boys downplayed it. For instance, within this school, notions of idealised body shapes intertwined with concepts of sporting prowess were prevalent. This was highlighted by a group of year 11 boys who talked about a boy who had been driven from the school: 'He was overweight, he wasn't very good at sport, he wasn't very good at anything really, I think he just, you know, wanted to be included so he was doing things to try and be cool, and just got jarred for it.' Another year 11 boy in another interview also spoke of this student:

> *Simon*: There was a boy who actually left at the end of last year, who was a little bit overweight boy, his voice hadn't dropped yet, he was a little bit – have you seen the Simpsons?
> *Martin*: Yeah.
> *Simon*: His nickname was Ralph, he's that little kid, you know. That was the kind of boy he was and he used to do silly things like, if he knew that people were bullying him, like I guess in his mind he would have made the decision that he didn't want them ruining his life, and so he'd just go around and pretend things were normal. And so he'd do things like try and interact with other people, like having mock fights with them like other people would, and then he'd just get knocked down.

So even attempting to act 'normal' and to engage in mock fights was no guarantee that a student would become accepted at this school as a 'normal boy' by his peers. Other boys who described this boy indicated that such bullying was a rare event and that often the victim brought it upon himself:

> There's been cases that I know of. I've been class captain I think every year, then I've had a few boys approach me and want me to say a few things to the form teacher at the end of the year, but not really. I mean, there was one little problem with a boy who had a lot of trouble at this school and some guys didn't make it extremely easy for him, but he often brought it upon himself, you know, he just didn't really fit in. He's gone now. But in general, no, well not, I haven't had any troubles with anybody myself.

> You get the occasional people who don't have the guts to sort of say no to it, but in general I think most people, they try to stamp it out a bit. I mean, obviously there's going to be a bit of name calling, but a lot of it's just out of just no-one really takes any notice of it, people who say it, you don't really care about them anyway, and everyone

sort of has their friends that they're really – it doesn't affect them too much. I mean, it's pretty good at this school.

Martin: So that boy who brought it on himself, what would he do to bring it on himself?

He didn't have much, many social skills sort of thing and didn't sort of take part in any activities, you know, but yeah, he made some sort of comments that no-one really appreciated and didn't get on extremely well with any people. But yeah, that was – I don't think he probably should have been in that grade. I think he could have been in the grade below. But yeah, no, he's gone, I think he's very happy now. I think he just didn't quite adjust to – and he didn't like the competition. He wasn't hugely intelligent and he found the work very tough and it's a bit of a shame, but – there's a competitive environment at this school, it's quite tough, they've got a lot of students out there wanting to do very well and a lot of smart people out there, so you know, I don't think he handled that too well.

Here this boy indicates that the 'victim' who had to be excluded to the point of leaving the school was not masculine enough. Within this school, dominant forms of masculinity contrasted with those found in some of the poorer government schools in that acceptable masculinities did not require anti-school behaviours. Indeed he was in part driven out because he 'wasn't hugely intelligent'. Within this school there was an expectation that boys would be highly competitive, intelligent and be able to demonstrate they had the toughness to survive in this, if somewhat denied, very hypermasculine environment.

Homophobia

Within both the working-class and the privileged high schools, homophobia was a central discourse in the policing of boys' behaviours. The hatred that many boys display towards gays and those perceived as gay is a warning to boys of the dangers of being constructed as such. For instance, at English Queen's, whilst many of the boys indicated that there were not significant levels of violence at the school they did indicate that the potential for violence was there and that this was especially the case in relation to those boys who appeared to be gay. This was evident in the comments of one year 11 boy who stated that it would be 'dangerous' for a person to be openly gay at English Queen's private school:

I think it would be very dangerous for them to be openly gay. There are people who, in their mannerisms, seem to be gay, like the boy who left the school last year, he spoke with a bit of an accent and, you know, was not very academic and didn't play sports and didn't enjoy sport, and so people used to question whether or not he was gay. . . . but it would be very difficult if you were to admit that you were homosexual.

Similar attitudes were expressed by a group of year nine boys from Tamville, a middle-class city school, who made the following comments in relation to what would happen if one of their classmates stated that he was gay: 'I won't play with him any more', 'I would tell him to fuck off', 'I'd probably beat him up' and 'I pretty much hate them all'. One year 11 boy, John, at St Adams, a working-class high school, was quite articulate about the oppression he had faced as the result of being labelled gay:

I copped it every minute of the day when I got, when I came here, copped it every day, I still get called failure, people still think I am gay. . . . I'm not going to say that I'm gay or I'm heterosexual because I don't think that you know what you are at my age, and I think, I mean, I could be gay now, I could be heterosexual when I'm older, I could be this when I'm older.

There are three boys in this school that really shit me to tears. And no matter how hard they try, they even did it at the formal, they can't just leave it, they have to pay me out, they have to do it. . . . people like D. and B. and everyone like that, they're really, really, really harsh, they're really mean, . . . high school's really hard and I don't see what they get out of making someone's life miserable. I try and see it from their direction. . . . That's what makes my life miserable at this school. I don't even want to be here today. I'm only here today because I have to practice the dance for the thing on Friday and I have to do an English assignment.

The experiences of John are not dissimilar from those found in other research (see, e.g., Martino & Pallotta-Chiarolli, 2005; Robinson, 2005c). However, within many schools there is an avoidance of efforts to address issues of homophobia (see, e.g., Mills, 1996). There can be a multiplicity of reasons for this, fear of opening up discussions around sexuality, being perceived to legitimise gay and lesbian sexualities, attracting public attention to the school, and teachers' and school administrators' own homophobia. The silences within equity and social justice discourses within schools around the issue of homophobia are often grounded in discourses that construct homophobic behaviours as boys just joking around. This was the case with Julian, a year 11 boy from Tamville High School who stated that:

> I've...you know I've called my mates poofters and that. You know it doesn't mean nothing. It doesn't mean they are a poofter but it just...it's just a joke. That's all we consider it. And it never goes any further than that you know it just. Like that Sam he gets a bit of flak. Because he just does things everybody else doesn't do and they just make fun of him....Ah they...they're going on about him going to the gay Mardi Gras. (Laughter) You know. Mainly Isaac. You know that's it (laughter). It just happens. It's just all part of growing up. It's always going to happen.

However, the grade 11 boy Sam, who Julian referred to above, when interviewed broke into tears when describing these 'jokes'. At the elite English Queen's school, 'just joking' was used to suggest that bullying did not occur at this school. As one year 11 boy from this school tried to explain:

> Even though a teacher might think that a kid is bullying another kid, it's like having a joke between each other, you know what I mean, like it's not bullying, but if the teacher saw it they'd think it's bullying, you know what I mean, it's just like more of a joke and like everyone just laughs about it. Even like, when we have like a sports event, so you've got the rowing tomorrow, there's all posters around and nicknames, and like you just stereotype someone and we just joke about it.

Such explanations for various aggressive and violent behaviours are not uncommon (see, e.g., Kehily & Nayak, 1997; Robinson, 2005c). They are particularly prevalent when justifying homophobic (and misogynist) behaviours. The role of 'just joking' in policing particular gender constructions requires significant critique.

The politics of survival

For many boys the negotiation of their school years is a matter of survival. This negotiation can involve them avoiding violence, sanctioning violence or being violent themselves. In some cases this occurs through forming alliances with other violent boys, staying away from potential victims, making others victims or by being prepared to fight those who threaten and intimidate them. In a very few cases some boys do take a stand against the bullying of marginalised boys. For instance, Mark, the boy who experienced racial violence at Irish Saints School, talked about how 'a couple of times' his friends had stood up for him. One of his friends indicated how he had done just that:

> I have stuck up for Mark, 'cos they don't want him to play sport 'cos he's slow and not very good at it and I said let him play.

However, other boys in his year level suggested that this is not a regular occurrence as such a stand is often fraught with danger. They suggested that supporting boys who are the recipients of violence in schools can also make them targets because, 'You might get picked on then, 'cos they might be bigger and there's a lot more of them.' Furthermore, they also indicated that out of fear they are also likely to participate in the bullying of Mark:

> *Grant*: And like one person might be picking on Mark, and even if they're friends of Mark, they have to join in.
> *Martin*: What happens if they don't join in?
> *David*: Well they probably would get them (his other friends) to come over and join in too.

This survival through failing to stand up for one's friends out of fear of becoming the target of bullying oneself is closely aligned with that of seeking out another victim in order to deflect attention away from oneself. This was apparent at English Queen's where one grade 12 boy reflected on the practices at the school:

> What I hear happens everywhere is rejection of one person to make everyone else feel good. It was like this in grade eight because everyone pretty much knowing another person, everyone was looking for a friend and they needed to group together and expel someone else to make them look bad, etc. It's typical. I found in my class two people who were rejected.

Some boys take a path of avoidance, like that of the boy who left English Queen's. Few seek out support from authority figures. For instance, when asked what the teacher did when he was bullied, the boy who had told of other kids farting on his school work replied, 'I didn't tell him'. For many of the boys who experience this kind of continual harassment, appeals to authority are seldom used, as this is likely to bring further retribution. The only way out is to usually 'fight back'.

For many boys, survival requires being perceived to be 'hard', especially in low socioeconomic locations (see, e.g., Reay, 2002; Skelton, 2001). Such perceptions about one's hardness can come about through being violent to others or standing up to threats. Thus, for many boys who experience harassment and bullying at school they succumb to the pressure to be a 'real boy' by participating in fights. For example at Irish Saints, the group of year seven boys spoke of how an act of racism provoked a violent incident at the school: 'Like there's a boy in the school he's from another country, and they picked on him about his name and he never liked it and one day everyone kept saying it, and he just got up and they just started fighting.'

This fighting is not to be unexpected; it is a common response on the part of those who have been bullied. For example, a year 11 boy from a country high school, Mountainview, spoke of the ways in which he had been bullied when he first arrived at the school. He explained how he had finally become sick of the teasings of one boy in particular and had finally lashed out and hit him. He stated that, 'I just did it because I didn't see any other way to stop this.' And, according to this boy, it worked, for as a result the bullying stopped. His seeming willingness to engage in violent behaviour in his own defence had marked him as a 'real boy' and therefore not in need of regular sanctioning. The grade 11 boy from St Adams who was regularly being bullied because he was perceived to be gay also indicated that the only way that he could see the violence stopping was by fighting back:

> If someone's going to start me and mess with me, I'm going to mess with them because I'm sick of being picked on. . . . I don't care if I lose in a fight, I don't care whether I lose or not, I'm going to stick up for myself. That's the way I think of things.

As with Mark, the primary school boy from Irish Saints, above who had been good at school work and who 'didn't see any other way to stop' the violence, this boy was preparing to engage in violence to stop the bullying he was facing.

Conclusion

This chapter has sought to indicate some of the ways in which violence structures communities of masculine practice within schools. Implicit within this chapter is an understanding that whilst within dominant communities there is a privileging of some boys over others, violent practices amongst boys also underpin a gender order that works in the interests of men as a social group. Thus, whilst the focus of the chapter has been on boys' violence towards each other, this has not meant to downplay the experiences of violence experienced by girls in schools by both boys and other girls. This is clearly a serious issue (Robinson, 2005c). The focus on violence amongst boys in schools is also not to suggest that violence is never committed by teachers. For instance, in some schools some male teachers enter into 'blokey' violence with some boys (see, e.g., Duncan, 1999, p. 111). Nor does this focus suggest that boys cannot be violent towards or harass female teachers (see, e.g., Robinson, 2000). However, the ways in which violence in schools is utilised amongst boys requires an analysis of how such violence is deployed in ways that entrench particular forms of privilege.

The denigration and harassment of boys who engage positively with the schooling process in many working-class schools clearly works against the interests of boys from low socioeconomic backgrounds. Fear of violence and the exclusion of boys who do engage positively work to construct a warning to boys in some schools not to be too enthusiastic in their academic engagement with the school curriculum. Such anti-schoolwork attitudes are not solely responsible for some boys' 'failures' within school, as Jackson (2006) indicates, boys' anti-school behaviours can also be a means of diverting attention away from their own perceived inability to navigate the demands of the academic curriculum. However, a failure to address this culture and associated violence continues to ensure that the benefits of successful engagement with the academic curriculum remain in the hands of the already privileged.

The experiences of the boy who was bullied out of English Queen's is one example of the ways in which schools that reproduce class privileges use meritocratic discourses to justify their academic success. The implications of this exclusion are that the environment at the school is only suitable for those boys who are able to match it intellectually with the expectations of the school culture. Interestingly, the departed boy was constructed as now being 'happy', with the implication that he had found his place in an environment where he belonged, presumably a less academic school. Further, discourses also operate within these privileged schools to create 'other' schools as dangerous places because they do not have the same academic expectations. Such discourses are partly grounded in assumptions about dangerous working-class masculinities

(Cannan, 1996; Fine et al., 1997). However, whilst the schools considered in this chapter had very different academic cultures, underpinning the communities of masculine practice within the various schools were common discourses about masculinity. Boys were expected to be tough emotionally and physically, and have at least a liking for, if not be good at, sport. When boys could demonstrate such attributes then going against the grain of the dominant culture within the school was possible, although not necessarily easy (Reay, 2002).

When boys did not perform their masculinities according to the dominant cultures of the school, homophobic discourses were regularly deployed to punish such boys. Homophobic, along with misogynist, discourses are integral to the policing of the borders protecting communities of masculine practice. Within some working-class schools engaging in school work, especially dance and singing, and not being tough or sporty meant a boy's sexuality could be brought into question. Similarly, boys who were neither competitive academically nor athletically could be constructed as gay at the elite boys' private school. In each of these differing environments, such a construction is fraught with dangers.

Many boys within schools are faced with the task of surviving the dangers associated with the dominant politics of masculinity operating within their schools. This can mean forming alliances with those who have the potential to protect, demonstrating a willingness to access those forms of violent practices which reinscribe hegemonic forms of masculinity or attempting to fly below the radar of dominant expectations of masculine cultures. These various politics of survival work in ways that reinforce violent behaviours in schools. Whilst it needs to be recognised that schools are not isolated entities unshaped by the discourses that work within a range of other sites to produce idealised forms of masculinity, schools are key sites for the shaping of masculinities, and thus have to be one site where such disruptions are attempted. As such, they are sites where the relationships between violence, masculinities and privilege have to be considered and where necessary disrupted.

Implications for practice

Addressing issues of gender, violence and privilege in schools can appear to be an overwhelming task. Discourses that construct boys, and working-class boys in particular, as violent are widespread beyond, as well as within, school walls. However, schools and teachers can make a difference to the ways in which boys learn to interact with each

other, and with girls and women, by disrupting normalised constructions of masculinity. Strategies designed to cause such a disruption need
to happen at all levels of schooling: policy, links to the community,
school organisation and within the classroom through curriculum and
pedagogy. The focus in this section is on the classroom.

In order to undertake change, understanding the communities of masculine practice operating within the school is critical. Questions have to
be asked about which boys (and indeed male teachers) are valued and
profiled and which are vilified and abused; and why and how. Likewise
responding to questions about how some boys manage to successfully
negotiate schooling will be insightful for developing strategies to address
gendered violence in schools. Answers to these questions may be very
different depending upon the context and locality of the school. Small
action research projects undertaken by either staff or students (or both)
can help to answer these questions within the local context (see, for
instance, Atweh et al., 1998; Cammarota & Fine, 2008). Such research
projects can then provide important insights into the kinds of strategies
that need to be developed at various levels within the school.

Whilst action research projects within schools are often undertaken
by small groups of staff, many such research projects can be developed as
part of the regular classroom curriculum. For instance, research projects
that explore and respond to the issue of violence in schools can draw
upon social sciences research skills and knowledge for collecting data,
mathematical skills and knowledge for interpreting statistical data, and
various English curriculum expectations can be met through the pre-
sentation of findings and recommendations. In planning activities for
such projects there is a wealth of material available on the Internet.
Two excellent sources include, in Australia, Bullying. No Way! (www.
bullyingnoway.com.au/) and, in the United Kingdom, Beatbullying
(www.beatbullying.org/). Sites such as these often provide video clips,
advice to teachers, links to special programmes, worksheets, further
reading and other useful materials. They also provide advice on how to
deal with sensitive issues such as homophobia, racism and faith-based
violence (See also Martino & Pallotta-Chiarolli, 2005).

Underpinning such work with students have to be pedagogical practices that align with the intent of disrupting existing gendered relations
of power. The productive pedagogies research provides insights into
the kinds of practices that can work to do this in classrooms, whilst
at the same time rejecting deficit models of students from disadvantaged backgrounds (Hayes et al., 2006). The productive pedagogies
approach suggests that classrooms need to be supportive, connected to

students' worlds, value and engage with difference, and be intellectually challenging.

Such a classroom would, for instance, ensure that all students are encouraged to engage with classroom tasks without fear of put downs, whether such put downs be based on, for example, homophobic discourses or on derogatory comments about ability. These classrooms would take account of students' interests, although not reinforce particular constructions of gender, and enable students to impact on their environment through meaningful tasks. They would encourage students to understand, problematise and challenge privilege by asking questions such as who wins and who loses from particular sets of power relations, and what needs to be done to change oppressive power relations. These classrooms would also ensure that *all* students are intellectually challenged regardless of perceived abilities. For instance, negative assumptions about the level of intellectual complexity that boys (and girls) from disadvantaged backgrounds can engage with often means such students are not provided with the opportunity to demonstrate high-level outcomes. Failing to provide students who traditionally do not do well at school with an intellectually challenging classroom perpetuates privilege, as such students are denied opportunities to develop those skills and understandings of knowledge valued within the formal curriculum and post-compulsory education (for greater detail on productive pedagogies and gender, see Keddie & Mills, 2007; Lingard et al., 2002; Mills & Keddie, 2007).

The implications for practice of the material presented in this chapter are many and varied. In this section the focus has been on the classroom and on students. However, successful gender reforms will also require school policies to align with classroom approaches in order to ensure that teachers' class work is not undermined through contradictory messages elsewhere in the school. Further, there is no suggestion here that students are *the* problem. Many adults within schools have invested interests in maintaining exiting patterns of privilege. These interests will also have to be challenged as part of any successful programme to address issues of masculinities, violence and privilege within schools.

6

'I'm not scared of the teacher – I can hold him – I can hold him with my bare hands': Schoolboys, Male Teachers and Physical Violence at a Durban Secondary School in South Africa

Robert Morrell, Deevia Bhana and Vijay Hamlall

Violence that occurs in schools is antithetical to the function of schools as places for educating children and young people in conditions of safety, tolerance and reverence for knowledge. Ever since the English public schooling system was described by Thomas Hughes in *Tom Brown's School Days* (1857), the existence of robust, hierarchical and often violent relations between schoolboys has been acknowledged. In recent decades, violence between school students has become a central concern for studies of gender in schooling, with bullying, sexual harassment and physical violence linked in a number of studies to issues of masculinity and patriarchal privilege. However, an issue that has been less well-documented and that is still poorly understood is the phenomenon of violence between students and teachers. In this chapter, we draw on empirical research conducted in a secondary school in Durban, South Africa, to explore the ways in which masculinity is implicated in physical violence that occurs between schoolboys and their male teachers in the South African context.

Our interest here is threefold. Firstly, we want to consider issues of physical violence between schoolboys and teachers against the backdrop of South Africa's extensive history of social and political violence. We understand violence in schools, in this sense, as a manifestation of broader cultural, institutional and social beliefs and practices in which masculine authority and power are often expressed in physically violent ways. Secondly, we want to consider physical violence that schoolboys at times direct at their teachers as attempts to exercise agency within a hierarchical institutional setting, in which students feel the need to protect their dignity from teacher infraction. As the quote from which the chapter of the title is taken vividly illustrates, student masculinities perceived as being under threat are at times defended with violent aggression in the South African school setting. Thirdly, we consider acts of teacher violence against male students as a means of establishing and maintaining masculine authority over students. This, we argue, is violence intended to ensure adult authority and its primacy over learning needs and student entitlements, despite legislation and policy developments aimed at altering such practices.

Violence in South African schools

South Africa is a country in transition, and the volatility of schools needs to be understood against the national backdrop. As a country, South Africa manifests very high levels of sexual and other forms of physical violence. Levels of homicide in South Africa are amongst the highest in the world, and according to Seedat, 'A dominant feature of the violence is the disproportionate role of young men as perpetrators and victims' (Seedat et al., 2009, p. 69). Young people are particularly affected by violent crime, with high numbers of rape victims amongst young women (CIET, 2000; Human Rights Watch World Report, 2001), and homicide fatality statistics dominated by men in the 15–29-year-old age category (Seedat et al., 2009). Two recent studies of men and rape in South Africa support these claims with respect to sexual violence, finding that approximately 25 per cent of men interviewed in large samples of young men in the Eastern Cape and slightly older men in the Eastern Cape and KwaZulu-Natal, admitted to having raped a woman (Jewkes et al., 2006, 2010).

It is hardly surprising, in light of such figures, that the violence experienced within the broader community should also be experienced within school settings. This is not to suggest that violence is a recent phenomenon, however, and it is important to note that schools in South Africa and more generally on the African continent have long been sites of widespread physical violence. Rape, murder and sexual assaults are not uncommon (Dunne et al., 2006). While much of this violence involves attacks on female learners (both by male teachers and by male learners) (Jewkes et al., 2002; Niehaus, 2000), the phenomenon of violence between males is also a serious problem, taking the form of gang violence in some schools (Glaser, 2000; Griggs, 1997; Vetten, 2000).

Both in its culture and its social and political institutions, however, shifts are consciously being promoted to address the legacy of apartheid, to promote democracy and to foster racial and classed redress. While many of these shifts have been broadly welcomed, they have nonetheless instigated widespread changes to ways of being and doing, with which institutions such as schools must grapple in an ongoing way. For example, previous institutional structures and practices in schools have been destabilised with the introduction of new curricula (Chisholm, 2004), the banning of corporal punishment, the introduction of new democratic forms of governance (Harber, 2001), and a sense that teachers have lost the authority and aura previously associated with their roles (Bloch, 2009).

These changes have occurred within a policy context that has explicitly sought to achieve gender equality. While efforts may not have been all that successful (Morrell et al., 2009), conditions have been created for posing new challenges to authoritarian forms of male authority. While such challenges are necessary in order to transform South African schools into more equitable and socially just institutions, for many, masculinity is seen as having undergone a kind of crisis. In the wake of policy and institutional reforms, masculine power and authority are called into question, at times with violent consequences.

Explanations for violence have focused on constructions of masculinity and the place of poverty, homophobia and misogyny within these (Bhana, 2005; Kimmel, 2000; Messerschmidt, 1993; Morrell, 1998a). There are many reasons advanced to explain the violence of young men (Barker, 2005; Hearn, 1998; Seidler, 2006), including gender inequalities and men's perceived necessity in patriarchal societies to assert their power over women and younger men. Among the explanations that men in South Africa give to explain their violence is that they have not been respected. This is the explanation offered, for example, by young men who gang raped a girl who had slept with men other than her boyfriend, and was thus considered by her attackers to have disrespected him (Wood & Jewkes, 2001). A perceived lack of respect is also a factor in violence by older men, who explain their hostility towards what they refer to as the 'cheek' of younger men (Campbell, 1992; Carton, 2000).

The focus of this chapter is on physical violence as expressed between older and younger men. Violence between men occurs along a number of fault lines, including those of sexual orientation and race.

The violence itself is often located within discourses of exclusion by which hegemonic ideals are established, protected and reproduced. This often occurs by specifically denigrating and 'othering' males who do not meet or show opposition to hegemonic ideals (Ferguson, 2001; Martino & Pallotta-Chiarolli, 2003; Sewell, 1997). In the process of creating and maintaining a hierarchy of masculinities, power is created and mobilised. In the school setting, this power is conventionally wielded as legitimate authority by teachers. In the study whose findings are presented in this chapter, this wielding of power and authority was most obvious, symbolically and physically, in the use of corporal punishment by teachers on learners.

The frequent use of violence by teachers, together with boys' investment in violent cultures, produces a climate of hostility, anger and resentment. Adult male teachers in such a climate may relate to boys not from positions of pastoral care givers or as authority figures who keep professional distance, but rather as elder males who use physical power to assert their dominance. Teachers, however, do not have a monopoly over violence – older school boys or groups of boys may retaliate violently or even initiate violence against male teachers perceived as challenging their self-concept as young autonomous males.

Physical conflict that occurs between teachers and learners in these ways stems from competing versions of masculinity, with fights occurring in schools where the violence of learners and teachers is part of a status quo that the school is unable to diffuse. But fighting that takes place in schools can also be seen in light of wider social processes that are unfolding in South Africa. These involve the renegotiation of racial identities and relationships which were set on unequal and competitive terms by colonialism and apartheid. Another important factor is poverty which charges school life with uncertainty and future insecurity. The claim that teachers and learners, adult and younger men, make for respect permits both to resort to physical force. Violence is, after all, a resource available to all men though not all choose to use it (Messerschmidt, 1993).

Race is also significant in the construction of masculine identities within school and community settings alike. International research such as school-based ethnographies concerned with boys and masculinity (e.g., Mac an Ghaill, 1994; Sewell, 1997) has shown how gender intersects with race in the formation of masculinities. Such studies have demonstrated that individual identities are produced, in part, through collective practices associated with negotiating connections centred around more broadly perceived racial and ethnic identities. In a country such as South Africa, which has a history of legalised and insti-tutionalised racism, and in which race still overlaps strongly with socio-economic status, racial and ethnic identities can place considerable emphasis on being tough and being able to use violence.

Particular shared constructions of masculinity in school can and do bring boys and male teachers into violent confrontation on grounds of physical equality rather than on structured grounds where author-ity and age establish hierarchy and inequality. Violence is thus used in situations of protest to challenge power inequalities and to assert particular readings of youth masculinity. Historically, precedents for vio-lence used in this way exist on the gold mines where white and black miners, separated by a vast gulf of authority, were attracted by 'the allure of violence'. As discussed in the following sections of this chapter, however, we see how violence centred around notions of masculin-ity and authority is played out in a school setting, in which violence became the language by which struggles over power were conducted (Breckenridge, 1998).

The context of the research study

The research for this paper was conducted at Sunville Secondary School,[1] a technical high school located in Chatsworth in the city of Durban, South Africa. The research was undertaken by Vijay, who has taught for a number of years at the school. The partic-ipants in this qualitative research were male teachers and learn-ers at Sunville, all of whom had been involved in incidents of teacher–learner confrontations. Chatsworth had been created by the apartheid state as a township exclusively for Indian habitation, although Chatsworth is no longer exclusively Indian. With the abolition of the Group Areas Act in 1991, an increasing number of African and Coloured[2] people have moved into Chatsworth. Most of these peo-ple are concentrated in informal settlements that have mushroomed in vacant spaces within Chatsworth, which is densely populated with a largely working-class population. The unemployment rate is over 50 per cent (Desai, 2000), the crime rate is high and many youth are involved in gangs. Alcohol and drug abuse is common, and boys and men frequent local *shebeens* (informal bars) where violence is common.

Sunville is a co-educational, racially mixed, school with a large major-ity of boys. The gender regime of the school celebrates a tough and rough masculinity with an emphasis on heterosexuality. Intimidation, bullying and violence are often used by the boys to produce and reproduce the dominant, or hegemonic (Connell, 1996), masculinity at this school. As described above, race and socioeconomic status intersect with masculinities in this particular school setting.

Methods used to collect and analyse data

Our research data was primarily gained from in-depth semi-structured interviews conducted by Vijay with teachers and learners of Sunville. An interview schedule utilised questions pertaining to teachers' and learners' experience of violence in the school, inquiring about what happened in the school when learners who were confronted by teachers acted out and attacked by hitting back. Interviews with learners asked them about how they felt when they had been embarrassed, ridiculed or physically punished by teachers. Still other questions inquired about the process of escalation to physical aggression and the conditions under which such escalation occurred. Teachers were interviewed about their experiences of violence in the school, and in particular about their views regarding corporal punishment and the relationship of corporal punishment to learners reacting violently.

In some cases, boys were interviewed immediately after an incident of violence against a teacher had come to Vijay's attention. The boys were encouraged to tell stories in response to questions, an approach described as 'good practice' (Holstein & Gubrium, 1995). Because Vijay was also a teacher in the school, and the learners being interviewed were formally under his authority, a power gradient existed between teacher and learner, interviewer and research participants. In order to establish an empathetic environment for the learners, Vijay used an approach of strategic self-disclosure, relating, for example, an incident from his own past in which he had been punished as a pupil in school by a teacher, and describing how the incident had made him feel. This approach not only provoked and produced further interview talk from the respondents but also served to establish greater freedom to talk about the incident in which the learners had been involved.

All the interviews were conducted in English and transcribed. The analysis and selection of the transcriptions was based solely on the subjective meaning and interpretation of the respondents' experience (Denzin, 1989). Comparisons and contrasts allowed us inductively to draw composite themes that reflected shared experiences, reactions, feelings and common meanings (Lincoln & Guba, 1985).

Boys and male teachers negotiating violence at Sunville school

Our findings indicate that male teachers at Sunville do not tend to relate to boys from positions of professional distance, but rather as elder males who use physical power to establish their authority. Boys at the school, on the other hand, are not passive recipients of teacher violence, and some boys actively and physically resist teachers. As discussed elsewhere in this chapter, many teachers' notions of authority have been challenged by laws that limit their right to punish students and give children new rights (Children's Amendment Act, 2007). The abolishment of corporal punishment by the South African Schools Act (1996) is seen by teachers as presenting a particular challenge, removing as it does the ultimate sanction from teachers, one which many had previously used to confirm an age- and rank-based hierarchy of masculinities in the school (see Mac an Ghaill, 1994). However, legislation is not the sole factor leading to changes in the ways that teachers exercise authority. Chatsworth, like other areas that share South Africa's divided history, has been left with a highly complex mix of regimes, cultures, value systems and traditions, which in turn shape the cultures of schools such as Sunville. Thus we see the manner in which teachers handle disciplinary issues in schools as being constituted, on the one hand, in dialogue with (and at times contrary to) legislation, and on the other, within the complex interplay of race, social class and geographical location.

Male teachers and violence

At Sunville, male teachers often deploy overt physical action in order to restrain, control and dominate boys, and examples of this are especially observed outside the classroom. These teachers often use their bodies to block the path of boys, to bump them into line, to knock them against walls. At other times, direct aggression is used to control a volatile situation. The following extract is taken from Vijay's fieldnotes:

> During ground duty I witnessed a scuffle between two boys. A few of the teachers on duty rushed to the scene to intervene....Mr. Desmond a male teacher caught these two boys by the throat and pinned them against the wall in order to separate them. This show of overt aggression immediately resulted in these boys succumbing and the other boys were all suddenly silent and slowly dispersed. Mr. Desmond then dragged them to the office.

It is common for male teachers at Sunville to use violence to stop violence. Teacher violence is normalised under the guise of intervention. Ironically, interventions by teachers such as Mr. Desmond give legitimacy to violent learner masculinities. Vijay observed that it was male teachers who always intervened in these conflicts, whereas female teachers did not participate in dealing with boy-on-boy violence. It is thus important to recognise that teacher intervention (and non-intervention) in schoolboy violence provides an important space in which particular forms of teacher masculinity and femininity are confirmed and maintained.

In the absence of non-violent mechanisms for dealing with male schoolboy violence, male teachers at Sunville remain particularly complicit in entrenching the cultural context where violence is seen to be the most appropriate means to end conflict in the school. In the words of one male teacher: 'This is the only language they understand...you have to clobber one or two.' It would be overly simplistic to assume that violence is simply engendered by dominating male teachers. Schools as institutions are significant places where violence is enacted, and boys have been identified as being particularly likely to engage in violence and crime (Morrell, 1998a), a concern that resonates beyond South Africa (see, e.g., Barker, 2005; Mills, 2001). We therefore acknowledge that violence in schools is far more complex than simply what male teachers do to innocent schoolboys.

Despite the culturally entrenched violence that permeates the Sunville context, the use of violence by male teachers occurs within a broader policy context in which their authority is neither unquestioned nor unquestionable. The policy discourse of children's rights, freedom and agency is in turn reinscribed within the power relations of the school. Authoritarian teaching styles and unbridled teacher authority that may once have been accepted are now contested by the knowledge that teachers may be prosecuted for infringing the rights of children (Morrell, 2007). Schoolboys now challenge the limits of teacher authority and do not passively accept teacher violence. As we see in the extract below, legislation that promotes learner entitlement provides a source of tension between schoolboys and male teachers, which sometimes leads to violent confrontations:

Mr. Naidoo: This boy continued to walk up and down the corridor with the music loud on his cell phone. I asked him to put the music off in a polite manner. He did not say anything. He just lunged at me, put his hands onto my chain – pushed me into the classroom, broke my glasses. He is a big boy and a strong boy too. I toppled over the desks and onto the floor. Then his other comrades came and the whole lot of them. I could feel a few kicks and so on while I was on the floor from the other boys.

Vijay: How did you react?

Mr. Naidoo: I am happy that I remained tolerant and calm. I did not use violence by punching him and so on. I could have punched him and opened up a cut in his mouth or somewhere...I could really hurt this boy and I will lose my job....

In this case Mr. Naidoo's authority is openly challenged with physical violence, which the boys have come to understand as being their main source of power (Garbarino, 1995). Mr. Naidoo's account of this violent episode reflects the complex difficulties experienced by teachers caught up in the tensions between policy discourse, professional practice and violent contexts. There is an uneasy interplay between his concerns about what he sees as professionally appropriate – to be polite, tolerant and calm in his dealings with learners – and his awareness of his own physical strength and potential for inflicting physical harm on them. However, he is ultimately overpowered by the violence of others who share neither concerns for his professional obligations nor his physical safety. Instead, these are used against him in a collective demonstration of the learners' masculine power.

Socioeconomic status may be seen as an additional factor in this case, as international research on school violence has shown that low-income youth who lack other means of affirming their identity often resort to violence as a chief means of exerting power and authority (Mac an Ghaill, 1994; Mills, 2001; Sewell, 1997). Humphries (1995) suggests that in certain contexts such violence is part of boys' transition to adulthood and an expression of a particular form of youth masculinity. As was the case in Humphries study, many of the boys at Sunville aspired to be seen as men, and therefore considered violence in particular circumstances to be a legitimate means of achieving this aspiration.

Violence in the Chatsworth community has become normalised and many men appear to have become de-sensitised to violence, often using it to settle disputes. Similarly, many boys from this area also resort to violence, particularly when they believe that their rights are being infringed. However in a school setting such as Sunville, teachers' and schoolboys' interpretations of and reactions to 'rights' legislation are shaped by power, age and race dynamics that at times reach boiling point. The example provided by Mr. Pasiya, the only African teacher on the staff at Sunville, helps us to better understand competing discourses and the fluid nature of power and generational differences between male teachers and boys:

> *Mr. Pasiya*: The boys in this school feel that they can do whatever they want. The discipline is getting out of hand. They know for a fact that no one can do them anything, they do whatever they feel. At some stage if they can dare you that much – they don't even care for you as a teacher. The only punishment they recognize is that punishment [meaning violence]. Chasing him out of class, suspension and so on does not work. That is what they want. Where we are today is because of that – soft type of discipline. When it comes to my culture and religion – it says straight away that if you spare the rod you spoil the child – it is our religion – it is in the Bible. There is a chapter in the Bible that says that.

Mr. Pasiya is not comfortable with the newfound freedom that boys express. He objects to their belief that 'no one can do them anything' and to what he sees as their diminished respect for teachers:

> *Mr. Pasiya*: ...I was once a boy, I know how to treat the boys. I am what I am and who I am because of the way I was treated as a boy. It is not an ill-treatment but a different way to discipline and it puts you on track.

Mr. Pasiya understands corporal punishment not in terms of physical violence or 'ill-treatment' but rather as a legitimate means to an end, a way to keep things 'on track'. Yet evidence from a number of studies internationally shows that aggressive forms of discipline lead to the construction of tough forms of pupil masculinity. When teachers adopt an aggressive violent type of 'discipline' with male learners they are helping to create macho modes of masculinity identified in practically all studies of masculinity and schooling (Connell, 1989; Corrigan, 1979; Mac an Ghaill, 1994; Walker, 1988; Willis, 1977). These writers argue that a violent discipline system invites competition in machismo among boys and sometimes between the boys and teachers.

As we have argued earlier, policy discourses promulgating children's rights and the abolishment of corporal punishment are implicated in what we see as increasing tensions between working-class youth and teachers in the South African context where racial tensions and systemic inequalities have yet to be adequately addressed. Yet violence between students and teachers in this context is not only perpetrated by students, but by teachers in response to student resistance to teacher authority. As the example of Mr. Pasiya demonstrates, his view that legislation promoting children's freedom and their right not to be punished only increases boys' challenges to authority furnishes the rationale for using physical punishment in response to such challenges from boys seen as 'daring' him to use violence against them. Mr. Pasiya presents himself within the gendered role of a disciplinarian whose violence is seen not as misguided, but rather as directed by a spiritual goal of keeping boys on the right track.

What Vijay has observed is that in the absence of any intervention strategies for addressing issues and cultural tensions associated with race, ethnicity, authority and power in the Sunville school setting, this pattern of boys' and teachers' behaviour has become cyclic.

Generational dynamics are also rooted in particular cultural practices that assert the power of the adult. In Zulu cultural practices, for example, 'ukuhlonipha' or respect for elders plays an important role in regulating relations between adult males and younger men and children. 'Ukuhlonipha' refers to customs of avoidance and deference that reflect generational hierarchies that are both contested and reinforced (Carton, 2001). Here again, corporal punishment has become a site where the rights of adult come into conflict with the rights of the child. The new legal framework in South Africa has the effect of depriving adult men of a major instrument used to police 'ukuhlonipha'. When Mr. Pasiya talks about school discipline he is defending his male authority and Zulu gender hierarchies (Mchunu, 2006), and thus he sees the boys as also looking for respect from their peers and from elder men. According to Morrell (1998b) discussions of African masculinity have to take into account both critical changes and continuities. In the decline of the Indigenous age cohort we find two important themes: the age-old challenge by the young of the old, and the emergence of new black masculinities in new (urban) contexts. This generational struggle involves open defiance of the authority of elders and flagrant disregard for custom, a process that is accompanied, particularly in the cities, with a rejection of traditional ways. Yet in many of these associations boys are still brought to manhood in a process that involves the teaching of ritual and respect.

The notion of respect has become key in the manner in which boys and male teachers interact with each other, and again, this can be understood against the backdrop of the broader cultural context. Mchunu's (2007) study of young Zulu males in KwaZulu-Natal, for example, found that there was a struggle between younger males and older males emanating from a competition for respect. He argues that respect is a key feature in constructions of traditional Zulu masculinity. This confrontation seems to have been similar to the sub-cultural opposition of the (White) Ducktails, in that it flouted convention and put a premium on independence rather than fealty. The Ducktail youth subculture that emerged in South Africa after World War Two operated as a vehicle for youth to indulge in and express their various and often ambiguous identities and develop their own code of respect (Mooney, 1998).

Mr Pasiya's views draw on his cultural and religious views, harnessing them for the purpose of resurrecting corporal punishment as an exercise of authority, reinforcing intergenerational hierarchies and simultaneously calling into question the abolition of corporal punishment in South African schools. He can no longer legitimately use corporal punishment as a vehicle to get respect from the boys, and resents this law for what he sees as giving learners too much latitude for challenging and disrespecting their teachers:

> *Mr. Pasiya*: These young people know that they have rights according to the constitution – that you can't touch them – you can't do this – you can't do that. If you give them a good hiding to discipline them – they are running home to tell that you have done this for nothing. They say that they did not do anything, 'he just hit me.'

Mr. Pasiya's comments reveal feelings of both frustration and hostility regarding the ways in which he sees rights discourses as at fault in eroding traditions of teacher authority and the once taken-for-granted power ascribed to adult men. Interestingly, the responses by Mr. Pasiya and Mr. Naidoo to learners' challenges to their authority differ markedly. Yet Mr. Pasiya, who advocates physical punishment, and Mr. Naidoo, who consciously avoids physical violence against learners even when under attack himself, are both mindful that their obligations under the legislation may be used as a tool by others to undermine their professional legitimacy.

'I am not scared of the teacher – I can hold him – I can hold him with my bare hands': Boys' responses to violence, race and male teachers

In this section, we turn to considering in greater depth some of the responses of boys to racial tensions and the violence that characterises their interactions with teachers and peers. As already discussed, the population of Chatsworth was initially exclusively Indian. However, the abolishment of the Group Areas Act in 1991, followed by the end of

Apartheid in 1994, saw the influx of increasing numbers of Africans moving into Chatsworth. However, this demographic shift was not universally welcomed, and the competition for employment and housing placed increased pressure on race relations between Indians and the new African residents in the area. These tensions are often played out in schools as well. Sunville provides an interesting example – under Apartheid, the school took only Indian learners, yet the increasing number of African students enrolled at the school since 1991 is reflective of the changing population of Chatsworth.

For teachers in the school, race relations within and beyond the school can have profound implications. As the only African teacher at the school, Mr. Pasiya is himself subject to violence and threats of violence that are indicative of broader racial tensions and conflicts in the Chatsworth community:

> *Mr. Pasiya*: The Indian boys challenge me more than the African boys. But it is the parents that sometimes also encourage them. There was a parent who came to our school – because his son was bunking classes, running away, running a mock in school, ducking and diving – I had to discipline him. His father came to school and gave his son the gun and said, 'go and shoot that fucking darkie man'. The boy took the gun and the whole class screamed and said no. So there is that racial conflict there.

This violent incident recounted by Mr. Pasiya takes place against the backdrop of racial tensions between working-class Africans and Indians, which has a long history that was further intensified by the racialised labour policies of the Apartheid era (Freund, 1995). The competition over economic space and for political rights between Africans and Indians has served to intensify tensions over the years. The communal violence between Indians and Africans in 1949 was an expression of these pressures and tensions (Chetty cited in Morrell, 1996). The violence in 1949 was concentrated mostly in Inanda and Cato Manor where a substantial Indian community lived among Africans. Since then, however, new sets of pressures continue to emerge, most of them around political rights, access to resources and competition for employment, which in turn fuels current tensions between Africans and Indians in the post-Apartheid era.

Against the background of this historical legacy, poverty among Indians living in Chatsworth has also intensified since 1994 (Desai, 2000). During this period affirmative action policies designed to provide opportunities for Africans have been perceived as a threat by Indians. This situation creates further racial tensions at Sunville, where many of the Indian learners experience social and economic distress, and regard the upward social and economic mobility of Africans with hostility. In a context where violence is common and there is a constant threat to all learners from male teachers and other boys, there are a limited number of options available. The school's authorities show little commitment or capacity to end the violence, and boys cannot remove themselves from the situation without leaving the school. While some boys might try and hide, make themselves invisible, refuse to be part of the violence (cf. Bhana, 2005), the more common response is to resort to understandings of masculine power as demonstrated through displays of violence.

Attributes such as hardness, readiness to confront antagonists and fighting prowess were key elements in the construction of hegemonic masculinity. The use of force and aggression to settle disputes was a key feature of the boys' micro-culture that served to validate and amplify their masculine reputations. Combined with the violent masculinities of some of the school's teachers, many of the boys' investment in violence or intentions of violence generated a great deal of volatility, anger and pain:

> *Shivern*: Why should they hit us? Mr. Pasiya hits first then talks. I don't like that. One day I will show him. He is coming from wherever and tries to control us. We will show him.

Shivern's contempt for Mr. Pasiya and his use of violence is clear. In the absence of any formal structure within the school through which issues can be raised or strategies designed, violence becomes for Shivern an 'obvious' solution. Shivern is vengeful and he demonstrates clearly that Mr. Pasiya's attempt to control breeds anger, hatred and further violence. 'We will show him' bears testimony to the collective significance that boys give to violent teacher masculinities. Shivern's comments are also racialised, and the reference to 'he is coming from wherever' is a strategy used by Shivern, as an Indian boy, to distance himself from Mr. Pasiya. This kind of social distancing and its particular racial construction of 'African' under Apartheid lives on as an aspect of racialised co-existence in South Africa. At Sunville, which remains largely Indian, there is racialised resentment of the presence of an African teacher who under Apartheid would have been prohibited from living in Chatsworth or teaching in the school. This resentment is further exacerbated by Mr. Pasiya's exertion of power through physical violence against both Indian and African boys in the school.

Impati, an African boy, also invoked race to explain the use of severe violence on African boys:

> *Impati*: With Mr. Pasiya he takes advantage because I am Black. He hits very bad. Sometimes I feel like holding him – but what he is doing is, he is making a great future for us – we must understand that. Mr. Pasiya hits the Black boys more – he does not hit the Indian boys so much. The Indian children don't treat Mr. Pasiya well. Indians respect each other, but they don't respect Mr. Pasiya.

Impati says that Mr. Pasiya 'takes advantage because I am Black' whilst 'he does not hit the Indian boys so much'. Racial and cultural configuring and associated meanings have implications for boys like Impati, who see themselves as even more vulnerable to Mr. Pasiya's attack than did Shivern. An interesting contradiction emerges between Impati's anger at Mr. Pasiya, however, in his belief that corporal punishment is 'making a great future for us-we must understand'. In contrast to the Indian pupil who responded to Mr. Pasiya's disciplinary efforts by bringing a gun to class, Impati shares a cultural understanding with Mr. Pasiya that attributes future academic success to the need for physical punishment. Despite his anger at receiving such punishment, Impati accepts that Mr. Pasiya is operating from a shared set of beliefs that are, as he puts it, 'for his own good'. In so doing, he reproduces gendered, racial and cultural assumptions regarding violence, demonstrating his respect for a set of cultural mores through submission to a regime of violence enacted by his teacher.

As an African boy he finds himself aligned to a cultural regime which circumscribes his relation with Mr. Pasiya, whereas Indian boys who neither share nor accept these cultural understandings are more inclined to show disrespect to an African teacher such as Mr. Pasiya. Impati provides similar explanations for Indian boys' respect for Indian teachers assuming that shared race and culture predispose one to show respect and to observe particular cultural practices. Yet as Vijay's interviews further reveal, just as the disciplinary action of an African teacher towards an Indian student can provoke a violent, indeed potentially lethal response, so too Impati's response to physical violence from an Indian teacher incites hostility and a threat of future retaliation:

Impati: He [Mr. Moodley] hit me there right in front of the classroom. He hit me about four or five times with the stick all over my body. I couldn't hold myself – there and then I told him 'what you did is wrong, you should not have done it' and I went for him. I still got that anger when I see him but I just hold myself. Maybe if I see him somewhere else I can catch him and something bad can happen. I mean I can catch him and hit him – somewhere else – not in the school. He embarrassed me and he must pay.

Vijay: Why do you feel this way?

Impati: I am too old to be hit. I am 18 years old now, I should not be hit. You rather talk to me because I am an understanding person, but if you hit me you are showing me disrespect. I am not scared of the teacher – I can hold him – I can hold him with my bare hands. I felt like holding him in front of classroom and I said to myself I will get you. He hit me with a thick stick. He saw that I was strong and he knew it was wrong – later he called me and spoke to me.

Impati is 18 years old, and is therefore considered a man. As such, he considers himself to be an adult with certain entitlements – to be seen as rational and as strong, and not be beaten or humiliated. In his view, to be humiliated by a teacher therefore demands retribution, if not immediately, at some later point in time.

The above examples provide insights into the way male power is negotiated and contested through the bravado of ritualised revenge. Boys resorted to violence as a way of taking revenge and affirming the norm of what it was to be a man. As a man, Impati felt ashamed to be hit in front of his peers. Carton (2001), in his research of Zulu men in the Thukela River valley in KwaZulu, found that the *isithombe sikababa,* the masculine bearing (alter ego), was (and remains) of utmost importance for Zulu men. Carton (2001) found that *ukuphindisela* (revenge attack) was a 'Zulu' reaction to strife and conflict and it was important for Zulu men to *wadla* (conquer) at all costs. For Zulu males it is very important to act like a man *(ukudoda)* and to do things worthy of praise. Revenge is often taken for reasons of *ukudoda* or male pride. *Ukudoda* is also a social and not just an individual feature. One's pride is damaged when respect is not shown, particularly in public, and such disrespect is held to be disrespect for the clan and ancestors, that is, an invisible collectivity is at work in constructions of revenge associated with *hlonipha* (respect).

Impati's anger is in part, then, a response to feeling disrespected and ridiculed, and he is further embarrassed because he knows that boys mock and tease others when corporal punishment has been inflicted.

Corporal punishment in the micro dynamics of the classroom can give rise to shame and humiliation. The infliction of corporal punishment allows for other boys to assert their masculine power and to question Impati's masculinity:

> *Vijay*: How do the other boys react when a teacher hits a boy?
> *Impati*: They laugh and tease you. They say that you caught hiding from a teacher and you did nothing. They say you are a sissy. They say if it was me I would have done something like this or that. Sometimes as a man you feel embarrassed and feel that you can do something.

Impati interprets the violence experienced at the hands of Mr. Moodley, who is Indian, as being differently motivated by comparison to the violence experienced at the hands of Mr. Pasiya. Mr. Moodley's attack is not seen as one that can create a 'great future' but as an attack on his masculinity and his sense of dignity. Strong emotions surface as Impati relives the experience of being beaten in front of the class, believing that the other learners will in turn impugn his masculinity as a consequence. His response in relation to the two teachers, however, reflects differences in the ways that Impati makes sense of their respective raced and gendered understandings. Whereas Mr. Pasiya is afforded the status of an adult in a position of authority and responsibility for his future success, Impati positions himself in relation to Mr. Moodley as an adult in his own right, with all the perceived status and power of an adult. Mr. Moodley has contravened that position and the result is anger and resentment.

Impati's appeal to a more humane way of dealing with teacher–youth struggles is nowhere echoed in any acknowledgement by teachers that pupil misconduct might be or could be rationally addressed. Impati points out, for example, that he is a reasonable person, for whom talking is a more acceptable form of persuasion than being physically attacked. Despite this observation, however, not one of the teachers interviewed in this study made any mention of addressing student conduct through rational conversation and reasoned discussion.

Conclusion and implications for practice

Violence is often used by teachers at Sunville to maintain power and authority, and it is used by the boys to challenge power inequalities. This results in a precarious school context where relationships between teachers and learners become blurred by the use of physical violence. In a climate where teachers do not automatically receive respect by virtue of their position, physical force is often used to command respect and confirm authority. Cultural factors also come into play, with some male teachers relating to boys not just as teaching professionals, but also as elder males who reserve the right to use physical power to assert their dominance. Yet teacher authority is situated in the volatile context of racial tensions and rights discourses whose implications in changing school relations have yet to be resolved. For boys, the use of violence remains a way of asserting their masculine identities in a complex and hostile school environment. Whilst interpreted differentially according to cultural understandings and racial hierarchies within and beyond the school, the boys' experience of violence at the hands of teachers is a source of physical pain, humiliation, and at times, an incitement to violent retribution. At Sunville, both teachers' and learners' masculine investments in violence afford high status to 'tough' forms of masculinity, and contribute to a school culture of hostility, anger and resentment that is reflective of the broader racial and cultural tensions in a changing South Africa.

Notes

1. Pseudonyms have been used for names of participants and schools.
2. We use the racial terminology that was developed under apartheid to distinguish between people on grounds of race. While the country's constitution specifically protects people against racial discrimination the legacy of apartheid is such that racial labels still reflect sociological, race-based realities.

Part III

Language, Representation and Practice

7
Speaking Violence: Homophobia and the Production of Injurious Speech in Schooling Cultures

Cristyn Davies and David McInnes

In this chapter, we explore the ways in which homophobic violence is understood and recognised both in society more broadly and particularly within schooling cultures. We also examine the discourses through which same-sex attraction is constructed, and the impact of these discourses in addressing the ongoing problem of homophobic violence in schools. While physical forms of violence are most salient and most visible – that is most visibly injurious – forms of linguistic violence (direct or indirect name calling and verbal abuse) and emotional and psychological violence also have severe detrimental effects (Davies, 2008; Hillier et al., 1998, 2005; Mason, 2002; Mason & Tomsen, 1997; McInnes, 2008; McInnes & Davies, 2008; Rasmussen, 2006; Robinson & Ferfolja, 2008). All too frequently within school environments, this kind of violence either goes unrecognised (or in some cases is ignored) by educators or is shut down with little room for the perpetrators of such harassment and violence to reflect on their own subject position within relations of power. In our earlier work that examined homophobic and gendered violence within schooling cultures (Davies, 2008; McInnes, 2008; McInnes & Davies, 2008) we outlined an approach to educational ethics that resists the reproduction of normative ideas of the coherent subject. By educational ethics we mean the response of educational institutions such as schools to situations such as homophobic violence, so that students, teachers, parents and the wider community are educated about the engagement of homophobic violence to reinforce normative subjectivity across gender, sexuality, race, class and ability. In order to re-think school violence, we argue that those involved in incidents of homophobic violence would benefit from understanding the effects of their behaviour through the process of *circuits of recognition* that operate when individuals are involved in incidents of homophobic violence.

Through examining two media texts, we consider the process of circuits of recognition in which same-sex desire and homophobia are discursively constituted. In addition, we provide examples of pedagogical approaches that can act as potential *circuit breakers* – that is, methods and practices that intervene in homophobic violence within schooling contexts. Most significantly, it is critical that educators intervene in homophobia when it occurs by engaging students in a process of deconstructing the *circuits of recognition* – that is, the discursive constructions that inform their behaviours and attitudes. We demonstrate how this is also achieved in a student-led initiative. Another more planned approach we discuss is performed ethnography. The methods that we see as critical in these approaches focus on multiple techniques for encouraging students to learn about and explore different positionalities, and also utilise deconstruction as a method for teaching students to interrogate their own and other subject positions within particular discursive regimes. Deconstruction is an approach that was introduced by philosopher Jacques Derrida (1976); it exposes contradictions and internal oppositions within texts including social practices and interactions, showing that those foundations are irreducibly complex, unstable or impossible. The methods that we propose are situated within poststructuralism, and differ from the more commonly employed liberal humanist approaches used in education that tend to focus on pathologising or celebrating individuals, rather than changing systemic cultures, practices and policies.

Initially we briefly outline some of the key scholarship regarding homophobia in schools, which is followed by a concise explanation of the Australian socio-political context with regard to homosexuality and the law, and school policy in the Australian state of Victoria. Most of the examples in this chapter are specific to the Victorian context. Keeping this in mind, our approach takes into consideration the politics of location and socio-political and cultural context. Policy around homophobic and other school violence in Australia, like many other countries, differs across states and territories. However, our approach is designed to be broadly applied in educational contexts.

Scholarship around homophobia in schooling cultures

Homophobia refers to the fear or hatred of homosexual people and to anti-homosexual beliefs and prejudices (Flood & Hamilton, 2008). More specifically, the term represents the attitudes, beliefs, stereotypes and the cognitive and affective (anxiety, disgust, aversion, anger, discomfort, fear) responses based on hostility to or fear of same-sex attracted people (Flood & Hamilton, 2008; Mason & Tomsen, 1997). Same-sex attracted young people are all too frequently subject to homophobic violence perpetrated not just by fellow students, but also by teaching staff. Being subjected to such violence contributes to higher rates of drug and alcohol use, self-harm, depression and attempted suicide among same-sex attracted young people (Hillier et al., 1998, 2005). We argue that employing a *circuits of recognition* approach requires subjects involved in instances of homophobia not only to engage in self reflexivity, but also to think critically about the power relations mobilised when dominant discourses of homophobia are used to recognise the 'other'.[1]

There is a significant and growing body of scholarship that examines homophobic violence in schooling environments through ethnographic research – that is a strategy employed for gathering empirical data on human societies and cultures. Data collection is often conducted through participant observation, interviews, focus groups and questionnaires. In recent years, anti-homophobia education and recognition of sexual diversity within schooling cultures have become a critical focus for Australian and international researchers. Much of this research has focused on same-sex attracted youth within a secondary school context (Davies, 2008; Hillier & Harrison, 2004; Hillier et al., 1998, 1999b, 2005; McInnes, 2008; McInnes & Davies, 2008; Rasmussen, 2006); homophobic violence and harassment experienced by lesbian teachers (Ferfolja, 2008, 2009, 2010); providing pre-service teachers with training around anti-homophobia education (Robinson & Ferfolja, 2001, 2008); gendered (homophobic) violence (Martino, 1999, 2000; McInnes & Couch, 2004; Mills, 1999, 2001, 2006, see chapter in this book; Robinson, 2005a, see chapter this book); gender and sexuality in primary school (Renold, 2005, 2006; Robinson & Davies, 2008a); or sexuality education and family diversity in early childhood settings (Davies & Robinson, 2010; Robinson, 2005a, 2002; Robinson & Davies, 2007, 2010; Robinson & Jones Diaz, 2006).

Homophobic violence in schools does not exist in isolation from the wider national and international socio-political climate. While students are produced, shaped and constrained by various educational and other related government policies, so too is the broader citizen *body* regulated by and constructed through legal reform relating to same-sex populations. The socio-political climate also impacts on the school curriculum, which constitutes students as heteronormative (Robinson & Davies, 2008b). Schools offer a microcosm of broader society in which homophobic, heterosexist, racist and other offensive discourses are replicated in various forms through relations of power that operate through individuals and institutions. Recently, Portugal, Mexico City and Iceland have joined Holland, Belgium, Spain, Canada, South Africa, Sweden, Norway and six U.S. states in allowing same-sex couples to marry. In addition, the number of places where same-sex marriages are either soon to be allowed or are already recognised from elsewhere is even larger and more diverse, ranging from Argentina through Slovenia and Israel to Nepal (see Croombe, 2010). Julia Gillard, the current Prime Minister of a Labour minority government in Australia, opposes same-sex marriage despite '60 per cent of Australians who believe same-sex couples should be allowed to marry and the 80 per cent of same-sex partners who believe they should have the right to marry' (Croombe, 2010). The issue of same-sex marriage entered public debate again in 2010 with an upcoming federal election in which leaders of both the Australian Labour Party (ALP) and the Liberal Party of Australia (Tony Abbott) expressed their disagreement with gay marriage. In 2011, the ALP amended its official policy platform to advocate same-sex marriage during the party's national conference, despite Prime Minister Gillard's continued opposition. The party's Members of Parliament will be allowed a conscience vote on the issue in the federal parliament, but this is unlikely to pass without support from the Coalition.[2]

In 2004, when Australia was under the leadership of Liberal Prime Minister, John Howard, former federal Attorney-General Philip Ruddock introduced the Marriage Amendment Bill which modified the Marriage Act 1961 to define marriage as 'the union between a man and a woman'.[3] After the House of Representatives and the Senate passed the bill, it became the Marriage Amendment Act 2004, and received little effective opposition in parliament (Davies & Payne, 2008). Not only is same-sex marriage currently not permitted under Australia federal law, but Australian law also specifies that unions between same-sex couples that take place outside the country are not to be recognised as marriage in Australia. Representatives of the Australian Democrats and The Greens introduced three bills in the Australian parliament between 2006 and 2009, but these proposals have either been stalled or rejected.[4] We are not interested here to debate the politics of same-sex marriage, or to critique the institution of marriage more broadly, but rather, we are interested in the ways in which the wider socio-political national and international landscape inform the attitudes, beliefs and practices around same-sex populations within schooling cultures.

Other significant changes with regard to same same-sex entitlements took place in Australia following the report, *Same-Sex: Same*

Entitlements – National Inquiry into Discrimination against People in Same-Sex Relationships: Financial and Work-Related Entitlements and Benefits (2007). The Australian Human Rights Commission recommended that the Australian Government amend laws that discriminated against same-sex couples and their children. At the end of 2008, the Australian Government, then under the leadership of Labour Prime Minister, Kevin Rudd, amended 84 discriminatory laws including those related to taxation, social security, employment, Medicare, veteran's affairs, superannuation, worker's compensation and family law.[5] These reforms include same-sex couples within the category of 'de facto relationship' in all federal laws (previously limited to unmarried heterosexual couples), extend the definition of 'parent' and 'child' in much federal law to include lesbian parents who have a child through assisted reproductive means and, in more limited circumstances, include parents who have children born through surrogacy arrangements (Milbank, 2009, p. 160). Some of the laws commenced immediately, while others commenced on 1 July 2009.

Circuits of recognition

Circuits of recognition is a theoretical framework that we use to foreground the way in which social subjects are constituted interdependently. A moment of homophobic abuse serves as a moment of recognition. The perpetrator of homophobic violence is involved in 'othering' the abused through the use of hate speech, in a concerted effort to make the recipient of this abuse recognisable as a marginalised queer person. 'Othering' refers to defining and securing one's own positive identity through the stigmatisation of an 'other' through markers of social differentiation such as sexuality, gender, ethnicity, location, ability and socio-economic class. The perpetrator of this kind of violence attempts to shore up his/her own identity as (hetero)normative. In such instances of linguistic violence, the perpetrator of the violence is attempting to determine the terms of recognition, generally by citing dominant discourses of heterosexuality, and the individual/s being hailed by this linguistic violence is/are temporarily interpellated through discourses that can and frequently do cause injury. In such instances, a perpetrator is shoring up his/her (hetero)normative place in the grid of intelligible social positionings while casting the abused as more vulnerable and less valued.

A typical educational response to homophobic abuse in the school environment has been the deployment of the liberal humanist discourses of tolerance and pride. We argue (McInnes & Davies, 2007) that these discourses that attempt to relocate the power of the recipient of homophobic violence also operate as an attempt to secure the place of the gender non-conforming, or queer subject, by producing the perpetrator of the abuse as ignorant so that each person involved in the incident can *know* who s/he is. As we have argued (McInnes & Davies, 2007), these kinds of interactions work to fix recognition in an axis that moves from self to other (I know who/what you are and can make such claims because through them my *self* appears stable), shutting down reciprocal address and ignoring the interdependencies of meaning that operate within *circuits of recognition*. This move towards pride and declarations of coherent identity rework broader cultural meanings about what it is to be human and leave unproblematised the normative and normalising logics of these liberal humanist frameworks. What gets left out of this approach is the mutual dependence each person has on the other, particularly the perpetrator's dependence on the recognition dynamic for his or her sense of self.

We use a feminist and queer poststructuralist approach, using 'poststructuralist theories of language, subjectivity, social processes and institutions to understand existing power relations and to identify areas and strategies for change' (Weedon, 1987, pp. 40–41). We argue that subjectivity – that is, our perceptions of the world, our sense of *self*, and our relations to our environment and to others – is constituted in and constructed through language and discourse. In direct contrast to liberal humanist assumptions of a unified, rational *self*, poststructuralism proposes a subject that is fragmented, inconsistent and contradictory (Gavey, 1989). This theoretical approach offers a contextualisation of experience and an analysis of its constitution and ideological power (Weedon, 1987, p. 125) with particular attention to the performativity of gender and sexuality. We are particularly interested in linguistic violence, and engage Judith Butler's understanding of hate speech as a 'site of injury', but also as a potential moment of a counter-mobilisation (Butler, 1997). We argue that engaging *circuits of recognition* as a theoretical framework to underpin pedagogical approaches that intervene in and address homophobic violence is an opportunity to initiate the kind of counter-mobilisation Butler advocates. This kind of response refuses simplistic approaches by schools and educational institutions that attempt to simply shut down or forbid homophobic violence. Rather, our approach reveals power as central to producing particular kinds of knowledge about gendered and sexual subjectivity. Power, in this formulation, is not the possession of an individual but works to shape and constrain social relations.

A Foucauldian idea of the constitution of subjectivity suggests that subject positions are made possible in and through discourse, that is, the knowledge and power formations that provide shape and meaning to the world. In such a figuring, discourse enables and constrains how it is possible to be in the world and we, social subjects, speak and are spoken by discourse. Our subjectivities, and our identities, are implicated in and made possible by *circuits of recognition* through what Butler (2004), following Foucault (1978), would call a grid of intelligibility – we are all dependent on what the circuits provide for our formation or enactment of ourselves. In this way, all life, all 'selves', are precarious. We are also, always, dependent on one another for the discursive potential of our subjectivities because the circuits, the grid of intelligibility, depend on our speaking to and reproducing the systems of value and meaning as much as we depend on being 'spoken' by discourse. Engaging *circuits of recognition* as a theoretical approach to intervening in and addressing homophobic violence is an opportunity to initiate forms of counter-mobilisation. *Circuit-breakers,* such as those that deconstruct homophobic discourses, or resignify terms or signs of abuse, act as opportunities for collective reflection and systemic transformation rather than for simply silencing homophobic linguistic violence. Before examining potential *circuit-breakers*, we turn to two incidents of homophobic violence reported by the Australian media, focusing on the dominant discourses through which homophobia is produced and understood.

'Lesbian student teacher axed'

This section of our chapter will explain our understanding of the *circuits of recognition* that operate to give discursive shape and meaning to public discourse about same-sex desire and homophobic violence in schools. We follow the media reporting of an incident involving 'Jane' (a pseudonym used in the media reporting of this incident), a trainee teacher from The University of Melbourne, at an undisclosed primary school in Victoria in 2004. During this time, Jane had accompanied years five and six students to a school camp, and on returning to the school, went home with her female partner. The following week, curious students repeatedly questioned Jane about her relationship with the woman who had picked her up after the school camp. Finally, Jane made a decision to tell the students that her partner had picked her up after school camp. According to Jane, a 5-minute discussion ensued in which one 'girl told the group she had an aunt who was gay and [the student exclaimed] "I think she's great". Later, several students admitted they already knew Jane was gay' (Green, 2005). After claiming to have received complaints from parents, Jane was accused by the principal of discussing gay issues with children, and also, for conducting sex education lessons (Green, 2005b). At this point, Jane's internship was terminated.

A feature article, 'Lesbian student teacher axed', written by Shane Green, published in *The Age* newspaper on 7 March 2005 reports on and fashions this incident as a violent one. The use of the metaphor 'axing' speaks simultaneously to the way the incident was violent – Jane was wounded by the response of the school principal – and to the way in which discourse *about* homophobic abuse tends to shape such a moment as violent. In our earlier work, we identified the *discourse about homophobia* as a second-order discourse, and as an educational discourse produced about homophobic discourse (McInnes & Davies, 2007). The *discourse about homophobia* is drawn from a complex arena including gay liberation, discourses of diversity, tolerance and acceptance, and is produced across a range of fields including legal, legislative, political and community bodies (McInnes & Davies, 2007). The *discourse about homophobia* produces understandings of *homophobic discourse* and generates imperatives and strategies for use in schools and other contexts. Green's article is an example of the *discourse about homophobia* because it contributes to public discourse and knowledge about homophobia. *Homophobic discourse* refers to the set of things that are possible to say about sexuality and those things that should not be said because they are 'homophobic' (McInnes & Davies, 2007). In Green's article, the primary example of homophobia is the school principal's response to Jane disclosing her sexuality to her students, and the accusations of conducting sex education classes that followed.

Green's account of the incident (2005b) presents discourse about homophobic violence within a narrative structure. The most basic narratives are linear sequences that present information as a connected sequence of events (Lacey, 2000). Employing emotive language such as 'shocked' and 'deeply troubled' in his recount of the incident, Green signals the key moment of homophobia through the principal's response to the effects of Jane's declaration of her relationship to the students (parents' complaints), and the effect of this response on Jane's circumstances (the termination of her *final* [our emphasis] teaching internship):

In a case that has shocked educators and 'deeply troubled' the Government, the woman was summoned to the principal's office. She was told parents had complained she had discussed gay issues with her grade 5 and 6 students, and conducted sex education classes. Despite strong denials about the latter allegation, the school terminated the teacher's internship – her final teaching round as part of her studies at the University of Melbourne.

(Green, 2005a)

The article provides an opportunity for discourse about homophobic violence to circulate through media discourse so that this critical issue can be reflected on and reconsidered. This ongoing dialogue contributes to the *second-order discourse about homophobia*. This second-order discourse about homophobia redeploys the narrative as a stimulus for a more general discussion and integrates existing elements of the discourse about homophobia by quoting academics, research reports, giving accounts of educational initiatives and their evaluation. Distinguishing between these two levels of discourse, that is, *discourse about homophobia* and *homophobic discourse*, provides opportunities to examine the dominant *circuits of recognition* in each of these discourses so as to rethink homophobia as a form of violence in schools. An examination of the *circuits of recognition* operating in this context reveals a perfect example of systemic homophobia, and the way in which the individual becomes pathologised. We argue that recognition and deconstruction of the discourses that lead to systemic homophobia are critical to anti-homophobic practices in educational contexts.

Throughout Green's article, fear is rhetorically linked to the *discourse about homophobia*, offering insights about how understandings of power and responsibility are inhibited. According to Silvan Tomkins (1995, p. 111) fear is a response that 'is very toxic even in small doses. Fear is an overly compelling persuader designed for emergency motivation of life-and-death significance.' Tomkins categorises fear as a negative affect, which is grouped on a continuum: fear–terror, which is featured throughout Green's article. In the context of this chapter, we are interested in the ways in which institutions such as schools have historically frequently been positioned, or have positioned themselves, in public discourse about homophobia in relation to this affective continuum. Inline with our *circuits of recognition* theoretical approach, Tomkins argues that 'increased skill in *recognition* may change' responses to fear [our emphasis] (1963, p. 6). Anne Mitchell, an academic quoted by Green, claims that 'schools are running scared', and that 'there is a climate of fear around the issue – fear of parental or wider community backlash'. The WayOut (Rural Victorian Youth and Sexual Diversity Project) report, quoted by Green, states that 'many school staff were afraid of a backlash if they became involved in addressing homophobia in the school'. Jane is also quoted as saying, 'Kids get taught by gays all the time but they don't know it ... For them to know it, that's the fear. If they know that their teacher is gay, then people have got this idea – I don't know what they think is going to happen. They're terrified of it.' Applying affect theory to this example demonstrates that the fear–terror continuum is a key feature of the discourse about homophobia in schools. In some of these instances fear is about backlash, retribution and moral panic both within and outside the school.

Schools are heteronormative institutions – they are gendered and gendering, and they are sexed and sexualising. They are necessarily sites wherein discourses circulate and provide the models or frames for recognition, some of which are injurious and violent. In addition to perpetrators of homophobic violence confronting their fear of the 'other' and considering their investment in projecting gendered and homophobic violence towards others, our approach demands that schooling cultures invite students and the wider school community to reflect on the discursive construction of this knowledge. Perpetrators are not the originators of their fear nor are they solely invested with or responsible for the power enacted through their injurious acts. Perpetrators of homophobic harassment and violence accumulate the power to injure through the repetition or citation of a prior set of practices – in this case, a set of practices that are understood to cause injury to the intended recipients.

We argue that the discursive construction of knowledge becomes the object of anti-homophobic violence pedagogy such that teachers and students can critically reflect on the operation of power relations in social practices. Deconstructing these modes through which we come to understand the 'other' is critical if any circuit-breaking interventions are to be successful. Another media example provides insights about the discourses that constrain anti-homophobia interventions.

Out and proud – *60 Minutes Australia*

The Australian version of *60 Minutes* – a news and current affairs programme that screens on the Nine Network – featured a segment in September 2010 on gay students and homophobia in schools. While it is significant that a mainstream current affairs programme is prepared to address this topical issue, the discourses through which the queer students are understood in this media segment, and often more broadly within schooling cultures, are situated within liberal humanist ideals. Examples of key tropes within liberal humanist discourses about homophobia include individuals overcoming ongoing systemic violence, or individual students or teachers being relocated to seemingly atypical school environments that are progressive with respect to gender and sexuality issues. While it is positive that a few schools have taken the lead in addressing homophobia, this should be common practice rather than the exception. We argue that the systems in which this kind of violence takes place need to critically reflect on the links between policies and everyday practices, and the ways in which power relations are operating in the school environment, rather than on individualising and pathologising individual behaviours. We do not mean to suggest that individuals should not take responsibility for their behaviour, but rather that addressing homophobic violence is a systemic rather than just an individual issue.

In our earlier work (McInnes & Davies, 2007), we identified a call to 'pride' within the *discourse about homophobia*. As an antonym to shame–humiliation, affects often experienced by same-sex attracted populations because of homophobia, pride has been employed as an educational imperative that has sought to combat homophobic harassment and violence in Gay, Lesbian, Bisexual, Queer, Transgender, Intersex campaigns post the Stonewall riots, and also within schooling contexts.[6] Through the discourse of pride, which has frequently been taken up within the context of anti-homophobia initiatives in schooling contexts, same-sex attracted young people are encouraged to declare their 'real' selves, thus being proud in the face of the attempts to shame them that are part of the violence of homophobic discourse operating within *circuits of recognition*. In the *60 Minutes* segment titled 'Out and Proud', the discourse of pride is mobilised by the current affairs programme both in the title and more broadly throughout the segment, and by schools as a way of negating and responding to homophobic violence:

MICHAEL USHER: Principal John Stone says changing attitudes takes time, but at Princes Hill the entire school – students and teachers – know homophobia will be met with zero tolerance.

PRINCIPAL JOHN STONE: It really is terrific. The kids can feel safe and explore who they are and their relationship with their community. It's my hope that all schools should be like this though. But, yeah, I feel particularly good about this school and proud of it …

MICHAEL USHER: 16-year-old Sam Rodda is thriving at Princes Hill.

SAM RODDA: It's a very open school, very accepting sort of school.

MICHAEL USHER: After four schools in four years, he's found an environment where he can finally be himself – openly gay.

While we acknowledge the excellent efforts and intentions of the school with regard to addressing homophobic violence, we argue that the dominant *discourse about homophobia* relies on the liberal humanist demand for coherent, authentic selfhood. Michael Usher uses this dominant discourse to describe Sam's current situation 'where he can finally *be himself* – openly gay' (our emphasis). This sense of an authentic, coherent self operates normatively, reproducing idealised understandings of *self* and *self*hood that underpin heteronormative alignments of the categories: sex, gender and sexuality. As well as normalising and essentialising sex (male/female), gender (masculine/feminine) and sexuality (heterosexuality), these liberal humanist discourses normalise the idea that we are coherent (sexually and otherwise) and that we can know ourselves and make ourselves known. In contrast, we seek to 'decentre the subject' – that is, to shift emphasis away from the individual as the origin and guarantor of meaning and as a 'fully aware and self present agent' (Gavey, 1989; Sampson, 1989, p. 14). We do not mean for individuals to be relieved of responsibility for their actions; rather we are keen to deconstruct broader schooling contexts in which homophobic violence takes places, so as to effectively intervene in such systemic violence.

Another dominant discourse that emerges in the 'Out and Proud' segment is the discourse of schools as safe spaces. The implicit expectation that schools are safe places is a recurring trope in the research and interventions around gender and sexuality in schools (Davies, 2008; Rasmussen, 2006). 'Safe Schools' initiatives have been and continue to be employed internationally as a response to and for the prevention of ongoing violence in schooling contexts (see Rasmussen, 2006; Szalacha, 2003). While the constitution of schools as safe spaces dominates the dominant discourse in policy and strategy documents, research in this field demonstrates that homophobic violence is still prevalent in schooling contexts (Ferfolja, 2009; 2010; Hillier et al., 1998, 2005) and that the idea of a safe space is a pervasive myth (Davies, 2008). In the 'Out and Proud' *60 Minutes* segment, Michael Usher interviews Australian model and MTV video jockey, 24-year-old Ruby Rose Langenheim, who describes her experience of schooling as very unsafe as a result of ongoing homophobic violence:

MICHAEL USHER: It's hard to believe, but this current queen of cool was once a favourite victim for school bullies, targeted because she was gay. How hard was it for you at school?

RUBY ROSE LANGENHEIM: The hardest time of my life, definitely.
MICHAEL USHER: You weren't safe?
RUBY: Oh, no, I wasn't very safe at school at all. I was often bullied, you know, verbally. I was physically bullied. There was a toilet in the P.E. area that had a whole wall dedicated to people writing how much they hated me.[7]
MICHAEL USHER: How bad did the bullying get?
RUBY ROSE LANGENHEIM: I was put into hospital once. And I went to the doctor – I had lots of lumps on my head. They were throwing chairs – they had metal chairs at the cafe and they were just throwing them, they were pelting them, there was [sic.] five of them.
MICHAEL USHER: I mean, Ruby, that sounds like hell.
RUBY: It was hell.

Ruby Rose describes her experience of ongoing verbal and physical homophobic violence at the hands of her peers, but does not outline any teacher or institutional interventions. Despite narratives of homophobic violence such as this, the dominant discourse of schools as safe spaces prevails through policy documents and strategies. This is not unlike the dominant discourse of the constitution of 'family' as a safe space (in contrast to 'stranger danger' campaigns which still prevail in schooling cultures), even though most child abuse is perpetrated by a person within the family, or known to the child. The National Safe Schools Framework, a collaborative effort by the Australian Commonwealth and State and Territory government and non-government school authorities and other key stakeholders (released in January 2003), claims that 'Schools are among the safest places in the community for children and young people' (p. 4), despite evidence of homophobic violence (Davies, 2008; Ferfolja, 2009, 2010; Hillier et al., 1998, 2005; McInnes 2008; McInness & Davies, 2008; Rasmussen, 2006) and other kinds of violence in the school environment which suggests that this is not the case. Mary Lou Rasmussen argues that 'there is a sense that everyone can enter into a safe space, but these heterotopic spaces may only offer the illusion of inclusivity' (2006, p. 162). Following Foucault (1986, p. 26), she argues that 'safe spaces' might be described as heterotopic 'in so far as they "presuppose a system of opening and closing that both isolates them and makes them penetrable" '. Foucault (1986) used the term 'heterotopia' to refer to spaces outside everyday social and institutional spaces, such as colonies, brothels, and even boats, which are floating spaces with often-precarious relationships to place. The power relations inherent in these spaces suggest that some subjects are safer than others.

Some research in this field adopts the safe schools imperative, evaluating and measuring the degree of success or failure particular safe school interventions have had (Szalacha, 2003). The safe schools rhetoric thus frames and determines the discourses through which violence might be recognised or understood. For instance, in the Australian National Safe Schools Framework, the term 'homophobia' is not mentioned. Instead, the term 'sexuality' is used within the context of a list of other potential descriptors including: 'gender', 'race', 'disability' and 'other factors' through which students may experience or perpetrate violence (National Safe Schools Framework, p. 8). The exact terms of reference and specifications of safe school interventions differ internationally, and produce different results depending on whether homophobic harassment and violence is named, or whether broad and more generalised behaviours are employed instead (Szalacha, 2003).

In *Writing Themselves In Again*, an Australian report conducted with same-sex attracted young people, Hillier and her colleagues conclude that, 'School remains the major place where same-sex attracted young people experience verbal and physical violence' (2005, p. 83). According to Twenty10, which offers community-based housing, advocacy and support for GLBTQI youth under 26 years of age in New South Wales,

> it would be fair to say that bullying in schools has been one of the most common causes of disadvantage and homelessness, particularly when it has led to disengagement from school and the depression that results in self harm or suicide. Too often, these stories involve the inaction of school staff and parents to address the bullying and assure the young person that they are welcome and accepted.
>
> (Twenty10, http://www.twenty10.org.au/about-twenty10)

Schools are disciplinary regimes in the Foucauldian sense: they are hierarchically organised institutions that demand the regulation of conduct and the production and selective distribution of knowledge. Schools can be intrinsically violent places: they demand compliance and they are, whether passively or actively, disciplinary mechanisms (Harber, 2004). Such awareness yields a critical realistic and reflective perspective that can facilitate responsive pedagogy.

Discussion: Towards a reflexive educational ethics

To begin our summary and discussion, we'd like to engage with Judith Butler's observation:

That words wound seems incontestably true, and that hateful, racist, misogynist, homophobic speech should be vehemently countered seems incontrovertibly right.

(Butler, 1997, p. 50)

And we agree. But, on the heels of this statement Butler also offers a set of cautioning and critical questions:

But does understanding from where speech derives its power to wound alter our conceptions of what it might mean to counter the wounding power? Do we accept the notion that injurious speech is attributable to a singular subject and act?

(Butler, 1997, p. 50)

Butler suggests that a complex view of the formation and operation of speech and speakers is necessary to provide thoughtful reconsideration of the violence of speech and violence more generally. The speaker who engages in violent homophobia is not the originator of the speech or the violence that it inflicts. Violent or injurious speech, like any violent or injurious act, can be seen as performative speech acts wherein the naming that inflicts injury pre-exists the subject who speaks; the speaker and what is spoken are products of homophobic discourse. For example, the perpetrators of homophobia who directed their violence towards Ruby Rose or the primary school principal who, more subtly, engaged in homophobia by accusing 'Jane' of discussing gay issues with children, and also, for conducting sex education lessons, are citing and recontextualising dominant homophobic discourses within their own schooling context. For these reasons, Butler (1997, p. 51) argues that 'power is not the function of an originating will but is always derivative'. While individuals mobilise homophobic discourse, the origins of this dominant discourse are already established, and it is precisely the accumulative force of this power that can be used to injure others.

This apparent contradiction – that power precedes the speaker and yet is enacted by the speaker in their speech – is precisely the contradiction that we feel opens out reflexive, ethical potential in thinking about homophobic violence. It is especially crucial that we consider the question of agency as it is captured in these last quotes from Butler. We argue that the identification of a violent act often too quickly moves towards identification of the perpetrator and the victim without proper consideration of how each is constituted and implicated in the precarious production of their 'selves' within the domain of the school. Resisting a sole focus on locating individual responsibility will lead to alternate ways of responding in educational contexts.

It is necessary to vehemently contest injurious speech. But, can we sustain an understanding of the charge of homophobic violence and, *at the same time*, engage an ethics that resists the individualising of power and culpability? Butler (1997, p. 69) recommends resignification as a strategy of bringing norms and their reproduction through injurious acts to the foreground whereby they might be made politically malleable or educationally useful for reflection and reconsideration. All injurious acts emerge from a system of social meanings and are the resources used for making and remaking those meanings. In this sense, injurious acts 'exceed' the moment of iteration, and citation. In as much as homophobic discourse is a citation, it is also malleable and available for reconsidering and reshaping.

Pedagogical implications

Critical to intervening in circuits of recognition are *circuit-breakers*. These are methods that encourage students to learn about and explore different positionalities, as well as utilise deconstruction as a method for teaching students to interrogate their own and other subject positions within particular discursive regimes. *Circuit-breakers* need to be 'responsive' pedagogies that exploit the teachable moment by taking moments of linguistic homophobic violence as opportunities to deconstruct dominant homophobic and heterosexist discourses and practices. Another more planned *circuit-breaker* includes performed ethnography. This approach involves developing ethnographic research data into playscripts that are either read aloud by a group of participants or performed before audiences. This methodology has been employed by writers, researchers and educators in the disciplines of sociology and anthropology, and in the fields of performance studies, theatre studies and arts-based inquiry in education (see Deavere Smith, 1993, 1994; Denzin, 1997; Ensler, 1998; Goldstein, 2001; Langellier, 2000; Mienczacowski, 1997; Sykes & Goldstein, 2004).

Davies (co-author) employed this method, using *A Book with Heart* – which is an unpublished performed ethnography that addresses homophobia, written by Tania Ferfolja, Kerry Robinson and Tara Goldstein – with trained and untrained early childhood educators in a disadvantaged area of rural Victoria. This pedagogical approach is particularly useful because it allows educators to engage with a variety of discourses about homophobia without personalising the incidents.

Participants are able to engage in the narrative at an affective level because the experiences are familiar, but distant enough for the educators to gain a sense of critical distance and perspective. In addition, the experience of reading aloud a character that holds dissimilar views to that of participants often provides the grounds for a transformative experience for individuals and the group because they are able to observe more clearly the *circuits of recognition* in operation when homophobia takes place in schooling contexts. At the end of particular scenes throughout the reading, participants were invited to pause, and were asked a series of questions that engaged them in critical reflection. This discussion was pivotal in guiding participants through the multiple discourses, power relations and *circuits of recognition* operating when a homophobic incident occurs. This is an educator-initiated pedagogy that can be used with pre-service teachers, teachers and other educators as well as with students in schooling contexts.

Another example of a *circuit-breaker* involves a student-based anti-homophobia initiative. A grade 9 boy at a Rural High School in the small community of Cambridge, Canada, was harassed and physically threatened for being perceived to be gay because he wore a pink polo shirt on his first day of school (CBC News Online). Two of his fellow students, David Shepherd and Travis Price, took action. They went to a nearby store and bought 50 pink shirts to wear to school. Then Shepherd and Price went online to e-mail classmates to get support for their anti-bullying cause – 'sea of pink'. The next day, dozens of students were outfitted with the discount tee-shirts and hundreds of students showed up wearing their own pink clothes.

This moment of homophobic violence is responded to without a focus on prosecution. There was no administrative or policy-led strategy that sought to identify and punish the perpetrator for this violence. This incident is not simply about a show of solidarity or support as it might initially be figured to be in the discourse about homophobia. Instead, we are interested in the ethics revealed by this response. By wearing pink shirts, the students had taken the symbols and tokens of homophobic violence and used them as 'an instrument of resistance in the redeployment that destroys the prior territory of [their] operation' (Butler, 1997, p. 163). The shirts did not neutralise the homophobic violence; they *resignified* it. The students used the pink shirt as a sign to destabilise meaning. To speak or act differently with words that wound is a form of resistance that deconstructs, makes visible and rewrites normative power relations. This student-led initiative made the *circuits of recognition* operating around homophobic harassment and violence visible, before designing an effective and performative speech act, which served as a *circuit-breaker*. This approach was particularly successful because it was not focused on the prosecution or shaming of an individual perpetrator, and not focused on inviting the student to proudly declare himself as GLBTQI. Instead the students intervened in the circuits of recognition so that these discourses were less predictable and foreclosing. This act or *circuit-breaker* opened space for the unpredictable fashioning of selves, reducing the impact of violence.

Notes

1. Please see 'Circuits of recognition' section in this chapter for an explanation of 'othering'.
2. The Labour Government also agreed to set up a special ministerial advisory group on gay issues, and is also likely to issue 'certificates of no impediment' for gay couples who want to marry in other countries.
3. The amendment specifies the following: 'Marriage means the union of a man and a woman to the exclusion of all others, voluntarily entered into for life. Certain unions are not marriages. A union solemnised in a foreign country between: (a) a man and another man; or (b) a woman and another woman; must not be recognised as a marriage in Australia.'
4. The Australian Democrats 30-year representation in the Parliament of Australia ceased on June 30th 2008 after the loss of its four remaining seats in the Senate.
5. These included the following: Family Law Amendment (De Facto Financial Matters and Other Measures) Act 2008 (Cth); Same-Sex Relationships (Equal Treatment in Commonwealth Laws – Superannuation) Act 2008 (Cth); Same-Sex Relationships (Equal Treatment in Commonwealth Laws – General Law Reform) Act 2008 (Cth) and Evidence Amendment Act 2008 (Cth).
6. The Stonewall riots were a series of spontaneous, violent demonstrations against a police raid that took place in the early morning hours of June 28, 1969, at the Stonewall Inn, in the Greenwich Village neighbourhood of New York City. They are frequently cited as the first instance in American history when people in the homosexual community fought back against a government-sponsored system that persecuted sexual minorities, and they have become the defining event that marked the start of the gay rights movement in the United States and around the world.
7. P.E. is an abbreviation of Physical Education.

8
Random School Shootings, Teen Culture and the Representation of Violence

Sara Knox

> ...don't blame my family, they had no clue and there is noth-
> ing they could have done, they brought me up just fucking
> fine, don't blame toy stores or any other stores for selling us
> ammo, bomb materials or anything like that because it's not
> their fault.... don't blame the school.... just because we went
> on a killing spree doesn't mean everyone else will.... (From the
> journal of Eric Harris)[1]

The names of those small American towns in which multiple-victim
random school shootings have occurred over the last ten years are not
hard to recall: Pearl, Paducah, Jonesboro, Springfield, Littleton, Santee,
Red Lake and Blacksburg, to name but a few of the more infamous.[2]
Yet some of these place names misidentify the community suffering the
immediate impact and the long aftereffects of the violence. Heath lies
on the western outskirts of Paducah, and it was at Heath High School
that Michael Carneal opened fire on classmates assembled for morning prayer. Westside, too, is the rural/suburban satellite of a larger town,
Jonesboro, Arkansas, and it was in that community's Middle School that
Andrew Golden and Mitchell Johnson set off the alarm and – from
the safety of the tree line above the school – laid down sniper fire
at the students and teachers evacuating.

The responsibility for such small errors of association – Paducah for
Heath, Jonesboro for Westside – can be laid at the foot of the media,
perhaps because the identity of the specific community to which the
schools belonged was less legible to the media personnel arriving to
cover the crimes than the jurisdiction integral to the response to the

disaster; the town with the local paper, radio station, hospital, courthouse and Sheriffs' Department. The actual locale of the disaster was glossed, even though shooters and victims, parents, friends and neighbours may have seen themselves as Westside residents, or as 'Heatherans' (Newman et al., 2004, p. 16).

This minor flaw in the accuracy of the reporting of the Kentucky and Arkansas spree shootings is not surprising; the narrative imperatives of crime reporting routinely lead to factual colouring more lurid than this, even by the most sober of media outlets. Nevertheless, the slippage tells. Tensions over identity are a central characteristic of the context to school shootings. Those tensions may be described as developmental, a property of the psychological 'pathology' of the individual shooter. Then there are the cultural tensions inherent in the adolescent culture of suburban or rural high, middle or elementary schools in the United States, and not least of all those normative codes of masculinity so punishing that kids who feel they are 'failing at manhood' (Newman et al., 2004, p. 143) might see a demonstration of hyper-masculine violence as the only acceptable out.

There are also tensions over identity that might be described as social and inter-subjective: the relationships between students and teachers, between adolescents and their siblings and parents and between responsible adults in a specific community. In regard to this definition of identity tensions, what school shootings may demonstrate is the distance between the *expected* benefits of social capital in tightly knit communities (where everyone knows everyone else's business) and its actual dividends. And finally, there are tensions over identities projected, virtual and mediated; the 'confusions between semblance and substance' (Young, 1996, p. 112) escalated to the category of crisis in, or as the result of, an act of extreme violence.[3]

In the chapter to follow I explore to explore three of the four tensions of identity and identification noted above, with particular emphasis on the last. To discuss as fully as possible those tensions over identity around which school shootings pivot, the chapter will move from an analysis of actual school shootings – 'real events' – to the analysis of mediation/representation of these rare events: from the attempts of individual teen killer's to style their killings (prior to, during or after the act) to the representation of such killings in film, popular culture and literature. The dynamic relationship between both these mechanisms of representation will also be stressed. The chapter only lightly explores the pathological character of school shooters – a subject well canvassed elsewhere, and one of negligible value beyond the realm of the forensic. Michael Kimmel suggests there has been an 'analytic blindness' (Kimmel & Mahler, 2003, p. 1442) in discussions of school violence that tend either to individualise/pathologise or to reach for meta-explanations that make anomalous violence part of some larger social trend (most typically, the impact of a culture of gun ownership, and of media violence). For Kimmel, such explanations pick apart the 'form' of the event without considering the complexity of its discursive and ethnographic content: 'the stories and narratives that accompany the violence, the relationships and interactions among students, and local school and gender cultures' (p. 1440). Notwithstanding the months Katherine Newman and fellow researchers spent living in communities traumatised by major school shootings, and the careful scholarship produced by that research (National Research Council and Institute of Medicine, 2003; Newman et al., 2004), much still remains to be said about the 'content' of school shootings. Much remains to be said, even if what we learn has no power to predict outbreaks of such violence, or to 'profile' those most likely to offend.

The 'implications for practice' section at the end of this chapter accordingly stresses the need for careful attention from educators and professionals to the *local* and *particular* context to school shootings. An understanding of the discrete cultural content of such rare events – a Foucauldian husbandry of *local knowledge* – will help practitioners self-reflexively shape the institutional cultures of the schools and communities they best know, and are most responsible for.

Fact and myth

This section aims to provide basic definitions of rampage school shooting, to canvas the essential facts that give a context to rampage school shootings and to outline those persuasive explanatory models, phrased in a language of individual and social pathology, made by claims-makers in an era of moral panic.

If we are to talk about the content, and not the form of school shootings, a definition that captures social and cultural contexts to the event is essential. The definition used by Newman et al. (2004) uses the following criteria:

- The shooting took place on school grounds or at a school event
- The shooting claimed two or more victims
- The killers were enrolled (or recently enrolled) at the school in which the shooting occurred
- Individuals were randomly targeted.

These criteria highlight the social and cultural location of the shooter (local school and peer group culture; the relationship of a given community to its core institutions) while simultaneously enabling focus on the symbolic character of the violent act. The location of the shooting is central to the act's meaning: Newman et al. (2004) suggest that rampage attacks – like workplace mass killings, with which they share a number of key characteristics – are aimed in part at the institution: the school as an entity is a discrete 'victim' of the violence. Extending that logic, we should more properly count as victims both the school *and* the community to which it belongs; schools being the chosen 'site for a rampage because they are the heart and soul of public life in small towns' (Newman et al., p. 15).

Shootings like those at Virginia Tech or Northwestern University should be considered as analytically distinct from the rampages that occur in middle, elementary and high schools. The institutional culture of higher education institutions is quite different from that of secondary schools, as is the experience and 'rules' of attendance for students of such institutions. Peer and gender cultures are also significantly different for elementary/high school age, and college age students. It might also be argued that colleges are less 'local' institutions than secondary schools, in terms of both the demographics of the student body and their relationship to the communities in which they are sited.

School shootings are a rare form of violence. Indeed, the percentage of the rates for teen-on-teen homicide accounted for by school shootings (including those with single victims, in urban schools) is very small. In the United States, as in Australia, teens are more vulnerable to violence outside of schools than in them. Using data for the years 2004–2005, the National Center for Educational Statistics suggests that American teens – whether urban, suburban or rural – are 50 times more likely to die at another's hands away from school than at school (Dinkes et al., 2007, p. 6). School shootings form but a small proportion of school homicides, and school homicides account for only 2 per cent of the total teen homicide rate. *The rampage shooting at school is therefore an extraordinarily rare event.*

We should bear this in mind when turning to the issue of moral panic. In the later 1990s, such was the level of political anxiety that even the normally temperate Colin Powell called 'the problem of troubled youth the biggest threat to the future of the United States' (cited in Alter, 1998, p. 27).[4] More accustomed to the inflammatory mode, George W. Bush coined the phrase 'juvenile superpredator', calling such teens 'fatherless, jobless, fearless and Godless' (*Harpers Magazine* 'Index',

August 1999, p. 13). In a book written after the Jonesboro shootings, Mike Huckabee (then Governor of Arkansas, and in the 2008 election round a Republican hopeful for presidential nomination) suggested school shootings were proof that things were going from 'bad to worse' (Huckabee, 1998, p. 16). He then predicted (wrongly) that the 'violence is going to intensify, and the body count' get higher as American communities fell progressively prey to the 'youngest, biggest, and baddest generation any society has ever known'; 'social monsters' who may 'actually make us long for the relative quiet and security of the 1990s' (Huckabee, 1998, p. 17).

As part of a wider anxiety about teen violence, the furor around school shootings in the later 1990s is tied to logics of moral panic that oppose adult predator to vulnerable child. Social constructionist historian Philip Jenkins (1998) suggests that the historical and demographic preconditions for the teen killer and child abuse panics are the same: the age distribution of populations, and – specifically – the bulge in the age range correlated with parenting, and the bulge (to come) in the numbers of teens in the United States: by 2010, 35 million or so anxious demographers predicted in the year of the Columbine High shootings (Kantrowitz & Wingert, 1999, May 10, p. 36). Countries in the developed West are 'dominated by the vast cohort of the baby boomer generation' (Jenkins, 1998, p. 223). And those baby boomers are parents, politicians and school-teachers, a powerful parenting generation finding itself confronted by economic instability, high levels of stress and fewer hours to spend at home: 'compared to their parents generation, many adult baby boomers found that they had less domestic stability and less direct supervision over their own children' (Jenkins, 1998, p. 224). Ours is a generation of anxious parents. This demographic pattern holds true for Australia, as it does for many Western countries – one reason why cultures with different teen homicide rates have to some degree shared the moral panic around both child abuse and teen violence.

Social identity, gender and status-anxiety

> All of the rampage shooters are boys. . . . this is no accident, for in addition to failing at adolescence, they were – at least in their own eyes – failing at manhood.
>
> (Newman et al., 2004, p. 143)

The shared characteristics of rampage school shooting, as far as they can be determined, suggest that the shooters will be white, that they will be male, and that shootings are much more likely to occur in rural or outer suburban towns (places that, not coincidentally, have higher levels of gun-ownership[5]), in communities that are close-knit and have low rates of violent crime: 'Edens of social capital' (Newman et al., p. 116). In terms of predisposing factors of personality, or situation, one shared pre-condition in terms of the psychological/social situation of the shooter is a sense of status anxiety. From Newman's close analysis of the identity struggles of Mitchell Johnson, Andrew Golden and Michael Carneal (drawn from how the boys saw themselves, and how they were seen by their peers) what seems clear is that the killers sought to shoot their way out of a status limbo linked, implicitly or tacitly, to a 'failed' performance of masculinity. Masculinity theories draw from widely differently disciplinary inheritances (psychology, anthropology, social theory, poststructural theory), focus upon a variety of subjects of analysis (men, women and masculinity in different cultures and time periods) and turn analytic light upon the gendering of institutions, language and the symbolic realm (Butler, 1990, 1993, 2004).[6] However, it is the structuralist tradition in masculinity theory that is most useful for this chapter given its tendency to apprehend the 'problem' of masculinity (or, in the language of current anxiety, its 'crisis') as related to the formation and maintenance of *gender roles* and the operation of *masculinity as power* (Kahn, 2009, p. 52). R. W. Connell's contribution to the field of masculinity studies has been the broad and deep analysis of the shaping power – socially and individually – of descriptive and prescriptive gender norms, an analysis most famously applied to schools as 'heteronormative' institutions (Connell, 2005; Connell & Messerschmidt, 2005). As Messerschmidt puts it, school 'does not merely adapt to a natural masculinity among boys. Rather, it constructs various forms of masculinity (and femininity) and negotiates among them' (1993, p. 87). Michael S. Kimmel's work on adolescent masculinities suggests that school shootings violently operationalise that process of construction and negotiation. In regard to the 'failed' performance of masculinity of school shooters, Kimmel and Mahler suggest that '[a]ll or most of the shooters had tales of being harassed – specifically, gay-baited – for inadequate gender performance' (2003, p. 1440). It is *homophobic bullying*, they conclude, that makes adolescent male culture so testing for some individuals.[7] Marginal social and gender status may be a matter of self-perception, not a matter of where a boy actually stands in his social pecking-order (Newman et al., pp. 143–148), and in this way school shooters who did *not* have their gender performance materially policed (as in the cases of bullying) may still have felt an inadequacy remediable only by 'manning-up', Rambo-style. As one anti-bullying coach puts it, rampage school shooters have a 'diminished sense of self' (Haber, cited in Lee, 2005). This qualification notwith-standing, the performance of normative (heterosexual) masculinity is a pivotal stressor in the pressure-cooker of adolescent teen culture. In a teen culture where anything (the colour of a sweat-shirt or one's choice in music) or anyone (member of the school band, geek, Goth) can be dismissed as *that's so gay*, heteronormative codes of masculinity would seem to be a key discursive and social context for school shootings.

Another indicator that this might be the case is the too frequently overlooked, but obvious, fact that the overwhelming majority of student *victims* of school shootings are girls. The teen rampage killing performs hyper-masculinity in a complex layering of ways: by choosing the gun (a 'loaded' weapon, culturally and symbolically) as their weapon for striking back, by girls being the preponderant victim and by the killer seeking – in some degree – the approval, or even the participation, of his male peers in the killing. The Bethel, Alaska, school shooter Evan Ramsey, 'made his plans known' to his friends 'and then wavered', and it was not until a friend warned him that his shilly-shallying would make 'everybody think you're nothing' that he was pushed into following-through (Newman et al., 2004, p. 151). And during the Pearl, Mississippi, shootings in 1997, the shooter was said to have been egged on by his male friends, one of whom – when Luke Woodham took a bead on the ex-girlfriend who'd jilted him –'allegedly told him to stop whining and "shoot the bitch" ' (Egan, cited in Klein, 2005, p. 94). In this scenario the command that the killer 'stop whining' is as important an act of gender policing as is the suggestion that he 'shoot the bitch'. The latter gives context to the former, showing with brutal economy just how offensive the feminine can be: whether it comes in the guise of the sissy or the castrating bitch.

The violent resort to action of the rampage shooter is, therefore, a kind of radical performance of masculinity. But that it is a performance – and a pointed one – is clear.

Media cultures and the transmigration of styles of violence

If we are to understand school shootings as a contemporary form of violence, we must think through the performative qualities of the ram-page shooting. One killer's act builds upon, and provisions, the styles and scripts of killing available to others, while the stock elements of an event's rehearsal and performance take the media stage, never entirely to disappear (thanks to a half-life on YouTube, or as embedded video on Internet news sites or postings on the profile pages of Facebook and MySpace). This means taking seriously not so much the broad effect of media violence upon the young (its culpability), but the proposition that media logic makes the 'content' of school shooting events *exportable*, and that the style of one rampage will likely turn up in a subsequent event.

When Michael Carneal told interrogators that he didn't 'know why it happened, but it wasn't a movie' (Kimmel & Mahler, 2003, p. 1441)[8] he showed he knew the difference between the movies and real life, between mediated and direct experience. Carneal responds, without being asked, to a common objection to media violence: that it destroys the capacity of children and teens, particularly, to discriminate between real violence and its representations. But if we force the tense of his statement into the predictive so that it becomes: *it won't be a movie*, then another model for the relationship of violence to the media appears, and one that can't so easily be laid to rest. For it is almost certain that 'it' (the Paducah killings, or something 'like' it) *will* turn up in the movies. Carneal himself knew that something 'like' his own crime would turn up, sometime, somewhere else – in the years following the shooting at Heath High School, Carneal was tortured by a feeling that he was responsible for subsequent shootings (at Columbine High, particularly). The doctor treating Carneal at the Northern Kentucky Youth Correctional Center found him very distressed at hearing of the rampage at Littleton: he 'was a mess, an absolute mess. [He] felt a lot of responsibility for that.... takes a little responsibility for every school shooting that happened after his own' (as cited in Newman et al., p. 304). We can see, then, that Columbine Killer Eric Harris's journal jotting that 'we are kind of a select case here, so don't think this will happen again' was off the mark, as he himself probably knew – having begun the entry with the declaration that he wanted to 'leave a lasting impression on the world' (Harris, 2002). It is not that one shooting makes the statistical likelihood of another greater, but that 'media coverage effects the form and method of crimes' (Newman et al., 2004, p. 72). A given shooting – particularly one that had the impact Columbine did – inflects the style of those subsequent. Indeed, this definition of the 'copycat effect' (Newman, 2004) has greater subtlety than what is normally implied by the term 'copycat' (meaning spur to action) or 'contagion effect' (indicating the source of an epidemic [the term is debunked in Nichols & Good, 2004, p. 47]). Following this softer logic of the copycat effect, a layering of influences might be apprehended in the style of a single crime. And, given the global reach of media, the degree of media immersion of teen cultures, the sophistication of teens as users of media technologies and mobile communications (Katz & Aakhus, 2002), and the globalised nature of teen commodity culture, the copycat effect also means the diffusion of rampage *style* from one local, regional and national context to another.

Evidence of the layering of killing styles, and of their transmigration, can be seen in the two school shootings that took place in Finland in 2007.

Figure 8.1 is an image of 18-year-old Pekka-Eric Auvinen, culled from the final frame of a posting he made to YouTube just hours before opening fire on students at Jokela High School, in the town of Tuusula. Posting under the username of Sturmgeist89, Auvinen had titled his video 'Jokela High School Massacre – 11/7/07' ('Student kills 8'), and – borrowing from the style of the Virginia Tech shooter, Seung-Hui Cho – showed images of himself in martial poses, armed with the weapon he'd go on to use, and spouting his manifesto in sound-bite snatches – a manifesto in English, not his native language ('I, as a natural selector, will

Figure 8.1   Self-portrait posted on YouTube by Pekka-Eric Auvinen before he went on to kill 8 at Jokela High School, Finland

eliminate all who I see unfit' ['Student kills 8']). Although 'Sturmgeist89' differed from Seung-Hui Cho in directly posting to YouTube (Seung-Hui sent videotapes to NBC news, and these only later turned up on YouTube) he borrowed the generic style of the earlier killer's video manifesto, and the strategic style of his rampage: like Seung-Hui, Auvinen shot a number of his victims through closed schoolroom doors. But that was not the limit of the layering of influence. The audio track Auvinen chosen for his YouTube posting was 'Stray Bullet', by KMFDM, a song Eric Harris had posted on his own website. The reference was almost certainly deliberate on Auvinen's part. His posting was not merely his pitch at a killer's infamy – a Herostratus complex for the digital age – it was a self-conscious homage to shooters who'd come before him; homage in a medium for which the fan-posting is generically key (that is, the re-positioning of other media content in a user's own 'cut', and with their idiosyncratic choice of music). In the style of both the video 'announcement' and the killing itself, a genealogy of references can be traced: from the Columbine killings, through Virginia tech, to Auvinen's rampage.[9] Note, too, how that borrowing of style shrugs at region and nation: to look at, the killer could be a teen from anywhere.

Just ten months after Auvinen's rampage, an even bloodier shooting occurred at the Kauhajoki School of Hospitality in Western Finland. Like the Columbine killers, Matti Yahuni Saari supplemented firearms with the use of explosives. But his more important influences were referenced by, and in, video he'd posted to YouTube before the crime, videos depicting him posing with, and firing a handgun (Figure 8.2) – posing, and firing, as Klebold and Harris had videoed themselves doing before Columbine, as Seung-Hui had done in his 'suicide manifesto', and – more importantly for Saari – as his fellow countryman Auvinen had done just a year before. Like Auvinen's postings, Saari's video was quickly removed from YouTube, but (also like Auvinen's postings) extracted frames and sections of the video can still be found on other sites. On the day of the shooting, Saari turned up at the school, dressed in black, toting a large bag, as had Eric Harris and Dylan Klebold at Columbine. Before his account was de-activated, Wumpscut86 (Saari's YouTube username) listed his favourite YouTube video as the CCTV footage of Harris and Klebold in the Columbine High School cafeteria during the shootings ('Gunmen held by police just hours before massacre'). Like Auvinen, Saari borrowed the Columbine killers' style, both in his postings and in the way he staged the killing. But he also seems to have borrowed from the style of Auvinen's YouTube posting (despite the fact that his own posting was video, and Auvinen's was a

Figure 8.2   Self-portrait posted on YouTube by Matti Yahuni Saari before he went on his rampage at the Kauhajoki School of Hospitality, Finland

series of stills joined by wipes). The final frames of both postings show the killer – head, shoulders and torso – aiming a gun down at a camera slightly below them, they loom into a shot in which the mouth of the gun-barrel is center frame.

While the social and cultural context for the Finnish school shootings is necessarily different to that of the rural and suburban rampages in the United States, they are both 'media-mediated'. Media-mediated crimes, as Joel Black puts it, need 'to be understood in the historically unprecedented context of a hyper-aestheticized mass-culture' (Black, 1991, p. 136) within which 'horrible events' (Christopher Lasch, cited in Black, p. 137) are immediately translated into images and ultimately become inseparable from them. Media-mediation is an artefact of global media culture, and killings with discrete social and cultural contexts (in terms of school, community, region and nation) have a media context not so spatially bound. That said, one aspect of the shared social context for the rampage of Auvinen and Saari should be noted, as it supports the first of five 'necessary, but not sufficient factors for school shooting' identified by Harding et al. (2002, p. 198). Finland – like the United States and unlike much of the rest of Europe – has a strongly ingrained culture of gun-ownership, and high levels of gun-ownership, and hunting is a widely practised and valued sport there ('Gunman kills 10 in attack'). The easy availability of guns and the cultural power of the gun were key pre-conditions to the crimes of Auvinen and Saari, just as they were key to those American rampage shootings so commented on by the media. One peculiarity of Finnish culture that did not come to light in commentary on the crimes is, however, worth noting here. According to Puro, Finland has the highest level of mobile phone ownership in the world (2002), and that 'perpetual availability' (Puro, 2002, p. 22) is manifestly changing 'the manner in which Finns interpret and understand their everyday interactions and interpersonal relations' (p. 19). As might be expected, not every aspect to that change is positive. The value of connectedness – a feature of strong social capital – has its underside, given the erosion of the distinctions between leisure and work time, between personal and business communication. And in Finnish culture where silence is traditionally respected, and where values around talk (both face-to-face and on phones) show a low tolerance for mere 'chit-chat', the changes presented by mobile phone culture represent distinctive challenges:

> the mobile phone, in terms of everyday interaction, raises the possibility of being open and outgoing.... [it] encourages new contacts and enlarges one's social network.... *Each encounter increases the potential that the feelings and emotions of others must be dealt with at the time and anywhere.*
>
> (Puro, 2002, p. 26. Emphasis mine)

While the mobile phone augments social capital in a general sense, it is also an artefact of social connection (and, conversely, disconnection) in particular ways. Text messaging, the maintenance of contact lists and call blocking operate, as Campbell and Ling suggest, to demarcate 'relational boundaries' (2009, p. 597), so that 'in-group and out-group distinctions are reinforced'.[10] Connectedness raises the stakes of social success, and therefore increases the chances of social failure for some. The mobile phone's promise of greater social connectedness, then, demonstrates the virtues of strong social capital (that we may call upon, and be called on, by our fellows) and its 'dark underside', identified by Newman et al. (2004) in the context of the tightly knit suburban and rural communities in which the US school shootings they studied occurred. In situations when there are high expectations around social interaction, about 'knowing' one another, it may in fact be easier to miss or to misinterpret the warning signs of anti-social behaviour (Newman et al., 2004, p. 125); the 'discord beneath the placid surface of community life' is made invisible by those very qualities that define social capital: trust, expectation and reciprocity. In the case of Finland, where the uptake of the mobile phone has been so vigorous, what might a situation where social networks are enlarged and 'each encounter increases the potential that the feelings and emotions of others must be dealt with at the time and anywhere' mean for the socially marginal, those who feel themselves on the outer? Teens, according to Don Tapscott, see mobile phones 'as an indispensable social tool – like a friend in their pocket' (Tapscott, 2009, p. 46) – if we follow through on the logic of that image, we can see how devices (and technologies) for social networking might come to be seen by some as potential weapons in the arsenal of their vengeance. It is partly in this light that we should view the self-mediatisation of rampage shooters like Auvinen and Saari as elements of the act of violence itself.

Representing the teen killer

Just as the teen spree shootings of the later 1990s have set the stage for proliferations of a killing script for a subsequent generation of disgruntled American middle school, high school and university students, so too has it given rise to a spate of movies, special episodes of teen television dramas (such as the double episode 'Time stands still' in season 4 of *Degrassi High*), and both young adult and literary novels that figure the teen killer *ala* Dylan Klebold or Eric Harris. The troubled protagonists of these fictions of teen killing are middle-class, white kids from the suburbs; teens about whom the question of poverty seems relevant only in relation to the poverty of their powers of empathy, or that of their peers.

Philip Jenkins argues that parent's at the tail end of the baby boomer generation feel they have 'less direct supervision over their children': that their kids are satellites, caught in their own dark orbit, inscrutable (1998, p. 224). In its most severe form, this idea of 'out of control' youth, of the lack of connection and coherence between the world of adults and that of teens morphs into the figure of the affectless teen 'sociopath' so well imagined, recently, in films and books about teen killers. In contemporary literature, Dennis Cooper's *My Loose Thread* paints a complicated portrait of the teen killer, as does Gus Van Sant in his film about a Columbine style rampage shooting, *Elephant*. A less complex portrait of disaffected (or affectless) youth is Ben Coccio's *Zero Day*. What makes Cooper's book and Van Sant's film so disturbing is their use of point of view: Cooper locks the reader into the head of the deeply troubled central character, Larry, while Van Sant plays on what might be called the weakness of film compared to literature: its inability to show us the internal worlds of the characters. Van Sant's naturalism – long real time tracking shots that follow the characters – forces the viewer into the role of helpless observer, and we're forced to witness terrible events for which no pat answers are provided. While Cooper's use of first-person point of view throws us into Larry (his inability to sort out his own actions, feelings and motivations from those of the world, and people, around him) so that we *experience* his confusion, self-delusion and sociopathy, Gus Van Sant's objectivising camerawork filmically replicates the unknowable and hermetic world of the teen: as viewers we are cut-off, floundering; pulled along in the wake of the event. But we're also implicated as witnesses to it.

In *My Loose Thread* Cooper (2003) skilfully manipulates tenses, and employs passive verb tenses to show the reader, in a very direct way, Larry's paranoia, and aggression: for Larry, everything is someone else's responsibility, even his own actions. Larry fails in his efforts to differentiate his feelings from those of the people around him; in one scene when he's browbeating his brother, his moment of victory is utter confusion: 'I feel him give up, and get upset. I mean I do' (Cooper, 2003, p. 94). And in a scene when Larry is beating someone, he thinks they're crying because they're sad, not because he's hitting them. At other times, Larry see people give him 'confusing' looks, as if everything done by others in the world has to have its effect on him. Cooper portrays, in Larry, a kind of meta-affectlessness, an apathetic self-interest. For Larry, it's always everybody else being, or doing, something gay – never the violently self-hating homophobe Larry. Cooper's portrayal of an affectless teen killer is an instructive one precisely for the way it portrays the troubled teen's self-involvement, his experiencing of being reached out to, even, as a slight. In the light of Newman's et al. (2004) makes clear study of the psychological tensions and the resulting social marginalisation of would-be rampage killers, Cooper's portrait of Larry is instructive. And not least of all because of how uncomfortable Cooper makes it for the reader inhabiting Larry as the point of view character. Through Larry, the reader gets a very strong sense for what it is like to be shut out of the world, and to what terrible ends being shut out of the world might lead.

In *My Loose Thread* Cooper makes an almost throwaway reference to the kinds of places American schools have become post-Columbine: places policed by metal-detectors and CCTV. Larry walks down halls 'watched over by cameras...where students go when they need the school's help' (p. 27) – when in trouble, the kid's go not to the principal's office, nor to a teacher, but to put themselves under the watchful eye of a surveillance camera. This is surveillance as a form of preventative care, a kind of virtual nannying of dangerous and/or vulnerable teens. In the discourse of moral panic around the contributory effect of media to teen violence, media and technologies of virtual communication, one fear has been human husbandry will be replaced by some technical equivalent, some technology that stands in for the proper parental presence in children's lives: the TV as nanny or surrogate mother; irresponsible nanny, bad mother. In the final pages of *My Loose Thread*, we see this glossing of communication technology/human relationship. Larry and Jim are walking down their stairs at home, past the living room, where the dead bodies of their parents – whom Larry had shot an hour or so before – sit sprawled in their easy chairs: 'The TV's still on. I think if it was off, they'd be too dead' (p. 117). Here the television's lively bleating has to stand in for Larry's forever silenced parents – the TV is no longer a surrogate: it's the life of the home. Marilyn Manson is on at the moment the boys walk past the set, and its not the dead bodies of his parents, but Marilyn – in Goth mourning garb – that brings the fact of death home to Larry.

Conclusion

This chapter suggests that we should attempt to understand that rampage school shooting is a rare – even an exotic – form of violence. The very rarity of the school shooting ironically suits it to complex processes of mediatisation: from the self-mediatisation of the killers prior to, or after the act; to media and scholarly attention that stresses form, rather than content (exceptionalising the killers, and individualising their acts, rather than finding out what their act can tell us about teen culture, structures of masculinity, or the local cultures of school and community more generally); to the media-mediation of the crime (the circulation of recognisable exemplars, of killing 'scripts' and 'styles'); to, finally, the representation of the teen killer in literature and film.

Implications for practice

Educational leadership

For educators, the first lesson wisely learned about school shootings is their *rarity*. While the classroom may be a place waiting to explode, it is unlikely to be the site of a massacre. It is not possible to plan for the rare and random contingency, nor to prevent it – except in so far as predisposing cultures can be changed to make the *rare event* less likely still.

- The glacially slow process of cultural change can perhaps be speeded up by specific institutional innovations. Parent–teachers associations, School Boards, principals, teachers or counsellors – the leaders and managers who shape the working of schools as institutions – might better concentrate less on the technical aspects of security (surveillance cameras, campus 'police', metal detectors, etc.) than on the husbandry of wider institutional cultures (family, community and school) that defray the hermetic pressure-cooker that is teen culture. The camera or the cop in the hallway tends to send a message of mutual suspicion and hostility, deepening the very divide (between adults and teens) that fosters a situation where troubled teens don't tell their troubles, and when they do tell it is very often only to tell another teen, who feels they cannot breach the etiquette of teen group loyalty.
- Educational managers might profitably seek ways to break down the insular nature of school cultures, and to defray the divide between adults and teens by, for instance, building strong mentoring programmes.
- Schools, the communities they serve and the parents of teens should be mindful that how a school values certain activities and groupings over others impacts strongly on teen gender cultures: creative and intellectual pursuits and successes should be lauded, just as prowess on the track and field are.
- Educators need to remain mindful of teen cultures in which bullying and violence arise from sexual and gender prejudices, and go beyond formally proscribing behaviours (like the anti-gay slur) to the fostering of cultures of inclusiveness. Such work requires wider changes in the communities school serve. One aspect of such wider change that schools can encourage is greater recognition of the diversity of contemporary families. As the research of Newman et al. (2004) makes clear, the strong social capital of tightly knit communities is not an unproblematic good. Community stakeholders should carefully consider what values and ties and affinities join them – do those values, ties and affinities actively *exclude* in order to create belonging?

In the classroom

In the classroom, leveraging off the representation of the teen killer can be a useful strategy – films such as *River's Edge, Zero Day* and *Elephant*, or young adults fiction titles like *The Last Domino* are recommended for this. Hypothetical or fictional examples can engender discussion of the real-world issues of teens jockeying for social status, the impact of anxieties around the performance of masculinity, and the nature – more broadly – of teen peer cultures. The scene in *Elephant* when the soon-to-be-killers kiss in the shower on the morning before their rampage can be a useful springboard for a discussion of teen masculinity and of a heteronormative homophobia so pervasive that it inflects even critical representations of the teen killer.

Lively discussions on the messy ethical implications of peer group loyalty can be sparked by discussion of teen horror flicks such as *I Know What You Did Last Summer* – a film that deals explicitly with the perils of keeping a secret. If students can 'agree to agree' that a *fictional* character is wrong not to tell on a friend who might harm themselves or others, it may become easier for them to recognise and act upon real-world decisions of the same gravity.

Notes

1. 'As you were' [from the journal of Eric Harris], *Harpers Magazine*, February 2002, p. 14.
2. In the order noted: in Pearl, Mississippi, on 1 October 1997, Luke Woodham, aged 16, stabbed his mother and then went to school and shot and killed his former girlfriend and a friend of hers, wounding seven other students in the process; on 1 December that same year Michael Carneal, aged 14, opened fire on a group of students gathered in prayer, killing three and wounding five; on the 24 March 1998, Mitchell Johnson, aged 13, and Andrew Golden, aged 11, killed four fellow students and one teacher, and wounded 11 others (ten students and one teacher) by sniper fire; on the 21 May 1998, 15-year-old Kip Kinkel shot his parents then, at his Springfield, Oregon school, shot and killed two of his fellow students, and injured 22 others; on the 20 April 1999, Dylan Klebold, aged 18, and Eric Harris, aged 17, brought an arsenal of weapons to Columbine High School and over a period of hours killed 12 students, one teacher and then themselves; on the 5 March 2001 in Santee, California, 15-year-old Charles Williams, who'd joked about shooting people at his school, followed through, killing two and wounding 13; on March 21, 2005 at the local school on the isolated Chippewa reservation of Red Lake, Jeffrey Weise, aged 15, shot and killed seven people, five of whom were fellow students. The case of the Virginia Tech shootings at Blacksburg is slightly different, as neither the shooter nor his victims can (in the same way as those above) be designated as 'teens'. Seung-Hui Cho was 23 when, on 16

April 2007, in attacks separated by a matter of hours, he shot and killed 32 adults (27 students and five members of faculty).

3. Young explores the 'the rhetoric of visibility and invisibility, of images of the seen and unseen' (1996, p. 112) in the murder of two-year-old James Bulger by two older children, Jon Venables and Robert Thompson.

4. Quoted in Jonathan Alter, *Newsweek*, 6 April 1998: 27.

5. High levels of gun ownership does not necessarily equate to more people owning guns, it may mean more guns owned by single individuals. Arguably, the latter is even more strongly indicative of gun culture.

6. Following the work of Judith Butler and the impact of Queer Theory more generally, the theorising of masculinities in recent years has emphasised the performative nature of gender, decentring the focus on masculinity in men to enable the study of female masculinity, and of transgender. See for instance Judith Halberstam's *Female Masculinity* (Durham, NC: Duke University, 1998) and H. Rubin's *Self-made Men: Identity and Embodiment among Transsexual Men* (Nashville, TN: Vanderbilt University Press, 2003).

7. See also Kimmel's *Guyland; the Perilous World where Boys Become Men* (New York: Harper Collins, 2009), pp. 86–93. Heteronormative masculinity is not the only weapon for conformity in rural and suburban schools in areas largely populated by whites. In the Jonesboro school district, students could not decide whether it was worse to be 'taunted' for being gay or for being black (Newman et al., 2004, p. 337).

8. Note that Kimmel and Mahler play down the degree and extremity of Carneal's mental disorientation, and this colours their interpretation. The evidence presented in Newman et al. (2004, p. 25) suggests that Carneal was paranoid and delusive to the extent that he thought he was being watched, and was vulnerable to attack, through the air-vents in his bathroom, so covered them. Whereas Kimmel and Mahler interpret Carneal's covering of the vents as evidence of hypersensitive adolescent modesty: that he was afraid of others seeing him naked (Kimmel & Mahler, 2003, p. 1447).

9. In an 8 November 2007 story headed 'Youtube the medium-choice for killers', online news site news.com.au connected Auvinen's killing and media-style in just this way. The graphics for the story show frames from the manifesto-ranting, and gun-pointing videos of Seung-Hui next to those of Auvinen and Harris and Klebold. Retrieved from: http://www.news.com.au/technology/story/0, 25642, 22723572-5014108, 00.html.

10. Text messaging, contact lists and blocking functions are part of numbers of social networking *applications* (Skype, IM, Facebook, MySpace, etc. . . .), but the mobile phone is distinctive in that it has those functions that are inherent to the newest generations of the technology. The mobile phone is also the most portable of all the devices that offer users the capacity to everywhere harness both the inbuilt and the add-on social networking applications noted above.

9
Young People, Ethical Sex and Violence Prevention

Moira Carmody

Educating young people about sexual assault and other forms of intimate partner violence is a challenging area for school educators. This is despite the fact that young people self-report high levels of violence in early dating relationships. Historically this area has tended to be ignored in most personal development curricula and when it has been acknowledged, anti-violence workers from victim services have often been brought in to provide input. More recently in Australian and UK schools, additional curricula have been developed which attempt to educate young people about sexual consent and 'healthy' relationships. This chapter will explore these developments and argue that they often unwittingly foster a range of degendered discourses. This impacts on how sexuality, violence and intimacy are conceptualised. Unwittingly this can result in reinforcing traditional discourses of heteronormativity and excludes same-sex attracted young people. An alternative approach based on sexual ethics will be discussed based on empirical research with rural and city young women and men of diverse sexualities who have participated in the *Sex & Ethics* sexual assault prevention education programme developed by the author (Carmody, 2009b). This programme offers a framework for young people to explore knowledge and skills of ethical decision-making that balances both pleasure and danger in intimate relationships.

The international context of gender-based violence prevention education

The United Nations 2006 in-depth study on all forms of violence against women: Report of the Secretary-General (United Nations, 2006) indicated that surveys of 71 countries found that on average at least one woman in three is subjected to intimate partner violence in the course of her lifetime. Between 10 per cent and 30 per cent of women in other studies indicated that they had experienced sexual violence by an intimate partner (Heise et al., 1999). In many cases physical violence is accompanied by sexual violence. In the Australian context two large-scale prevalence studies provide insight into the local experience. The 1995 Women's Safety Survey found women in the 18–24 year age bracket were more likely to be assaulted than women in other age groups: 19 per cent of women aged 18–24 had experienced sexual violence in the past 12 months, compared with 6.8 per cent of women aged 35–44 and 1.2 per cent of women aged 55 and over. Only 15 per cent of women who identified an incident of sexual assault in the 12 months prior to the survey reported to police (ABS, 1996). A later study in 2005 estimated that there were 44,100 persons aged 18 years and over who were victims of at least one sexual assault in the 12 months prior to the survey; approximately 72,000 incidents of sexual assault were experienced by these victims (ABS, 2005). There is no argument about the extent and impact of sexual and physical violence. The challenge we face is how to prevent it.

The context of violence prevention education in school settings

Persistent efforts over the last 30 years (especially by feminists in Western contexts) have aimed to render sexual and other forms of intimate violence a visible concern of public and state by challenging the idea that it is a private matter (Carmody, 1992; Franzway et al., 1989). A key strategy used to challenge gender-based violence has been education (see Carmody & Carrington (2000) for a detailed overview of violence prevention education up to mid-1990s and Schewe (2004) and Breitenbecher (2000)). This has primarily taken the form of large-scale public awareness campaigns or specific educational programmes designed to be implemented in schools and other educational settings. Underpinning this strategy is a belief that increased knowledge and awareness of the extent and impact of violence will result in changing attitudes and behaviour, and therefore prevent its occurrence. A problem here is the assumption that awareness by women and men of the risk and impacts of sexual violence, whether as a potential victim or as a potential offender, will prevent it.

Since the 1990s there have been organised attempts in Australia to develop specific violence prevention educational programmes.

Organised violence prevention educational programmes implemented in schools are now recognised as the most prevalent form of doing sexual and domestic violence prevention in Australia (Mulroney, 2003). These programmes have most commonly developed as a result of collaboration between women's community-based organisations, and health or youth organisations (Chung et al., 2006). In relation to sexual assault prevention, these programmes typically involve curricula that include debunking rape myths, teaching consent (including providing information about legal statutes regarding sexual consent), teaching young women how to keep safe and providing information about services for victims. Similar to the US experience, many of the programmes in this period primarily targeted women to reduce their risk of experiencing sexual assault.

A key focus within the international field of prevention education is targeting young people (Wolfe et al., 2006, Butchart et al., 2004 for example). It is argued this is necessary because of the increased risk of young women aged 14–24 as victims of sexual assault and that young men are the most likely perpetrators (Buchart et al., 2004). An additional argument is made that young people are at a critical point in their personal and social development (Grealey et al., 2004; Jaffe & Wolfe, 2003; Victorian Health Promotion Foundation (VicHealth), 2007) and that their attitudes and behaviours are more easily influenced than adults (Butchart et al., 2004). Building from these arguments is the belief that schools are the most suitable setting in which to deliver sexual assault and other forms of violence prevention education (Quadara, 2008).

The VicHealth report, for example, argues that specific anti-violence/respectful relationships programmes targeting young people in secondary school is a 'priority approach' (VicHealth, 2007, p. 18). The Amnesty International Australia report (Fergus & Lappin, 2008, p. 7) argued for 'an education program for implementation in every high school across Australia and that it must be the cornerstone of the National Plan of Action'. Subsequent to this publication, a National Plan of Action was developed in 2008 by the National Council to Reduce Violence against Women and their Children. The National Plan launched by the Prime Minister of Australia Kevin Rudd in April 2009 identified six key outcome areas to achieve the prevention of intimate violence (National Council to Reduce Violence against Women and Their Children (Australia) & Australian Department of Families, Housing, Community Services and Indigenous Affairs, FaHSCIA (2009). One of these outcomes was that relationships should be respectful. To achieve this goal a commitment to funding was made for the roll out of prevention education based on building the skills of young women and men to have respectful relationships. Nationally, promising programmes (of which *Sex & Ethics* was one) received funding in 2009. The aims of this funding are to trial programmes and assess their effectiveness, thus building an evidence base of what works. At the time of writing, a second round of funding is being made available through an open call of expressions of interest for funding to commence in 2010. A key focus of the Respectful Relationships Program funding is to maximise the exposure of young people in schools and other settings to violence prevention knowledge and skills (FaHSCIA, 2009).

Why schools?

There is a strong rationale for undertaking violence prevention education in a school environment. Schools are sites in which children and young adults spend much of their time. Schools have scheduled sessions, ready-made groups, and in relation to evaluation, they allow the repeated collection of data over 'event-bounded timeframes' (Hilton et al., 1998, p. 737). For both primary and secondary prevention efforts, locating programmes in schools increases their accessibility and is less stigmatising than services provided, for example, in mental health settings (Hassall & Hannah, 2007).

Therefore, sexual violence prevention education in schools can reach young and diverse populations relatively easily, and can be linked to existing curricula, processes and pedagogy (Hassall & Hannah, 2007). However, there is little clarity as to whether work takes place with children in schools because it is convenient, it is where children are a mass and captive audience, or rather from the recognition that schools are in themselves a key institution in the production of normative gendered identities and the concomitant violence (Berkowitz et al., 2005; Butler, 1993a; Connell, 1995a). Schools can thus be conceptualised as both the producers of violence and the starting point for ending it (Harber, 2004; Ross Epp, 1996); school culture and practices are then as important as curriculum work (as cited Ellis, 2008, p. 125).

The obvious disadvantage with a too heavy focus on school-based programme implementation is the fact that some children and young people do not attend school or have disrupted or contingent attendance at school. These children may be more at risk of using or experiencing violence (Carmody, 2009a; Ellis, 2004; Jaffe & Wolfe, 2003; Powell, 2007a; VicHealth, 2007; Wolfe et al., 2006). Efforts should be made to reach populations of young people who do not attend school. These include homeless young people, children living in poverty or in families receiving welfare or with incarcerated parents, children leaving juvenile detention or foster care, young parents, and girls and young women under protective services care (Rosewater, 2003). Other population groups such as same-sex attracted young people often find school less than supportive and in fact many experience significant bullying and homophobia. For these young people, existing sexuality education is 'as useful as a chocolate kettle' as it does not address same sex attraction and focuses almost exclusively on heterosexual sex (Hillier & Mitchell, 2008). Given the invisibility of their desires in sexuality education, it is highly likely violence prevention education will also fail to address their needs.

In reaching diverse populations, it should be recognised that young people spend time in other locations such as sporting and community organisations; faith-based social groups, Scouts and other educational settings (e.g. vocational education and university). While schools remain a key setting for violence prevention education, the goal of bringing about a significant cultural change requires targeting young people and adults in a range of settings.

A further disadvantage of school-based prevention programmes can be resistance or ill-fit between violence prevention pedagogy and school pedagogy. Bradford (2006) observes that school principals and teachers can be uncomfortable and unfamiliar with the content of violence prevention education programmes, and that this can hamper prevention efforts. Related to this problem is evidence that schools can be resistant to using a gender analysis or feminist approach in programmes. Schools are also increasingly being asked to undertake welfare and well-being programmes additional to their curriculum content, which may have the effect of 'overburdening' in schools or schools having a lack of time and resources to contribute to violence prevention programmes (Weissberg & O'Brien, 2004).

Gender and violence prevention education

Gender remains a core issue of theoretical approach in many programmes internationally. How gender is conceptualised and how it impacts on programme design varies significantly. One example from Canada shows the impact of a move away from explicitly addressing the gender basis to intimate violence. A Canadian review of violence prevention programmes by RESOLVE Alberta (Tutty et al., 2002, p. 14) found that the majority of programmes do not identify the fact that girls

and young women are the most likely victims of many forms of intimate violence. Gender neutrality therefore obscures international data
indicating the gendered nature of these crimes (Carmody, 2009a, p. 70).

In 2004, a UK review of educational programmes addressing violence
against women and girls was conducted in England, Northern Ireland
and Wales (Ellis, 2004). Jane Ellis found that there had been a significant growth of programmes between 2000 and 2003, which seem
to have been driven by a Home Office focus on crime reduction and
young people, a commitment to reduce domestic violence and the creation of a children's fund with a strong prevention agenda. Most of the
programmes were aimed at young people aged 3–25 years of age, had
short-term funding and were primarily delivered in school contexts.
However, 38 per cent were delivered in community contexts aimed at
reaching marginalised and 'at risk' young people. Partnerships between
teachers and community organisations like Women's Aid delivered the
programmes. A gender analysis and feminist understandings of domestic violence and sexual assault was acknowledged by 66 per cent of
programmes. However, many programmes seemed to think this was too
controversial or not relevant and therefore reduced the discussion of the
precursors to violence to interpersonal conflict. Evaluation of the programmes was only evident in 36 per cent of programmes reviewed and
these focused on children and young people's knowledge, understanding and attitudes. None of the programmes reported in this study looked
at outcomes in relation to behavioural change. The influence of a public
health discourse was evident in a focus of 42 per cent of programmes on
'healthy' relationships from friendship to intimacy.

Healthy relationships?

This concept of 'healthy relationships' has global currency beyond
the United Kingdom. I have a number of concerns about this
approach. What exactly is a 'healthy relationship'? It seems to me to
reflect a medical discourse in which we are constantly being asked
to monitor or surveil our practices, from eating to sex, against some
predetermined barometer of what is acceptable. One might ask what
is acceptable, and to whom is it acceptable? Who determines this?
Is it the teachers, educators, parents, the state or young people? Even
more concerning is that often programmes using a 'healthy' relationship model focus on telling young people what isn't 'healthy'. Jane Ellis
found that though people in the UK programmes said the aim was to

identify positive and negative actions and feelings, the focus in reality was telling young people about 'unhealthy' relationships. Obscured here is the complexity and diversity of gender, sexualities and cultural and socio-economic difference which impacts differentially on the lives of young people. It also implies a static quality to relationships and sexual intimacy that is disturbing. Intimacy and indeed relationships change over time rather than following a fixed predetermined set of characteristics.

Inherent in all relationships are conceptions of power and how these are shaped by cultural and personal discourses. Rather than seeing power as always coercive or negative, it can also be productive, following Foucault (2002). This allows for a more fluid conception of power that shifts and changes between the individuals involved. It is these shifts that people in intimate relationships negotiate daily. This is very different from reducing relationships to a checklist of healthy or unhealthy behaviours. The moral imperative here implies that if young people understand the predetermined characteristics of a 'healthy relationship' this will result in them governing themselves and being better heteronormative citizens. How gender and sexuality are implicated in this model and the possibilities of this being open to transformation and shifting subjectivities is made invisible (Carmody, 2009a, p. 69).

Knowledge about relationships is therefore constructed within a truth discourse of a binary of healthy/unhealthy. This reflects a particular form of power relations between the object of the knowledge (young people) and those who define how they should behave. I would suggest that the UK experience highlights the collision of competing discourses of prevention. This involves feminist concern to reduce violence against women and girls, the power of Home Office crime reduction policies targeting 'the problem of youth' and the unacknowledged impact of prevention strategies utilising public health discourse as the technology to impart a conservative moral and political agenda (Carmody, 2009a, p. 70).

Both the Canadian and UK experiences show how prevention work is deeply implicated in how we understand the communities in which we live, and how we can deny women's experiences of sexual violence in the framing of prevention education strategies. How gender is conceptualised and addressed or not in programme design impacts on the messages given to young people and on achieving the goal of the primary prevention of intimate violence.

Background to the Sex & Ethics violence prevention programme

My concerns over many years about the way violence prevention education was conceptualised, and the poor outcomes internationally in preventing sexual violence, led me to embark on theoretical and empirical research to explore alternative approaches. In the following section I will begin by providing an overview of the theoretical underpinnings of my work based on ethical subjectivity (for a more detailed discussion, see Carmody, 2009a). This will be followed by an outline of the *Sex & Ethics* programme, and the main components of the approach taken and how it differs from other violence prevention approaches. Young people's responses to the programme to date will then be discussed.

Towards ethical sexual subjectivity

There is much debate in philosophical literature between the terms 'morality' and 'ethics'. Often these terms are used interchangeably. Continental ethical philosophers influenced by Nietzsche, including Foucault, tend to dismiss or move away from morality because of its long association with religion, duty and its prescriptive demands, especially in relation to sexuality. It is beyond this discussion to engage with the lengthy debates about morality/ethics (see MacIntyre, 1998 for a detailed discussion). However, I would say that my approach falls broadly within the tradition of continental philosophy.

This is concerned with determining the conditions for ethical exploration for different types of people, rather than establishing the borders of acceptable or unacceptable desires, thoughts and actions. I extend the continental approach to include feminist conceptions of ethics, including a conception of gender that acknowledges the possibility of multiple forms of masculinities. My approach to sexual ethics is therefore not about seeking new certainties in the sense of new moral codes. Rather it is about a transformation of personal existence, paying attention to the cultural, psychological, interpersonal and emotional conditions of personal transformation that make ethical choices possible (Shroeder, 2000).

In exploring the place of sexual ethics and violence prevention, it is important therefore to be clear on how I will use the concepts of subjectivity and ethics. Let me first explore the role of the subject and subjectivity. By the term 'subject', I'm not referring to a topic or merely how we speak about selfhood. I am instead using it to refer to the way our immediate daily life is already caught up in complex political, social and philosophical; that is, shared concerns (Mansfield, 2000, p. 3). This is different from understanding an individual as an autonomous, free-spirited rational individual that develops as part of our spontaneous encounter with the world (Mansfield, 2000). The term 'subject' acknowledges our relations with others and how we are shaped by cultural forces and in turn shape them.

Building from this backdrop I turn to Michel Foucault, the French philosopher. His work is seen as extremely useful by many scholars in challenging modernist conceptions of power as always repressive (Zalewski, 2000). He reminds us that there is a fluidity of ways in which individual subjects can produce a diversity of subjectivities (whether we are male or female) and that we can resist power/knowledge discourses. This is particularly important when we consider how knowledge has been historically constructed and what is seen as acceptable sexual behaviour has shifted over time. Foucault's work on ethical sexual subjectivities has particular relevance in thinking through alternate spaces and possibilities in working with young people. What I find useful in his ideas is the notion of mutuality and the constant state of reflection and renegotiation that we all require to assess and rework where we are in relation to living an ethical life. I will elaborate on this point below in relation to how it is used in the *Sex & Ethics* programme. Rather than assuming a fixed and stable feminine or masculine subject, a process of constantly becoming or performing gender, as Judith Butler (1993b) points out, is possible. Therefore difference is acknowledged and how we can conform or resist dominant discourses of gender and sexuality is made possible. These ideas provide hope of an alternative way of relating in intimate relationships that moves beyond deterministic views that see all women as potential victims of male violence, and all men as potential perpetrators of such violence towards women and other men.

One way to counter the moral or normative standards imposed by constructing relationships as healthy/unhealthy is to argue for prevention programmes that build or increase ethical subjectivity. This requires more than replacing the healthy/unhealthy binary with a discussion of ethical/unethical behaviours or relationships. Rather, encouraging young people to reflect on their own behaviour and provide them with a framework and skills to reflect on their own ethical stance in relation to themselves and others within a gendered social context opens them up to alternative possibilities and ways of being women and men. My own work in this area seeks to encourage this kind of reflective and reflexive stance as a strategy to reduce pressured, coerced sex within 'dating' contexts. This is not about replacing one set of moral codes with another but rather seeks to engage a dynamic and constantly shifting process of ethical reflection specific to each sexual or relationship encounter. These may vary between individuals and places, but mutual negotiation by both partners of their individual and joint desires and needs is seen as central to an ethical relationship (Carmody, 2009a).

The Sex & Ethics violence prevention programme

The theoretical approach discussed above was then followed by field work interviewing young people 16–25 years of age. This was made possible by funding from the Australian Research Council (2005–2008) and working with an industry partner, NSW Rape Crisis Centre. Fifty-six young women and men of diverse backgrounds from rural and metropolitan NSW were interviewed in 2007. The focus of the interviews was to talk to young people about the education they had received about sexuality and also violence prevention. We were also interested in how they negotiated sex in the context of casual or long-term relationships. The findings of the research interviews informed the subsequent *Sex & Ethics* prevention programme discussed below.

We found that many young people are not being well prepared by existing personal development programmes in schools or by families to deal with relationships issues that emerge around their developing sexuality, issues of consent, conflict and negotiation of their own and their partner's sexual needs and desires. Their sexuality education was limited to biological facts and safe sex in the government schools context, while in faith-based schools it was abstinence based. A notable exception to this is the Share programme developed by Shine South Australia that involves a comprehensive evaluated sexuality programme including material on sexual consent and relationships (Johnson, 2006). I found highly gendered expectations about sexual intimacy among young people. This is consistent with other research with young people by Hirst (2004), Hillier and Mitchell (2008), Powell (2007a, b) and Allen (2003, 2005). Their exposure to sexual assault prevention education was at best, limited, and at worst non-existent, except for occasional messages that 'rape is bad' and 'just say no' to manage the complexity of consent.

The inadequacy of much sexuality education and the limited exposure of young people to violence prevention education suggest a need for these areas to work much more closely together. The *Sex & Ethics* programme brings together research and practice knowledge from the fields of sexuality and violence prevention education, particularly sexual assault prevention. Traditionally these areas of work have developed separately and often been delivered by different groups of professionals. Some are teachers who implement personal development curricula; others are trained sexual health educators. Professionals delivering violence prevention education have often come from a direct service background of working with victims of sexual violence.

The programme is designed to be delivered over six weeks, with sessions of 2–3 hours per week. Pedagogically, it begins with locating discussions in the first session around a role play of young people with diverse views and experiences of sexual intimacy. It builds over the subsequent weeks to more personal knowledge acquisition and skill development (e.g., understanding your own and other's desires; alcohol, drugs and sex; skills in reading and giving non-verbal communication; skills in sexual consent and the legal context of decisions; dealing with conflict and pressure to be sexual) and concludes by focusing on skills of how to be an ethical bystander and challenge sexually risky or potentially exploitative behaviour within friendship groups and the wider community.

A unique feature of this programme is the introduction of a theoretical framework of ethical sexual decision-making in the second session. The need for prevention programmes to demonstrate a clear theoretical underpinning and coherence of the programme elements is consistently argued for in the best practice prevention literature (Ellis, 2008; Schewe, 2004). The framework has four elements and forms the theoretical backdrop to the subsequent activities over the following weeks.

The Sexual Ethics Framework

Care for myself

+

Be aware of my desires and wants and the possible impact on the other person

+

Negotiate and 'ask'

+

Reflect

Carmody, M © 2009a

The framework incorporates elements of Foucault's approach to ethical sexual subjectivity. With apologies to Foucault, it makes a complex philosophical argument into a simple framework that young people can grasp and gives them some navigation tools to actually develop skills in ethical reflection and sexual decision-making. Each of the elements is explained to young people attending groups and a series of reflective questions are posed at each step. Ethical decision-making is explained to them as being a dynamic and constantly shifting ground, within any encounter or relationship and it is not something that is done once and never considered again. Each element needs to be present for all ethical considerations to be explored. This is the reason for the + signs. The inverted commas around 'ask' are to highlight that communication is non-verbal as well as verbal. The framework is reinforced in subsequent activities over the following four weeks and in group discussions.

The framework provides a space and skills for young people to personally scrutinise their own value systems. Through carefully constructed activities and critical questioning from educators they explore how their beliefs and attitudes about women, men, sexuality and violence are shaped by the broader social and cultural context in which they live. Many enter the groups with little experience of critical reflection. Rather they are often convinced that their values are the 'truth' about issues and the group process reveals the quite different ethical stance people take on the same issue. There are others who have some experience of self-reflection, but the framework pushes them further to actively encourage them to move beyond a self-focused sense of care of themselves to consider the impact of their desires and beliefs on others. Through this method, ideas of mutuality and negotiation become central to developing ethical intimacy and an ethical life more broadly.

The use of this framework does not imply that it will always result in young people or others making ethical decisions in relation to sexual intimacy or that it will prevent sexual assault in every situation. Unlike a checklist of 'healthy' and 'unhealthy' relationships, the *Sex & Ethics* programme does not impose what is ethical. Rather, it is about encouraging young people to develop their own ethical code which does consider self-care but not at the expense of care of the other person. These personal reflections are not suggesting a retreat to an individualistic model of ethics. There are much broader issues such as cultural beliefs and practices that promote and condone sexual assault which need to be challenged. The framework and the programme are strategies amongst a multi-level approach to achieving the prevention of intimate violence.

However, the framework and the activities and related conversations that occur within the programme do provide a place for personal and cultural practices to be held up to ethical reflection considering the impact of decisions we make in sexual situations. Living an ethical life is an ongoing process and sometimes we don't always behave ethically. I argue that, if ethical dimensions are not considered, the possibility of coerced, pressured, unwanted and unfulfilling sex will be increased. If we leave aside sexual assault by strangers and focus on the vast majority of sexual assault that is committed by known people, there are some different challenges for education. Pressured, coerced and forced sex is common among many couples including young people (1991, 2005; Carmody, 2009a; Powell, 2007b). In the *Sex & Ethics* education groups 30 per cent of women and 15 per cent of men reported experiences of pressured and coerced sex.

This form of sexual assault is often not perceived by the men or women involved as a crime. For some it is seen as part of the bargain for maintaining the encounter or relationship and to pressure someone to have sex is part of the gendered dance of heterosex in which men pursue and women resist and gradually cede bodily territory. Young women also report feeling fearful of trying to end an encounter because they feel a physically stronger partner will harm them. There have been recent legislative moves in the United Kingdom, and in Australia, in the states of Victoria and New South Wales towards a more communicative form of sexual consent. This is based on mutual and free agreement and seeks to challenge traditional gender expectations. If a sexual assault matter is taken to court, the accused person will now have to demonstrate how they actively and consistently obtained consent throughout the sexual encounter. The *Sex & Ethics* programme is one opportunity to teach young people the skills they need to ensure that consent is actively mutual and that both parties' needs are being acknowledged.

From a pedagogical and political perspective, the framework is often challenging for educators. To deliver the accredited programme, they are required to participate in a five-day training programme. They are required to experience the programme they will subsequently deliver to young people. This was a conscious decision on my part to ensure that educators have actively engaged in holding their own beliefs and values up to scrutiny. For those educators who are used to delivering fact-based education or hold the view that they know the truth about what is 'right' for young people, the programme is often challenging. Educators who have a structuralist analysis of gender and violence are discomforted by the *Sex & Ethics* approach which acknowledges the dynamic and shifting nature of power relations and acknowledges that women and men can be ethical and can also be highly unethical. Further challenges arise from the conception of gender which acknowledges the highly gendered nature of many intimate encounters but moves beyond a deterministic model and argues that there are many ways to perform gender whether you are male or female.

The response of young people to the Sex & Ethics programme

The programme was piloted with 50 young people 16–25 years of age in 2007, in rural and city locations. The settings for the programme included youth services, vocational education and a university. Eighty-two per cent of participants were women and 18 per cent were male. Fifteen per cent were identified as culturally diverse with the majority indicating they were opposite sex attracted and 75 per cent indicating they were sexually active.

A comparison of young people's confidence levels around sexual negotiation taken before the group began and at the end of the six week group indicated statistically significant increases in the confidence levels of young people in articulating their own needs in a sexual encounter or relationship compared to how they felt at the beginning of the group. This was supported by their comments, for example:

It really helped me as I am just starting to enter a relationship so it gave me a good base to start from to know what I need and want and what my other half needs and wants.

(Jane, 17 as cited Carmody, 2009a, p. 136)

Even higher levels of improvement were found in relation to understanding their partner's needs. For example:

I have certainly been more aware of my girlfriend's body language since partaking in the group. At one time I noticed stiffness in her persona and was able to discern that she was not as ready as I was for some aspects of our relationship and we were able to talk it out and find a common ground.

(Dave, 24 as cited Carmody, 2009a, p. 137)

These changes were maintained at six months following completion of the programme with 82 per cent reporting using *ideas* learnt in the *Sex & Ethics* group and 74 per cent indicated that they used *skills* learnt in the group. Sixty-one per cent of participants indicated using ethical bystander skills since the programme ended taking up issues of community responsibility raised in the programme and being active participants in standing up against sexual violence.

Ethical reflection is a dynamic and constantly evolving process and this encouraged young people to see they could use it beyond the life of the programme. The uptake of the ideas and skills indicated by the 2007/2008 research findings indicate that participants found this useful in their own intimate relationships, but also as a resource to offer advice to friends. This means that participants increased their own capacity for ethical negotiation as well as within their friendship networks. Given the strong reliance young people place on their friendship groups, increasing the skills of some of the members has enormous potential for primary prevention.

A focus on sexual ethics provided a space for young people to explore a multiplicity of ways to respond to sexual intimacy. Some used the knowledge and skills to enhance ongoing relationships; others learnt how to better negotiate for safe and pleasurable casual sex; for others it meant decisions to not be sexual at that point until it felt okay for them. For another small group it meant that the framework gave them the confidence to hold firm on not having sex outside of marriage. This final group had been feeling peer and, in some cases, partner pressure to change their ethical stance. The sexual ethics framework gave all of these different groups an opportunity to reflect on what they wanted and how they might make it happen ethically. This process indicates that the outcome of what young people do with ideas about ethical sex is not fixed. Rather, it acknowledges the diversity of young people and a range of options they could draw on to use in sexual decision-making. For many educators and parents this may be a scary concept. Many 'adults' like to feel they know better than young people, whether out of concern to protect them or believing they have the right to control their lives. The reality is that many young people are having sex earlier and with more partners than previous generations. They therefore need opportunities and education that better equip them to deal with these issues in a way that reflects care of the self and an understanding of the impact of their needs and desires on others. The *Sex & Ethics* programme is one such opportunity.

Current funding in 2009 of the *Sex & Ethics* programme from the Australian federal government under the *Respectful Relationships Program* resulted in extending the programme into different geographical sites and also to explore the usefulness of the programme with young people with learning difficulties, with two groups of same-sex attracted women and men, and with footballers. The Ministry of Justice in New Zealand has also funded the implementation of the programme in four youth settings in Wellington with participation from Pacific Islander, Maori and queer identified young people. By the end of 2009, over 200 young people in Australia and New Zealand had participated in the programme from diverse backgrounds and locations. We now have a more equal involvement of women and men which we were not able to achieve in the original pilot. Pre and post group data are currently being analysed from these groups. Preliminary data analysis shows that the response of the young people continues to be extremely positive. At the time of writing, I am about to conduct the six-month follow-up study with young people to ascertain if they are still using the knowledge and skills learnt in the group. Data collected from all of these sites will help us to understand more about the effectiveness of the programme for diverse groups of young people and suggest any refinements needed.

Implications for addressing violence in schools

My focus in this discussion has centred on approaches to reduce violence between young people in intimate relationships. The age of first sex is continuing to decline and in my study 30 per cent of women and 50 per cent of men were sexually active by the age of 15 or 16. Thirty-two per cent of women and 15 per cent of men indicated experiences of pressured coerced sex or sexual assault. The latest Australian National Secondary Schools Survey (Smith et al., 2009) showed a 10 per cent increase in the numbers of young people reporting such unwanted experiences compared with 2002. These findings indicate that the call for violence prevention programmes early in young people's lives is greatly needed.

The Australian government's commitment to addressing this need through the funding of Respectful Relationships Education is an important initiative. However, there is a need to ensure that the programmes that are funded are focused on achieving behavioural change and not just awareness-raising. There is also a need to ensure that a gender analysis underpins the programmes and that programme design addresses best practice research issues such as a clear conceptual approach, demonstrating a theory of change, undertaking inclusive, relevant and culturally sensitive practice and programme development and delivery, that effective evaluation strategies are built into the programme design and that educators are fully supported through training and professional development (see *Framing Best Practice: National Standards for the Primary Prevention of Sexual Assault Through Education* (Carmody et al., 2009)).

Schools will probably remain a primary site for the introduction of such programmes. Given this factor, working with principals and teachers will be important to ensure that the programmes that are delivered are in line with international best practice research about violence prevention programmes. At the same time, we need to develop closer collaboration between violence prevention advocates and schools to work together to implement the programmes so that schools are not left unsupported or overburdened. However, we also need to consider alternative settings where young people can be reached to ensure all young people have an opportunity to consider alternative ways of relating. There also needs to be an increased focus on involving parents in the development of respectful and ethical relationships with their children and young people.

10
Conclusions: Rethinking School Violence: Implications for Theory, Policy and Practice

Kerry H. Robinson, Cristyn Davies and Sue Saltmarsh

The importance of viewing school violence through the lens of socio-cultural, political and historical discourses

Each of the authors in this book has highlighted the complexities involved in the manifestation of school violence in its multiple contexts. Integral and foundational to each of the chapters has been the importance of reconceptualising school violence through the lens of socio-cultural, political and historical discourses that impact on the ways in which violence is constructed, understood and situated. As discussed in the introduction to this book, to date, understandings of and approaches to school violence have continued to be largely dominated by psychological discourses that focus on individual pathologies, rather than in complex relations of power that underpin the interplay between individual identities, social, cultural and environmental factors. This has limited understandings of and approaches to dealing with school violence. Each of the chapters also highlights the ways in which violence is often normalised in young people's lives through the hegemonic socio-cultural and political practices that operate in different cultural contexts. What has been argued in this book is that the 'everydayness' of school violence in many young people's schooling experiences, and lives more generally, stemming from broad socio-cultural, political and historical discourses, is missing from many analyses of school violence, rendering much of this behaviour as invisible and/or unremarkable in the eyes of many students, teachers and educational researchers.

The significance of gender in the manifestation of school violence

A particularly significant aspect of the research on school violence that informs the discussions in this book is the critical role that gender plays in the many forms of violence that occur in school contexts. The research in this book overwhelmingly indicates that a significantly high proportion of the victims of harassment, sexual harassment and other forms of violence in schools are girls (and women), reflecting broader socio-cultural values around gendered power relations. In addition, boys who are gender non-conforming – that is those boys who do not perform their masculinity in a way that is culturally expected – are also frequently targets of violence. Gender is not just significant in understanding who might become the targets of school violence, but it is also critical in understanding who directs violence towards others, and why. The socio-cultural construction of masculinity and its relationship to power and identity is highly significant to understanding violence in schools. This is not to say that girls do not engage in harassment, sexual harassment or other forms of school violence, as some authors in this book point out, but a gendered analysis of these behaviours provides an understanding of the different or similar ways girls might mobilise these behaviours and why.

However, dominant discourses of school violence frequently taken up in schools by teachers, educators and administrators tend to either downplay the role of gender, often portraying violent attitudes, speech and conduct in 'gender neutral' terms, or as the 'natural' cause of the gendered perpetrator/victim binary associated with violence. That is, males are often perceived to be inherently aggressive and naturally the perpetrators, while females are considered to be the natural victims of violence, or as inherently more likely to engage in behaviours that are less physical and less confrontational. Failing to include an analysis of the socio-cultural, political and historical influences associated with gender and power results in reverting to biological and psychological explanations that do not tell the full story behind practices of violence. As pointed out throughout this book, such readings of gender and its relationship to violence have largely constituted current approaches to school violence, which has rendered current strategies largely ineffectual. However, the authors in this book have provided different readings of the various manifestations of school violence that occur, highlighting the critical impact of gender, youth cultures and other socio-cultural factors, on this pervasive social phenomenon.

Addressing systemic or institutionalised violence in schools

Another critical point highlighted by the authors in this collection is that systemic or institutionalised violence is an important factor in the perpetuation of violence in schools. Institutional practices and policies often perpetuate a culture in schooling that fosters unsupportive and inequitable environments, and that all too often renders invisible the violent nature of many normative assumptions and everyday practices. This in turn renders students and teachers alike vulnerable to exclusionary and aggressive attitudes and behaviours that may have become an accepted and unremarkable part of 'business as usual' in some school environments.

Schooling practices and policies, especially related to sporting cultures, can perpetuate hegemonic masculinities as the normalising benchmark of male identity and power, fostering aggression as a legitimate means of solving conflicts in the eyes of those taking up this form of masculinity. Within these contexts heteronormative discourses prevail, increasing the vulnerability of those boys and young men who do their gender differently and are perceived to be sexually 'suspect'. Further, dominant discourses of authority and discipline operating in many schools often reinforce disciplinary practices that are based on aggression, coercion and force that easily slip into abusive behaviours, resulting in escalating conflicts between students and teachers. Some male teachers in schools, for instance, utilise their position to exert their institutionalised power, violating and harassing students into compliance and as a means of controlling student behaviours. Some teachers also breach their positions of power, authority and trust to engage in sexual harassment of students, while others engage in labelling and pathologising students in ways that can establish negative patterns of school engagement that can be long lasting and have disastrous consequences in the lives of students.

Developing effective strategies for counteracting school violence

The remainder of this concluding chapter highlights the implications for educators, schooling policies, educational research and for other relevant professionals dealing with school violence raised by the authors in this collection.

General implications of this research for educators and others working to counteract school violence

(i) There are no quick-fix answers to dealing with school violence;
(ii) Focusing solely on perceived individual deficits or pathologies as the 'causes' leading to violent behaviours, extreme or otherwise, does not provide an understanding of the complexities involved in this phenomenon; and
(iii) A consideration of the influence of socio-cultural and geographical factors impacting on school violence is essential when developing intervention strategies – that is, the interplay between individuals, relational, social, cultural and environmental factors.

Specific chapter implications for educators and others working to counteract school violence

Part I: School Violence in Context

Chapter 1. In Chapter 1, **'The kid most likely': Naming, Brutality and Silence within and beyond School Settings**, Sue Saltmarsh raises several critical implications for theory, practice and policy around school violence:

(i) When students behave in ways that are difficult or confronting, educators need to be reflexive about what such conduct may be telling them about the school culture and environment;
(ii) Teachers and principals need to be vigilant about ensuring that everyday norms within their school neither implicitly nor explicitly enable exclusionary practices;
(iii) There is a need for school leadership that maintains high expectations of staff attitudes towards and engagement with students and their families; and
(iv) Teacher preparation and professional development need to provide models of practice that represent a decisive shift away from pathologising discourses of student behaviour.

Chapter 2. Ronnie Casella's chapter, **The Historical and Political Roots of School Violence in South Africa: Developing a Cross-National Theory**, raised some important implications for educational research and theory, particularly in terms of developing an international perspective on school violence:

(i) There is a need for more quantitative research that examines the correlation between school violence and political volatility/political history to ascertain if school violence is experienced in similar or different ways in politically volatile countries, or in countries with similar political histories;

(ii) An examination of whether theories developed to explain school violence are applicable internationally is required;

(iii) An awareness that international theories of violence may not only provide insights into better ways of understanding traditional forms of violence, but also alert educators to other forms of violence that may be dismissed in traditional, more localised analyses.

Chapter 3. Amy Chapman and Rachel Buchanan's chapter focusing on cyberbullying, titled 'FYI... **Virtual Space Has a Context: Towards Alternative Frames for Understanding Cyberbullying**', raises the following implications for dealing with cyberbullying in schools:

(i) There is a need to consider school-yard bullying and cyberbullying as a normalised component of young people's experiences of schooling cultures, rather than the pathological behaviours of individuals;

(ii) It is important to examine why young people spend so much time online and to examine what it is that they actually do – a gendered analysis is important to this examination;

(iii) It is critical to understood cyberspace as a series of networked relationships, especially when considering young people's online participation. Young people are increasingly dependent upon digital participation for inclusion in their peer groups – a gendered analysis is important to this examination;

(iv) Educators need to take into consideration, when developing intervention strategies, the influence of socio-cultural factors impacting on schoolyard violence and its extension into cyberbullying, that is the interplay between individuals, relational, social, cultural and environmental factors; and

(v) Educators need to examine the definitions of cyberbullying that underpin the policies and practices that operate in their schools, that is definitions can influence and restrict how cyberbullying is understood and approached.

Part II: Gender and School Violence

Chapter 4. Kerry Robinson's chapter, titled **Sexual Harassment in Schools: Issues of Identity and Power. Negotiating the Complexities, Contexts and Contradictions of this Everyday Practice**, raises a number of significant policy, curriculum and professional development implications for educators, researchers and other professionals dealing with sexual harassment in schools:

   (i) School policies need to address sexual harassment as a complex socio-cultural phenomenon that is integral to performances of gender and intersecting with other aspects of identity such as sexuality, race, class, age and so on;

  (ii) Common practices of understanding sexual harassment as instigated by problematic individuals with pathological problems, and subsuming this behaviour within the context of bullying, eclipse the complex discursive nature of this widespread practice;

 (iii) Approaches to sexual harassment need to consider its complexities and the contradictions associated with those who experience and perpetrate this behaviour. For example, it is important that policies demonstrate an understanding of the complexities of racialised sexual harassment or of heterosexist sexual harassment;

 (iv) It is critical to highlight the way that sexual harassment becomes normalised in the everyday lives of young people;

  (v) Sexual harassment needs to be addressed in the school curriculum to increase young people's awareness and understandings of the political nature of this phenomenon and of the ways that it becomes normalised in their everyday lives. Until the stereotypes of sexual harassment are critically deconstructed with young people, this behaviour will continue to be viewed within the 'boss/secretary' binary, or the problematic individual, and considered irrelevant to young people's circumstances;

 (vi) Educating individuals about sexual harassment also requires a focus on its intersections with homophobia and heterosexism, racism and classism, to name a few critical areas that influence how this behaviour is used as a technology of power; and

(vii) Increasing awareness and understandings of sexual harassment needs to be a critical compulsory component of teachers' and school administrators' professional development. Teachers also need to consider how sexual harassment operates in young people's everyday lives, as well as how it operates as a technology of power in regulating and policing organisational hierarchies of power. It is also critical that teachers examine their own practices in order to consider how their own perceptions and values can perpetuate sexual harassment.

Chapter 5. In Chapter 5, **Schools, Violence, Masculinities and Privilege**, Martin Mills, examining the ways in which some boys engage, negotiate and survive the violence associated with dominant forms of masculinity operating in schools, raises the following important implications for educators, researchers and other professionals dealing with school violence:

  (i) It is critical that educators are aware of the 'communities of masculine practice' operating in schools and the implications of these on boys and other members of the school community;
 (ii) An examination is required of the ways in which the violence utilised amongst boys is deployed in ways that reinscribe certain forms of privilege in schools;
(iii) An awareness is required of the ways in which many boys have to negotiate surviving the dangers associated with dominant forms of masculinity that operate in schools;
 (iv) Homophobic discourses are frequently mobilised against boys who do not perform their masculinities according to the dominant cultures of the school and this is fraught with dangers for those boys;
  (v) Survival strategies mobilised by boys can reinscribe dominant forms of masculinity and perpetuate violence; and
 (vi) Teachers and educational administrators need to develop effective strategies to disrupt the relationships between dominant masculinities and violence.

Chapter 6. Robert Morrell, Deevia Bhana and Vijay Hamlall, in Chapter 6, **'I'm not scared of the teacher – I can hold him – I can hold him with my bare hands': Schoolboys, Male Teachers and Physical Violence at a Durban Secondary School in South Africa**, highlight the importance of examining the intersections of gender and violence in specific schooling cultural contexts and across different relationships in schools – in this instance, schoolboys' violent practices directed towards teachers. Echoing a similar perspective to Casella in Chapter 2, Morrell, Bhana and Hamlall point out that school violence in South Africa needs to be viewed within the context of a long history of social and political violence in this country. Morrell, Bhana and Hamlall raise some critical implications for theory, practice and policy around school violence:

(i) A history of social and political violence and disruption in a country or region can impact on the way that violence is played out in schooling contexts;

(ii) Understanding the diversity of power relations operating in schools is critical to understanding school violence, for example gender, ethnicity, student–teacher relations;

(iii) Institutionalised violence in schools stems largely from historical, socio-cultural factors. For example, teachers can use violence against students to maintain power and authority, whilst students can use violence against teachers to challenge power inequalities that exist between students and teachers;

(iv) Teachers' violence against male students is a means through which masculine authority is constituted and maintained in schools;

(v) Violence perpetrated by schoolboys against teachers is an exercise in agency within a hierarchical institution in which some teachers can infringe on boys' sense of dignity; and

(vi) An analysis of the institutionalisation of dominant forms of masculinity in schooling is critical to understanding school violence.

Part III: Language, Practice and School Violence

Chapter 7. In Chapter 7, **Speaking Violence: Homophobia and the Production of Injurious Speech in Schooling Cultures**, Davies and McInnes argue that the identification of a violent act often too quickly moves towards identification of the perpetrator and the victim without proper consideration of how each is constituted and implicated in the precarious production of their 'selves' within the domain of the school. Davies and McInnes advocate for the use of *circuit-breakers*, arguing that it is critical for educators to intervene in the circuits of recognition that operate around homophobic violence. They raise some critical implications for theory, practice and policy for educators and other professionals challenging homophobic violence in schools:

(i) *Circuit-breakers* need to be 'responsive' pedagogies that exploit the teachable moment by taking moments of homophobic violence as opportunities to deconstruct dominant homophobic and heterosexist discourses and practices. It is critical that educators intervene in homophobia when it occurs by engaging students in a process of deconstructing the *circuits of recognition* – that is, the discursive constructions that inform homophobic behaviours and attitudes. Inviting students to critically reflect on their behaviours and attitudes encourages them to learn about and explore different positionalities, as well as utilising deconstruction as a method for teaching students to interrogate their own and other subject positions within particular discursive regimes;

(ii) Employing a *circuits of recognition* approach requires students/others involved in instances of homophobia not only to engage in self-reflexivity but also to think critically about the power relations (around gender, sexuality, ethnicity, socio-economic class, ability) mobilised when dominant understandings of homophobia prevail;

(iii) There is a need to critically reflect on the links between policies and everyday practices, and the ways in which power relations are operating in the school environment, rather than individualising and pathologising individual (student) behaviours. While individuals should take responsibility for their behaviour, homophobic violence should be addressed systemically, rather than just as an individual issue;

(iv) While the constitution of schools as safe spaces is the dominant discourse in policy and strategy documents, research in this field demonstrates that homophobic violence is still prevalent in schooling contexts and that the idea of safe space is a pervasive myth. Safe schools rhetoric thus frames and determines the discourses through which violence might be recognised or understood;

(v) Inviting students to take part in developing school-based anti-homophobia initiatives is more likely to engage participants because they are likely to feel a sense of ownership towards policies and practices, which they have been involved in developing and implementing; and

(vi) There is a need to identify opportunities within the school curriculum that are part of a whole-of-school approach to educating students about homophobia. Taking a whole-of-school approach to educating students, staff and administrators about homophobic violence is central to the effectiveness of individual initiatives operating within the school environment.

Chapter 8. Sara Knox in her chapter, **Random School Shootings, Teen Culture and the Representation of Violence**, points out that in terms of extreme forms of violence involving shootings or other weapons, schools have tended to adopt extreme punitive quick-fix measures that treat the problem at the individual behavioural level, at the expense of looking at the 'cultural tensions', that is, the broader socio-cultural, geographical and political factors that influence much of this behaviour in individual subjects. Knox raises the following implications for theory, practice and policy associated with dealing with extreme cases of school violence, such as shootings. However, these implications are equally relevant to manifestations of school violence more generally:

(i) The rarity of school shootings makes it virtually impossible to plan for the rare and randomness of this form of violence or to prevent it. However, changing school cultures in ways that enhance students' positive schooling experiences can make these *rare events* less likely to occur;

(ii) A close examination of *local knowledge* associated with the *particular* context of school shootings is critical to understanding the discrete cultural content relevant to these events;

(iii) A greater concentration is required on building more positive relationships between families, communities and schools that foster a supportive environment in which young people feel more able to openly discuss their fears, stressors and concerns, rather than focusing on technologies of surveillance (cameras, campus 'police', metal detectors) that tend to encourage and perpetuate mutual suspicion and hostility between adults and young people;

(iv) Building mentoring programmes between adults and young people in schools could lead to more open and supportive school communities;

(v) A greater awareness of how schooling cultures constitute and perpetuate heteronormative discourses of masculinity would provide critical insight into more effective interventions into the ways that some young men take up hypermasculine violent behaviours, perceiving that this would 'prove' themselves as powerful masculine figures in the eyes of their peers and others; and

(vi) Focusing on school and community programmes that foster inclusion and a respect for diversity and difference should be at the heart of intervention strategies into bullying and other forms of school violence – this needs to include a focus on counteracting issues such as gender and sexual prejudices, as well as encouraging greater recognition of the diversity of contemporary families.

Chapter 9. Moira Carmody in the final chapter of this book, titled **Young People, Ethical Sex and Violence Prevention**, raises some critical implications for theory, policy and practice associated with developing effective violence prevention programmes targeted at young people:

  (i) Violence prevention programmes need to be focused on behavioural change, not just awareness building;
 (ii) Violence prevention programmes need to be founded on a critical analysis of gendered relationships, a strong emphasis on best practice research, a clear conceptual framework, with an undertaking of inclusive, relevant and culturally sensitive practice and programme development and delivery;
(iii) Effective evaluation strategies and appropriate teacher training is critical to the success of violence prevention programmes;
 (iv) Schools need to work collaboratively with violence prevention advocates in order to build a network of support to ensure the ongoing success of school programmes; and
  (v) There is a need for the development of programmes involving parents that focus on building ethical and respectful relationships in the lives of children and young people.

Conclusion

The implications outlined above provide educators and other professionals dealing with school violence, with some critical points to consider when reviewing the practices, policies and strategies they may be currently employing to counteract the different manifestations of violence encountered in their schools. In addition to practical implications for schooling sectors, the aim of the editors and contributors of this book is also to engage in research dialogues concerned with the socially and institutionally situated and culturally produced nature of school-related violence. Our commitment is to understanding violence beyond the terms of individual or family deficit and dysfunction, turning our attention instead towards schooling environments and their discursive norms.

References

Akers, R. (1990) Rational choice, deterrence, and social learning theory in criminology. *Journal of Criminal Law and Criminology*, 81 (3): 653–676.

Akiba, M., LeTendre, G., Baker, D., and Goesling, B. (2002) Student victimization: national and school system effects on school violence in 37 nations. *American Educational Research Journal*, 39 (4): 829–854.

Allard, T. (2008) Women, your armed forces need you. *Sydney Morning Herald*, 24 March, retrieved 30 September 2010, from http://www.smh.com.au/news/national/women-your-armed-forces-need-you/2008/03/23/1206206927415.html.

Allen, L. (2003) Power talk young people negotiating (hetero)sex. *Women's Studies International Forum*, 26 (3): 235–244.

Allen, L. (2005) *Sexual Subjects: Young People, Sexuality, and Education*, London: Palgrave Macmillan.

Altbeker, A. (2007) *A Country at War with Itself: South Africa's Crisis of Crime*, Johannesburg: Jonathan Ball.

Alter, J. (1998, 6 April) Harnessing the Hysteria. *Newsweek*, 131 (14): 27.

American Association of University Women (AAUW) (2001a) *Hostile Hallways: The AAUW Survey on Sexual Harassment in America's Schools*, Washington, DC: AAUW.

American Association of University Women (AAUW) (2001b) *Hostile Hallways: Bullying, Teasing, and Sexual Harassment in School*, New York: Harris/Scholastic Research.

Apple, M.W. (2010) *Global Crises, Social Justice and Education*, New York: Routledge.

Astor, R., Benbenishty, R., and Marachi, R. (2006) Making the case for an international perspective on school violence: implications for theory, research, policy, and assessment. In S. Jimerson and M. Furlong (Eds.) *Handbook of School Violence and School Safety* (pp. 103–117). New York: Lawrence Erlbaum Associates.

Atweh, B., Kemmis, S., and Weeks, P. (Eds.) (1998) *Action Research in Practice: Partnership for Social Justice in Education*, New York: Routledge.

Australian Bureau of Statistics (1996) *Women's Safety Australia*, retrieved November 2006, from www.abs.gov.au.

Australian Bureau of Statistics (2005) *Personal Safety Survey* (Catalogue No. 4906.0), Canberra: Australian Bureau of Statistics.

Australian Communications and Media Authority (ACMA) (2008) *ACMA Communications Report 2006–2007*, Canberra: Commonwealth of Australia, retrieved 8 June 2011, from http://www.acma.gov.au/webwr/_assets/main/lib310631/0607commreport_complete.pdf.

Australian Communications and Media Authority (ACMA) (2010) Trends in media use by children and young people, retrieved 12 June 2011, from www.acma.gov.au/webwr/_assets/main/lib310665/trends_in_media_use_by_children_and_young_people.pdf.

Australian Government, Department of Families, Housing, Community Services and Indigenous Affairs (FaHSCIA) (2009) *Gender Equality for Women – Respectful Relationships Guidelines*, retrieved 13 September 2009, from http://www.fahcsia.gov.au/sa/women/pubs/general/RespectfulRelationshipsProgramGuidelines/Documents/RR_ProgramGuidelines.pdf.

Bailey, C. (2011) Virtual skin: articulating race in cyberspace. In D. Trend (Ed.) *Reading Digital Culture* (pp. 334–353). Massachusetts: Blackwell.

Ball, S. (1990) *Foucault and Education: Discipline and Knowledge*, London: Routledge.

Bandura, A. (1977) *Social Learning Theory*, Englewood Cliffs, NJ: Prentice-Hall Publishers.

Bandura, A. and Walters, R. (1959) *Adolescent Aggression: A Study of the Influence of Child-Training Practices and Family Interrelationships*, New York: The Ronald Press Company.

Barak, A. (2005) Sexual harassment on the internet. *Social Science Computer Review*, 23 (1): 77–92.

Barker, G. (2005) *Dying to Be a Man: Youth, Masculinity and Social Exclusion*, London: Routledge.

Bauman, Z. (2001) *Community: Seeking Safety in an Insecure World*, Cambridge: Polity Press.

Becker, H. (1963) *Outsiders: Studies in the Sociology of Deviance*, New York: The Free Press.

Belgrave, J. and Smith, M. (12 June 2007) *Ombudsmen Act 1975: Investigation by John Belgrave, Chief Ombudsman and Mel Smith, Ombudsman, of the Department of Corrections in Relation to the Transport of Prisoners*, New Zealand: Ombudsman of the Department of Corrections.

Berkowitz, A., Jaffe, P., Peacock, D., Rosenbluth, B., and Sousa, C. (2005) *Young Men as Allies in Preventing Violence and Abuse: Building Effective Partnerships with Schools*, Pennsylvania: VAWnet, from http://www.vawnet.org/DomesticViolence/PreventionAndEducation/Approaches/YoungMenAllies.pdf.

Beynon, J. (1985) *Initial Encounters in the Secondary School*, London: The Falmer Press.

Beynon, J. (1987) Ms. Floral mends her ways: a case study of the micro-politics of creative drama. In L. Tickle (Ed.) *The Arts in Education*. London: Groom Helm.

Bhana, D. (2005) Violence and the gendered negotiation of masculinity among young black school boys in South Africa. In L. Ouzgane and R. Morrell (Eds.) *African Masculinities* (pp. 205–220). New York/Pietermaritzburg: Palgrave/University of KwaZulu-Natal Press.

Bhana, D. (2006) 'Doing power': Confronting violent masculinities in primary schools. In F. Leach and C. Mitchell (Eds.) *Combating Gender Violence In and Around Schools* (pp. 171–179). London: Routledge Falmer.

Bhana, D. (2008) 'Girls hit!' Constructing and negotiating violent African femininities in a working-class primary school. *Discourse: Studies in the Cultural Politics of Education*, 29 (3): 401–416.

Bingham, S.G. (1994) Introduction: framing sexual harassment – defining a discursive focus of study. In S.G. Bingham (Ed.) *Conceptualizing Sexual Harassment as Discursive Practice* (pp. 1–14). Westport, Connecticut: Praeger.

Black, J. (1991) *The Aesthetics of Murder: A Study in Romantic Literature and Contemporary Culture*, Baltimore: Johns Hopkins.

Blakar, R.M. (2008) Changing societal ideologies: a backdrop for understanding ethical issues. In S. Robinson and J. Strain (Eds.) *Ethics for Living and Working* (pp. 31–38). Leicester, UK: Troubador Publishing.

Bloch, G. (2009) *The Toxic Mix: What's Wrong with South Africa's Schools and How to Fix It*, Cape Town: Tafelberg.

Boyd, D.M. (2007) Why youth (heart) social network sites: the role of networked publics in teenage social life. In David Buckingham (Ed.) *MacArthur Foundation Series on Digital Learning – Youth, Identity, and Digital Media Volume*, Cambridge, MA: MIT Press, retrieved 10 July 2011, from http://www.danah.org/papers/WhyYouthHeart.pdf.

Boyd, D.M. and Marwick, A. (2009) The conundrum of visibility. *Journal of Children & Media*, 3 (4): 410–414.

Bradford, M. (2006) Educating for positive gender relationships: excerpts from the promoting positive gender relationships report. *Queensland Centre for Domestic and Family Violence Research Newsletter*, 4 (4): 6–9.

Braithwaite, D. (2006) Police transfers over 'sex harassment'. *Sydney Morning Herald*, 24 July, retrieved 30 September 2010, from http://www.smh.com.au/news/national/police-transfers-over-sex-harassment/2006/07/24/1153593241825.html.

Breckenridge, K. (1998) The allure of violence: men, race and masculinity on the South African goldmines, 1900–1950. *Journal of Southern African Studies*, 24 (4): 669–694.

Breitenbecher, K.H. (2000) Sexual assault on college campuses: is an ounce of prevention enough? *Applied and Preventive Psychology*, 9 (1): 23–52.

Bright, R. (2005) It's just a Grade 8 girl thing: aggression in teenage girls. *Gender and Education*, 17 (1): 93–101.

Brown, J. (2005) 'Violent girls': same or different from other girls. In G. Lloyd (Ed.) *Problem Girls: Understanding and Supporting Troubled and Troublesome Girls and Young Women* (pp. 63–75). Abingdon: Routledge Falmer.

Brown, L.M., Chesney-Lind, M., and Stein, N. (2007) Patriarchy matters: toward a gendered theory of teen violence and victimization. *Violence Against Women: An International and Interdisciplinary Journal*, 13 (3): 1249–1273.

Brownmiller, S. (1976) *Against Our Will: Men, Women, and Rape*, Harmondsworth: Penguin.

Buchanan, R. and Chapman, A. (2010) Globalisation and social justice: the exploitation of the digital native. *Learning for Life: Sustainability, Global Citizenship and Social Justice. SEAA Biennial Conference with SASOSE Annual Conference*, Adelaide, SA (2010), retrieved 10 September 2011, from http://www.seaa.org.au/adelaide2010.html.

Butchart, A., Phinney, A., Check, P., and Villaveces, A. (2004) *Preventing Violence: A Guide to Implementing the Recommendations of the World Report on Violence and Health*. Geneva: Department of Injuries and Violence Prevention, World Health Organization, retrieved 11 August 2008, from http://www.who.int/violence_injury_prevention/violence/world_report/en/index.html.

Butler, J. (1990) *Gender Trouble: Feminism and the Subversion of Identity*, New York: Routledge.

Butler, J. (1993a) *Bodies That Matter: On the Discursive Limits of 'Sex'*, London: Routledge.

Butler, J. (1993b) Extracts from Gender as Performance: An Interview with Judith Butler, Interview by Peter Osborne and Lynne Segal. *Radical Philosophy*, 67 (summer 1994): 32–39.

Butler, J. (1994) Gender as performance: an interview with Judith Butler. *Radical Philosophy*, 67 (1): 32–39.

Butler, J. (1997) *Excitable Speech: A Politics of the Performative*, New York: Routledge.

Butler, J. (2004) *Precarious Life: The Powers of Mourning and Violence*, London: Verso.

Butler, J. (2005) *Giving an Account of Oneself*, New York: Fordham University Press.

Butler, J. (2009) *Frames of War: When Is Life Grievable?* London: Verso.

Cammarota, J. and Fine, M. (Eds.) (2008) *Revolutionizing Education: Youth Participatory Action Research in Motion*, New York: Routledge.

Campbell, C. (1992) Learning to kill: masculinity, the family and violence in Natal. *Journal of Southern African Studies*, 18 (3): 614–628.

Campbell, M.A. (2005) Cyberbullying: an old problem in a new guise? *Australian Journal of Guidance and Counselling*, 15 (1): 68–76.

Campbell, M.A., Butler, D.A., and Kift, S.M. (2008) A school's duty to provide a safe learning environment: does this include cyberbullying? *Australia and New Zealand Journal of Law and Education*, 13 (2): 21–32.

Campbell, S.W. and Ling, R. (2009) Effects of mobile communication. In J. Bryant and M.B. Oliver (Eds.) *Media Effects: Advances in Theory and Research*, New York: Routledge.

Cannan, J. (1996) 'One thing leads to another': drinking, fighting and working-class masculinities. In M. Mac an Ghaill (Ed.) *Understanding Masculinities: Social Relations and Cultural Arenas*. Buckingham: Open University Press.

Carmody, M. (1992) Uniting all women: a historical look at attitudes to rape. In J. Breckenridge and M. Carmody (Eds.) *Crimes of Violence: Australian Responses to Rape and Child Sexual Assault* (pp. 3–17). Sydney: Allen and Unwin.

Carmody, M. (2009a) *Sex and Ethics: Young People and Ethical Sex*, Melbourne: Palgrave Macmillan.

Carmody, M. (2009b) *Sex and Ethics: The Sexual Ethics Education Program for Young People*, Melbourne: Palgrave Macmillan.

Carmody, M. and Carrington, K. (2000) Preventing sexual violence? *Australian and New Zealand Journal of Criminology*, 33 (3): 341–361.

Carmody, M., Evans, S., Krogh, C., Flood, M., Heenan, M., and Ovenden, G. (2009) *Framing Best Practice: National Standards for the Primary Prevention of Sexual Assault Through Education*, National Sexual Assault Prevention Education Project for NASASV: University of Western Sydney, Australia.

Caro, N. (2006) *North Country*. Director. Warner Brothers.

Carton, B. (2000) *Blood from Your Children: African Generational Conflict in South Africa*, Charlottesville: University Press of Virginia.

Carton, B. (2001) Locusts fall from the sky: manhood and migrancy in KwaZulu. In R. Morrell (Ed.) *Changing Men in Southern Africa* (pp. 129–140). Pietermaritzburg: University of Natal Press.

Casella, R. (2001a) *At Zero Tolerance: Punishment, Prevention, and School Violence*, New York: Peter Lang.

Casella, R. (2001b) *Being Down: Challenging Violence in Urban Schools*, New York: Teachers College Press.

Casella, R. (2006) *Selling Us the Fortress: The Promotion of Techno-Security Equipment for Schools*, New York and London: Routledge.

Cassidy, W., Jackson, M., and Brown, K.N. (2009) Sticks and stones can break my bones, but how can pixels hurt me? Students' experiences with cyber-bullying. *School Psychology International*, 30 (4): 383–402.

Certeau, M. d. (1986) *Heterologies: Discourse on the Other*, London and Minneapolis: University of Minnesota Press.

Certeau, M. d. (1997) *Culture in the Plural* (T. Conley, Trans.), Minneapolis and London: University of Minnesota Press.

Certeau, M. d. (2002) *The Practice of Everyday Life* (S.F. Rendall, Trans.), Berkeley: University of California Press.

Chisholm, L. (Ed.) (2004) *Changing Class: Education and Social Change in Post-Apartheid South Africa*, Cape Town: HSRC Press.

Chung, D., O'Leary, P.J., and Hand, T. (2006) *Sexual Violence Offenders: Prevention and Intervention Approaches*, Australian Contact Children's Services Association (ACCSA) Issues No. 5 (June 2006).

Coleman, M. (2007). The abuse of children in Irish Charter Schools in the early Nineteenth Century. In A. Potts & T. O'Donoghue (Eds.) *Schools as Dangerous Places: A Historical Perspective*. Cambria Press: Youngstown, NY.

Collins, P.H. (1990) *Black Feminist Thought*, Routledge: New York.

Community Information Empowerment and Technology (CIET) Africa (2000) *Beyond Victims and Villains: The Culture of Sexual Violence in South Johannesburg*, Johannesburg: CIET.

Connell, R. (1987) *Gender and Power: Society, the Person and Sexual Politics*, Sydney: Allen & Unwin.

Connell, R. (1995a) *Masculinities*, Cambridge: Polity Press.

Connell, R. (1995b) *Masculinities*, Sydney: Allen & Unwin.

Connell, R. (2005) *Masculinities* (Vol. 1), Cambridge, UK: Polity Press.

Connell, R. and Messerschmidt, J. (2005) Hegemonic masculinity: rethinking the concept. *Gender & Society*, 19 (6): 829–859.

Connell, R.W. (1985) *Teacher's Work*, George Allen & Unwin: Sydney.

Connell, R.W. (1989) Cool guys, swots and whimps: the interplay of masculinity and education. *Oxford Review of Education* 15 (3): 291–303.

Connell, R.W. (1996) Teaching the boys: new research on masculinity, and gender strategies for schools. *Teachers College Record* 98 (2): 206–235.

Cooper, A., McLoughlin, I., and Campbell, K. (2000) Sexuality in cyberspace: update for the 21st century. *CyberPsychology & Behaviour* 3 (4): 521–536.

Cooper, D. (2003) *My Loose Thread*, Edinburgh: Canongate.

Cornish, D. and Clarke, R. (Eds.) (1986) *The Reasoning Criminal: Rational Choice Perspectives on Offending*, New York: Springer-Verlag.

Corrigan, P. (1979) *School the Sash Street Kids*, London: Palgrave Macmillan.

Couvillon, M. and Ilieva, V. (2011) A review of schoolwide preventative programs and strategies on cyberbullying. *Preventing School Failure*, 55 (2): 96–101.

Coyne, I., Chesney, T., Logan, B., and Madden, N. (2009) Griefing in a virtual community: an exploratory survey of second life residents. *Zeitschrift für Psychologie*, 217 (4): 214–221.

Cranny-Francis, A. (1995) *The Body in the Text*, Melbourne: Melbourne University Press.

Croombe, R. (2010) Australia lags shamefully on gay marriage. *The Age*, 2 July 2010, retrieved 03 July 2010, from http://www.theage.com.au/opinion/australia-lags-shamefully-on-gay-marriage-20100701-zqia.html.

Cross, D., Shaw, T., Hearn, L., Epstein, M., Monks, H., Lester, L., and Thomas, L. (2009) *Australian Covert Bullying Prevalence Study (ACBPS)*, retrieved 20 March 2010, from http://www.deewr.gov.au.

Crotty, M. (2007) Sporting violence in Australian Public Schools 1850–1914. In A. Potts & T. O'Donoghue (Eds.) *Schools as Dangerous Places: A historical perspective*. New York: Cambria Press.

Curtis, B. (2007) 'Illicit' sexuality and public education in Ontario, 1840–1907. In A. Potts and T. O'Donoghue (Eds.) *Schools as Dangerous Places: A Historical Perspective*. New York: Cambria Press.

Das, V. (2007) *Life and Words: Violence and the Descent into the Ordinary*, Berkeley and Los Angeles: University of California Press.

Davies, C. (2008) Becoming sissy: a response to David McInnes. In B. Davies (Ed.) *Judith Butler in Conversation: Analysing the Texts and Talk of Everyday Life* (pp. 117–133). New York: Routledge.

Davies, C. and Payne, R. (2008) Introduction: cultures of panic. *Cultural Studies Review*, 14 (2): 11–13.

Davies, C. and Robinson, K.H. (2010) Hatching babies and stork deliveries: risk and regulation in the construction of children's sexual knowledge. *Contemporary Issues in Early Childhood*, 11 (3): 249–262.

Davies, S. (2005) Power and knowledge: the making and managing of the 'unfit'. In J. Bessant, R. Hil, and R. Watts (Eds.) *Violations of Trust: How Social and Welfare Institutions Fail Children and Young People* (pp. 1–13). Aldershot, Hampshire UK: Ashgate Publishing.

Dawes, A., Kafaar, Z., de Sas Kropiwnicki, Pather, R., and Richter, L. (2004) *Partner Violence, Attitudes to Child Discipline, and Use of Corporal Punishment: A South African National Survey*, Cape Town: Child Youth and Family Development, Human Sciences Research Council (HSRC).

Deavere Smith, A. (1993) *Fires in the Mirror*, New York: Anchor Books/Doubleday.

Deavere Smith, A. (1994) *Twilight, L.A. 1992*, New York: Anchor Books/Doubleday.

Denborough, D. (1996) Power and partnership? Challenging the sexual construction of schooling. In L. Laskey and C. Beavis (Eds.) *Schooling and Sexualities* (pp. 117–129). Victoria: Deakin University, Deakin Centre for Education and Change.

Denzin, N. (1989) *Interpretive Interactionism*, Newbury Park, CA: Sage.

Denzin, N. (1997) Performance texts. In W.G. Tierney and Y.S. Lincoln (Eds.) *Representation and the Text: Re-framing the Narrative Voice* (pp. 179–217). Albany, NY: SUNY Press.

Department of Education (1996) *South African Schools Act No. 84*, Pretoria: Department of Education.

Department of Social Development (2007) *South African Children's Amendment Act No. 41*, Pretoria: Department of Education.

Derrida, J. (1976) *Of Grammatology* (1st American edition), Baltimore: Johns Hopkins University Press.

Desai, A. (2000) *The Poors of Chatsworth: Race, Class and Social Movements in Post Apartheid South Africa*, Durban: Madiba Publishers.

DiGiulio, R. (2001) *Educate, Mediate, or Litigate? What Teachers, Parents and Administrators Must Do about Student Behaviour*, Thousand Oaks, CA: Corwin Press.

Dinkes, R., Cataldi, E.F., and Lin-Kelly, W. (2007) *Indicators of School Crime and Safety: 2007*, Washington, DC: National Center for Education Statistics, Institute of Education Sciences, U.S. Department of Education, and Bureau of Justice Statistics, Office of Justice Programs, U.S. Department of Justice.

Dooley, J., Pyzalski, J., and Cross, D. (2009) Cyberbullying versus face-to-face bullying: a theoretical and conceptual review. *Zeitschrift für Psychologie*, 217 (4): 182–188.

Duncan, N. (1999) *Sexual Bullying: Gender Conflict and Pupil Culture in Secondary Schools*, London: Routledge.

Duncan, N. (2006) Girls' violence and aggression against other girls: femininity and bullying in UK schools. In F. Leach and C. Mitchell (Eds.) *Combating Gender Violence in and around Schools*. London: Routledge Falmer.

Dunne, M., Humphreys, S., and Leach, F. (2006) Gender violence in schools in the developing world. *Gender and Education*, 18 (1): 75–98.

Dyer, R. (1997) Heterosexuality. In A. Medhurst and S. Munt (Eds.) *Lesbian and Gay Studies: A Critical Introduction* (pp. 261–273). London and Washington: Cassell.

Eliasov, N. and Frank, C. (2000) *Crime and Violence in Schools in Transition: A Survey of Crime and Violence in Twenty Schools in the Cape Metropole and Beyond*, Social Justice Resource Project, Institute of Criminology, University of Cape Town.

Elliott, D., Hamburg, B. and Williams, K. (Eds.) (1998) *Violence in American Schools: A New Perspective*, Cambridge: Cambridge University Press.

Ellis, J. (2004) *Preventing Violence against Women and Girls: A Study of Educational Programmes for Children and Young People*, Final report for WOMANKIND Worldwide, retrieved online 03/05/2008, URL: www.womankind.org.uk.

Ellis, J. (2008) Primary prevention of domestic abuse through education. In C. Humphreys, C. Houghton, and J. Ellis (Eds.) *Literature Review: Better Outcomes for Children and Young People affected by Domestic Abuse – Directions for Good Practice* (p. 25). Edinburgh: Scottish Government.

Ellsworth, E. (1994) Why doesn't this feel empowering? Working through the repressive myths of critical pedagogy. In L. Stone (Ed.) *The Education Feminism Reader*. New York: Routledge.

Englander, E., Mills, E., and McCoy, M. (2009) Cyberbullying and information exposure: User-generated content in post-secondary education. *International Journal of Contemporary Sociology*, 46 (2): 213–230.

Ensler, E. (1998) *The Vagina Monologues*, New York: Villard.

Epstein, D. (1997) Keeping them in their place: hetero/sexist harassment, gender and the enforcement of heterosexuality. In A.M. Thomas and C. Kitzinger (Eds.) *Sexual Harassment: Contemporary Feminist Perspectives*. Buckingham: Open University Press.

Epstein, D. (1998) Real boys don't work: 'underachievement', masculinity and the harassment of 'sissies'. In D. Epstein, J. Elwood, V. Hey, and J. Maw (Eds.) *Failing Boys?* Buckingham: Open University Press.

Ferfolja, T. (2008) Discourses that silence: teachers and anti-lesbian harassment. *Discourse: Studies in the Cultural Politics of Education*, 29 (1): 107–119.

Ferfolja, T. (2009) Stories so far: an overview of the research on lesbian teachers. *Sexualities*, 12 (3): 378–396.

Ferfolja, T. (2010) Lesbian teachers, harassment and the workplace. *Teaching and Teacher Education*, 26 (3): 408–414.

Fergus, L. and Lappin, K. (2008) *Setting the Standard: International Good Practice to Inform an Australian National Plan of Action to Eliminate Violence against Women*, Sydney: Amnesty International Australia, retrieved 11 August 2008, from http://www.amnesty.org.au/svaw/comments/14454/.

Ferguson, A. (2001) *Bad Boys: Public Schools in the Making of Black Masculinity* (Ann Arbor: University of Michigan Press).

Fine, M., Weis, L., Addelston, J., and Marusza, J. (1997) In(secure) times: constructing white working-class masculinities in the late 20th century. *Gender and Society*, 11 (1): 52–68.

Flood, M. and Hamilton, C. (2008) Mapping homophobia in Australia. In S. Robinson (Ed.) *Homophobia: An Australian History*. Sydney: The Federation Press.

Foderaro, L. (2010) Students' suicide linked to on-line humiliation. *Sydney Morning Herald* (1 October), retrieved 30 September 2010, from http://www.smh.com.au/technology/technology-news/students-suicide-linked-to-online-humiliation-20100930-15zdv.html.

Foss, K.A. and Rogers, R.A. (1994) Particularities and possibilities: reconceptualizing knowledge and power in sexual harassment research. In S.G. Bingham (Ed.) *Conceptualizing Sexual Harassment as Discursive Practice*. Westport, Connecticut: Praeger.

Foucault, M. (1974) *The Archaeology of Knowledge*, London: Tavistock.

Foucault, M. (1977) *Discipline and Punish: The Birth of the Prison*, London: Penguin.

Foucault, M. (1978) *The History of Sexuality* (1st American edition), New York: Pantheon Books.

Foucault, M. (1979) *Discipline and Punish: The Birth of the Prison*, Harmondsworth: Penguin.

Foucault, M. (1986) Of other spaces. *Diacritics*, 16 (1) (Spring): 22–27.

Foucault, M. (2002) Truth and power (R. Hurley, Trans.). In J.D. Faubion (Ed.) *Michel Foucault: Power: Essential Works of Foucault 1954–1984* (Vol. 3, pp. 111–133). London: Penguin.

Franzway, S., Connell, C., and Court, D. (1989) *Staking a Claim: Feminism and the State*, Sydney: Allen & Unwin.

Freund, B. (1995) *Insiders and Outsiders: The Indian Working Class of Durban 1910–1990*, London/Pietermaritzburg/Portsmouth, NH: James Currey/University of Natal Press/Heinemann.

Friedman, R. (1973) On the concept of authority in political philosophy. In R. Flathmann (Ed.) *Concepts in Social and Political Philosophy* (pp. 121–145). New York: Palgrave Macmillan.

Frosh, S., Phoenix, A., and Pattman, R. (2002) *Young Masculinities*, Basingstoke: Palgrave Macmillan.

Fry, D. (1993) The intergenerational transmission of disciplinary practices and approaches to conflict. *Human Organization*, 52 (2): 176–185.

Garbarino, J. (1995) *Raising Children in a Socially Toxic Environment*, San Francisco: Jossey-Bass.

Garbarino, J. (2001) Making sense of school violence: why do kids kill? In M. Shafii and S.L. Shafii (Eds.) *School Violence: Assessment, Management, Prevention* (pp. 3–24). Washington, DC: American Psychiatric Publishing, Inc.

Gavey, N. (1989) Feminist poststructuralism and discourse analysis: contributions to feminist psychology. *Psychology of Women Quarterly*, 13 (4): 459–475.

Gillborn, D. and Youdell, D. (2000) *Rationing Education: Policy, Practice, Reform and Equity*, Buckingham: Open University Press.

Giroux, H. (2006) *The Giroux Reader*, London: Paradigm Publishers.

Giroux, H. (2007) Beyond neoliberal common sense: cultural politics and public pedagogy in dark times. *JAC: Rhetoric, Writing, Culture, Politics*, 27 (1–2): 11–61, retrieved 5 August 2011, from http://www.engl.unt.edu/~kjensen/practice/jaconline/archives/vol27.1-2/giroux-beyond.pdf.

Gittins, D. (1998) *The Child in Question*, Houndmills, Basingstoke: Palgrave Macmillan.

Glaser, C. (1998a) 'We must infiltrate the Tsotsis': school politics and youth gangs in Soweto, 1968–1976. *Journal of Southern African Studies*, 24 (2): 301–323.

Glaser, C. (1998b) Swines, hazels, and the dirty dozen: masculinity, territoriality and the youth gangs of Soweto, 1960–1976. *Journal of Southern African Studies*, 24 (4): 719–736

Glaser, C. (2000) *Bo-Tsotsi: The Youth Gangs of Soweto, 1935–1976*, Portsmouth, NH: Heinemann.

Goffe, L. (8 August 2003) Abused gays find refuge in schools of their own. *Times Educational Supplement*, 15/9 URL: www.tes.co.uk/article.aspx?storycode=382541.

Goldstein, T. (2001) Hong Kong, Canada: playwriting as critical ethnography. *Qualitative Inquiry*, 7 (3): 279–303.

Gonick, M. (2004) The 'Mean Girl' crisis: problematizing representations of girls' friendships. *Feminism and Psychology*, 14 (3): 395–400.

Goodall, H. and Huggins, J. (1992) Aboriginal women are everywhere: contemporary struggles. In K. Saunders and R. Evans (Eds.) *Gender Relations in Australia: Domination and Negotiation*. Sydney: Harcourt Brace Jovanovich.

Gottfredson, G. and Gottfredson, D. (1985) *Victimization in Schools*, New York: Plenum Press.

Gould, S. (1981) *The Mismeasurement of Man*, New York: W.W. Norton & Company.

Graham, L.J. and Slee, R. (2005) Inclusion? Paper presented at the *Creative Dissent, Constructive Solutions* conference, annual conference of the Australian Association of Research in Education, Parramatta, NSW Australia (27 November–1 December 2005).

Green. S. (2005a) Lesbian student teacher axed. *The Age*. March 7, retrieved 17 January 2010, from http://www.theage.com.au/news/National/Lesbian-student-teacher-axed/2005/03/06/1110044258576.html.

Green, S. (2005b) Don't ask, don't tell. *The Age*, March 7, retrieved 17 January 2010, from http://www.theage.com.au/news/Education-News/Dont-ask-dont-tell/2005/03/04/1109700685285.html.

Griggs, R. (1997) *Children at Risk: The Security Situation in Durban Schools*, Independent Projects Trust public information paper 3, Independent Projects Trust: Durban

Gruber, J.E. and Fineran, S. (2007) The impact of bullying and sexual harassment on middle school and high school girls. *Violence Against Women*, 13 (2): 627–643.

Halson, J. (1991) Young women, sexual harassment and heterosexuality: violence, power relation and mixed-sex schooling. In P. Abbott and C. Wallace (Eds.) *Gender, Power and Sexuality*. London: Palgrave Macmillan.

Hansen, J. (2010) Schoolchildren sexually assaulting each other in Queensland – issue 'ignored'. *The Sunday Mail* (QLD), 25th July, retrieved 30 September 2010, from http://www.couriermail.com.au/news/queensland/schoolchildren-sexually-assaulting-each-other-in-queensland-issue-ignored/story-e6freoof-1225896438223.

Haraway, D. (2000) A cyborg manifesto: science, technology and socialist feminism in the late twentieth century. In D. Bell and B. Kennedy (Eds.) *The Cybercultures Reader* (pp. 291–324). London: Routledge.

Harber, C. (1996) Educational violence and education for peace in Africa. *Peabody Journal of Education*, 71: 151–169.

Harber, C. (2001) *State of Transition: Post-Apartheid Educational Reform in South Africa*, Oxford: Symposium Books.

Harber, C. (2004) *Schooling as Violence. How Schools Harm Pupils and Societies*, Abingdon: Routledge Falmer.

Harding, D.J., Fox, C., and Mehta, J. (2002) Studying rare events through qualitative case studies: lessons form a study of rampage school shootings. *Sociological Methods Research*, 31 (2): 174–217.

Hassall, I. and Hannah, K. (2007) *School-Based Violence Prevention Programmes: A Literature Review*, New Zealand: Prepared for the Accident Compensation Corporation.

Haugaard, J. and Feerick, M. (1996) The influence of child abuse and family violence on violence in schools. In A. Hoffman (Ed.) *Schools, Violence, Society* (pp. 79–1000). Westport: Praeger.

Hawisher, G. and Selfe, C. (2000) *Global Literacies and the World-Wide Web*, London: Routledge.

Hayes, D., Mills, M., Christie, P., and Lingard, B. (2006) *Teachers Making a Difference*, Sydney: Allen & Unwin.

Hearn, J. (1998) *The Violences of Men*, Thousand Oaks: Sage.

Heise, L., Ellsberg, M., and Gottemoeller, M. (1999) *Ending Violence against Women*, Population Reports, XXVII (Number 4, Series L, Number 11).

Herbert, C. (1992) *Sexual Harassment in Schools: A Guide for Teachers*, London: David Fulton.

Herek, G.M. (1993) Sexual orientation and military service: a social science perspective. *American Psychologist*, 48: 538–549.

Higgins, C. (1980) *Nine to Five*. Director. Twentieth Century Fox, 19 December 1980.

Hillier, L., Dempsey, D., Harrison, L., Beale, L., Matthews, L., and Rosenthal, D. (1998) *Writing Themselves In: A National Report on the Sexuality, Health and Well-Being of Same-Sex Attracted Young People*, Monograph Series No. 7, National Centre in HIV Social Research, Australian Research Centre in Sex, Health and Society Faculty of Health Sciences La Trobe University 215 Franklin Street Melbourne 3000.

Hillier, L. and Harrison, L. (2004) Homophobia and the production of shame: young people and same sex attraction. *Culture, Health and Sexuality*, 6 (1): 79–94.

Hillier, L., Harrison, L., and Dempsey, D. (1999a) Stories of life on the wild side: same sex attracted young people document their lives. *Health Education Australia*, Summer 1999: 12–14, Melbourne: Health Education Association of Victoria.

Hillier, L., Harrison, L., and Dempsey, D. (1999b) Whatever happened to duty of care? Same-sex attracted young people's stories of schooling and violence. *Melbourne Studies in Education Special Issue Sexualities and Education*, 40 (2): 59–74, Melbourne: Arena.

Hillier, L. and Mitchell, A. (2008) 'It was about as useful as a chocolate kettle': Sex education in the lives of same-sex attracted young people in Australia. *Sex Education*, 8 (2): 211–224.

Hillier, L., Turner, A., and Mitchell, A. (2005) *Writing Themselves In Again: 6 Years on, the 2nd National Report on the Sexuality, Health & Well-being of Same Sex Attracted Young People in Australia*, Melbourne, VIC: Australian Research Centre in Sex, Health and Society, Monograph Series No. 50, Australian Research Centre in Sex, Health & Society (ARCSHS), Faculty of Health Sciences, La Trobe University, 215 Franklin St, Melbourne 3000.

Hilton, N.Z., Harris, G., Rice, M., Krans, T., and Lavigne, S. (1998) Anti-violence education in schools: Implementation and evaluation. *Journal of Interpersonal Violence*, 13 (6): 726–742.

Hinduja, S. and Patchin, J. (2008) Cyberbullying: an exploratory analysis of factors related to offending and victimisation. *Deviant Behaviour*, 29: 129–156.

Hinduja, S. and Patchin, J. (2011) A review of the legal issues facing educators. *Preventing School Failure*, 55 (2): 71–78.

Hirschi, T. (1969) *Causes of Delinquency*, Berkeley and Los Angeles: University of California Press.

Hirst, J. (2004) Researching young people's sexuality and learning about sex: experience, need, and sex and relationship education. *Culture, Health & Sexuality*, 6 (2): 115–129.

Holdstock, T. (1990) *Violence in Schools: Discipline.* In B. McKendrick and W. Hoffman (Eds.) *People and Violence in South Africa* (pp. 348–349). Oxford: Oxford University Press.

Hollway, W. (1984) Gender difference and the production of subjectivity. In J. Henriques, W. Hollway, C. Urwin, C. Venn, and V. Walkerdine (Eds.) *Changing the Subject: Psychology, Social Regulation and Subjectivity* (pp. 227–263). London: Methuen.

Holstein, J.A. and Gubrium, J.F. (1995) *The Active Interview*, Thousand Oaks: Sage.

hooks, B. (1990) *Yearning: Race, Gender, and Cultural Politics*, Boston: South End Press.

Howard, A. and England Kennedy, E. (2006) Breaking the silence: power, conflict, and contested frames within an affluent high school. *Anthropology and Education Quarterly*, 37 (4): 347–365.

Huckabee, M. (1998) *Kids Who Kill: Confronting Our Culture of Violence*, Nashville, TN: B&H Books.

Hughes, T. (1857) *Tom Brown's School Days: By An Old Boy*, Cambridge: Palgrave Macmillan.

Human Rights and Equal Opportunity Commission (2007) *Same-Sex: Same Entitlements – National Inquiry into Discrimination against People in Same-Sex Relationships: Financial and Work Related Entitlements and Benefits*, retrieved 20 July 2007, from http://www.humanrights.gov.au/samesex/index.html.

Human Rights Watch World Report (2001) *Scared at School: Sexual Violence against girls in South African Schools*, New York: Human Rights Watch

Humphries, S. (1995) *Hooligans or Rebels: An Oral History of Working-Class Childhood and Youth 1889–1939*, Oxford: Blackwell (first published 1981).

Irwin, J., Gregoric, M., and Winter, B. (1997) Violence against homeless young lesbians. In G. Mason and S. Tomsen (Eds.) *Homophobic Violence*, Sydney: The Hawkins Press.

Ito, M. (2008) Migrating media: Anime Media mixes and the childhood imagination. In M. Gutman and N. Coninck-Smith (Eds.) *Designing Modern Childhoods: History, Space, and the Material Culture of Children* (pp. 301–315). New Brunswick: Rutgers University Press.

Jackson, C. (2006) *Lads and Ladettes in School: Gender and a Fear of Failure*, Maidenhead: Open University Press.

Jaffe, P.G. and Wolfe, D.A. (2003, January) Prevention of Domestic Violence and Sexual Assault. Harrisburg, PA: VAWnet, a project of the National Resource Center on Domestic Violence/Pennsylvania Coalition Against Domestic Violence, retrieved 8 August 2008, from http://www.vawnet.org/.

Jamal, N. (2010, 13 October) Fraser-Kirk to keep David Jones settlement money. *Sydney Morning Herald (SMH)*, retrieved October 28, from http://www.smh.com.au/business/fraserkirk-to-keep-david-jones-settlement–money-20101018-16pjd.html.

Jenkins, P. (1998) *Moral Panic: Changing Concepts of the Child Molester in Modern America*, New Haven, CT: Yale University Press.

Jewkes, R., Dunkle, K., Koss, M.P., Levin, J.B., Nduna, M., Jama, N., and Sikweyiya, Y. (2006) Rape perpetration by young, rural South African men: prevalence, patterns and risk factors. *Social Science & Medicine*, 63: 2949–2961.

Jewkes, R., Levin, J., Mbananga, N., and Bradshaw, D. (2002) Rape of girls in South Africa. *The Lancet*, 359: 319–320.

Jewkes, R., Sikweyiya, Y., Morrell, R., and Dunkle, K. (2010) Why, when and how men rape. Understanding rape perpetration in South Africa. *South African Crime Quarterly*, 34: 23–31.

Johnson, B. (2006) *An Evaluation of the Trail Implementation of the Sexual Health and Relationships Education (SHARE) Program 2003–2006*, Adelaide: University of South Australia.

Jones, C. (1985) Sexual tyranny: male violence in a mixed secondary school. In G. Weiner (Ed.) *Just a Bunch of Girls* (pp. 26–40). Milton Keynes: Open University Press.

Jones, K.B. (1988) On authority: or, why women are not entitled to speak. In I. Diamond and L. Quinby (Eds.) *Feminism and Foucault: Reflections on Resistance* (pp. 119–134). Boston: Northeastern University Press.

Jones, K.B. (1993) *Compassionate Authority: Democracy and the Representation of Women*, New York: Routledge.

Jürgens, U., Gnad, M., and Bähr, J. (2003) New forms of class and racial segregation. In R. Tomlinson, R. Beauregard, L. Bremner, and X. Mangcu (Eds.) *Emerging Johannesburg: Perspectives on the Postapartheid City*. London and New York: Routledge.

Kalantzis, M., Cope, B., Noble, G., and Poynting, S. (1990) *Cultures of Schooling: Pedagogies for Cultural Difference and Social Access*, London: Falmer Press.

Kantrowitz, B. and Wingert, P. (1999, 10 May) How well do you know your kid? *Newsweek*, p. 36.

Katz, J.E. and Aakhus, M.A. (2002) *Perpetual Contact: Mobile Communication, Private Talk, Public Performance*, Cambridge: Cambridge University Press.

Kaye, M. (2004) Skool's out. *Teaching Education*, 15 (1): 113–115.

Keddie, A. (2003) Little boys: tomorrow's macho lads. *Discourse: Studies in the Cultural Politics of Education*, 24 (3): 289–306.

Keddie, A. (2005) On fighting and football: gender justice and theories of identity construction. *International Journal of Qualitative Studies in Education*, 18 (4): 425–444.

Keddie, A. (2006) Fighting, frustration, anger and tears: Matthew's story of hegemonic masculinity. *Oxford Review of Education*, 32 (4): 521–534.

Keddie, A. (2007) Issues of power, masculinity, and gender justice: Sally's story of teaching boys. *Discourse: Studies in the Cultural Politics of Education*, 28 (1): 21–35.

Keddie, A. and Mills, M. (2007) *Teaching Boys: Classroom Practices That Work*, Sydney: Allen & Unwin.

Kehily, M.J. and Nayak, A. (1997) 'Lads and laughter': humour and the production of heterosexual hierarchies. *Gender and Education*, 9 (1): 69–87.

Kenway, J. and Bullen, E. (2005) Globalising the young in the age of desire: some educational policy issues. In M.W. Apple, J. Kenway, and M. Singh (Eds.) *Globalising Education* (pp. 31–45). New York: Peter Lang.

Kenway, J., Willis, S., Blackmore, J., and Rennie, L. (1997) *Answering Back: Girls, Boys and Feminism in Schools*, Sydney: Allen & Unwin.

Kimmel, M.S. (1994) Masculinity as homophobia: fear, shame, and silence in the construction of gender identity. In H. Brod and M. Kaufman (Eds.) *Theorizing Masculinities* (pp. 119–141). Sage: Thousand Oaks.

Kimmel, M.S. (2000) *The Gendered Society*, New York/Oxford: Oxford University Press.

Kimmel, M. and Mahler, M. (2003) Adolescent masculinity, homophobia, and violence: random school shootings, 1982–2001. *American Behavioral Scientist*, 46 (10): 1439–1458.

Klein, J. (2005) Teaching her a lesson: media misses boy's rage relating to girls in high school shootings. *Crime, Media, Culture*, 1 (1): 90–97.

Klein, J. (2006) An invisible problem: Everyday violence against girls in schools. *Theoretical Criminology*, 10 (2): 147–177

Kosciw, J.G. and Cullen, M.K. (2002) *The GLSEN 2001 National School Climate Survey: The School-Related Experiences of our Nation's Lesbian, Gay, Bisexual and Transgender Youth*, New York: Gay, Lesbian, and Straight Education Network.

Kowalski, R. and Limber, P. (2007) Electronic bullying among middle school students. *Journal of Adolescent Health*, 41: 522–530.

Lacey, N. (2000) *Narrative and Genre: Key Concepts in Media Studies*, London: Palgrave Macmillan.

Lahey, K. (2010, 4 August) 'No' gets no firmer than a $37 million lawsuit. *The Age*, 4 August 2010, retrieved 30 September 2010, from http://www.theage.com.au/business/no-gets-no-firmer-than-a-37-million-lawsuit-20100803-115el.html.

Lamont, L. (2007) He was bullied at school – now he'll walk away with $1M, (17 May). *Sydney Morning Herald*, retrieved 8 November 2010, from http://www.smh.com.au/articles/2007/05/14/1178995079788.html.

Langellier, K. (2000) Personal narrative, performance, performativity: two or three things I know for sure. *Theatre and Performance Quarterly*, 19: 125–217.

Larkin, J. (1994) *Sexual Harassment: High School Girls Speak Out*, Toronto: Second Story Press.

Larkin, R.W. (2009) The Columbine Legacy: Rampage shootings as political acts. *American Behavioural Scientist*, 52 (9): 1309–1326.

Laub, J. and Lauritsen, J. (1998) The interdependence of school violence with neighborhood and family conditions. In D. Elliott, B. Hamburg, and K. Williams (Eds.) *Violence in American Schools* (pp. 127–155). Cambridge: Cambridge University Press.

Laura, R. and Chapman, A. (2009) The technologisation of education: philosophical reflections on being too plugged in. *International Journal of Children's Spirituality*, 14 (3): 289–298.

Lave, J. and Wenger, E. (1991) *Situated Learning: Legitimate Peripheral Participation*, Cambridge: Cambridge University Press.

Lawrence, R. (2007) *School Crime and Juvenile Justice* (2nd edition), New York and Oxford: Oxford University Press.

Leach, F. (2006) Gender violence in schools in the developing world. In F. Leach and C. Mitchell (Eds.) *Combating Gender Violence In and Around Schools* (pp. 23–32). Sterling, USA: Trentham Books.

Leach, F. and Mitchell, C. (Eds.) (2006) *Combating Gender Violence in and around Schools*, London: Routledge Falmer.

Leach, F. and Sitaram, S. (2007) The sexual harassment and abuse of adolescent schoolgirls in South India. *Journal of Education, Citizenship and Social Justice*, 2 (3): 257–277.

Leadbeater, C. (2008) *We-Think*, London: Profile Books.

Le Bon, G. and Boddy, J. (2010) Working with vulnerable primary school aged children and their families: a review of the Australian literature on key principles, issues, and community level approaches. *Journal of Social Inclusion*, 1 (1): 53–73.

Lee, R. (2005) Boy-code a factor in fatal school shooting. *Washington Blade* [Online edition], retrieved 15 April 2005, from: http://www.washblade.com/print.cfm? content_id=5349.

Leoschut, L. and Burton, P. (2006) *How Rich the Rewards? Results of the 2005 National Youth Victimisation Study*, Monograph Series No. 1 pp. 9–11, Cape Town: Centre for Justice and Crime Prevention.

Li, Q. (2007) Bullying in the new playground: research into cyberbullying and cyber victimisation. *Australian Journal of Educational Technology*, 23 (4): 435–454.

Lincoln, Y.S. and Guba, E.G. (1985) *Naturalist Enquiry*, Beverly Hills, CA: Sage.

Lingard B., Martino, W., and Mills, M. (2009) *Boys and Schooling: Contexts, Issues and Practices*, Basingstoke: Palgrave Macmillan.

Lingard, B., Martino, W., Mills, M., and Bahr, M. (2002) *Addressing the Educational Needs of Boys, Research Report*, Canberra: DEST.

Linn, E., Stein, N.D., Young, J., and Davis, S. (1992). Bitter lessons for all: sexual harassment in schools. In J.T. Sears (Ed.), *Sexuality and the Curriculum: The Politics and Practices of Sexuality Education* (pp. 106–123). New York: Teachers College Press.

Lombroso, C. (1876, 2006) *Criminal Man*, Durham, NC: Duke University Press.

Mac an Ghaill, M. (1994) *The Making of Men: Masculinities, Sexualities and Schooling*, Buckingham/Philadelphia, PA: Open University Press.

MacIntyre, A. (1998) *A Short History of Moral Philosophy from the Homeric to the Twentieth Century*, London and New York: Routledge.

Mahony, P. (1985) *Schools for the Boys?* London: Hutchinson in association with The Explorations in Feminism Collective.

Mahony, P. (1989) Sexual violence and mixed schools. In C. Jones and P. Mahony (Eds.) *Learning Our Lines: Sexuality and Social Control in Education* (pp. 157–190). London: Women's Press.

Maitse, T. (1999) Political change, rape, and pornography in post-apartheid South Africa. In C. Sweetman (Ed.) *Violence against Women* (pp. 55–59). Oxford: Oxfam Publishing.

Mallan, K. (2009) Look at me! Look at me! Self-representation and self-exposure through online networks. *Digital Culture & Education*, 1 (1): 51–66.

Mansfield, N. (2000) *Subjectivity: Theories of the Self from Freud to Haraway*, Sydney: Allen & Unwin.

Marks, M. (2001) *Young Warriors: Youth Politics, Identity and Violence in South Africa*, Johannesburg: Witwatersrand University Press.

Martineau, S. (1996) Dangerous liaison: the eugenics movement and the educational state. In J. Epp and A. Watkinson (Eds.) *Systemic Violence: How Schools Hurt Children*. Washington, DC: Falmer Press.

Martino, W. (1999) 'Cool boys', 'party animals', 'squids' and 'poofters': Interrogating the dynamics and politics of adolescent masculinities in school. *The British Journal of the Sociology of Education*, 20 (2): 239–263.

Martino, W. (2000) Policing masculinities: investigating the role of homophobia and heteronormativity in the lives of adolescent boys at school. *The Journal of Men's Studies*, 8 (2): 213–236.

Martino, W. and Pallotta-Chiarolli, M. (2003) *So What's a Boy? Addressing Issues of Masculinity and Schooling*, Buckingham: Open University Press.

Martino, W. and Pallotta-Chiarolli, M. (2005) *Being Normal Is the Only Way to Be: Adolescent Perspectives on Gender and School*, Sydney: University of NSW Press.

Mason, G. (2002) *The Spectacle of Violence: Homophobia, Gender and Knowledge*, New York: Routledge.

Mason, G. and Tomsen, S. (Eds.) (1997) *Homophobic Violence*, Leichhardt, NSW: Hawkins Press.

Mchunu, M. (2007) Culture change, Zulu masculinity and intergenerational conflict in the context of civil war in Pietermaritzburg. In Shefer, T., Ratele, K., Strebel, A., Shabalala, N., and Buikema, R. (Eds.) *From Boys to Men: Social Constructions of Masculinity in Contemporary Society* (pp. 225–240). Cape Town: University of Cape Town Press.

Mchunu, M.R. (2006) Discipline, respect and ethnicity: a study of the changing patterns of fatherhood of three generations of Zulu fathers and sons in Inadi, Vulindlela area of Pietermaritzburg, KwaZulu-Natal from the 1930s to 1990s, MA thesis, University of KwaZulu-Natal, Durban.

McInnes, D. (2008) Sissy-Boy melancholy and the educational possibilities of incoherence. In B. Davies (Ed.) *Judith Butler in Conversation: Analysing the Texts and Talk of Everyday Life* (pp. 95–116). New York: Routledge.

McInnes, D. and Couch, M. (2004) Quiet please! There's a lady on stage: boys, gender and sexuality non-conformity and class. *Discourse: Studies in the Cultural Politics of Education*, 25 (4): 431–443.

McInnes, D. and Davies, C. (2008) Articulating sissy boy queerness within and against discourses of tolerance and pride. In S. Driver (Ed.) *Queer Youth Cultures* (pp. 105–122). New York: SUNY.

Medical Research Council (2000) The South African demographic and health survey of 1998. In Hirschowitz et al. (Eds.) *Quantitative Research Findings on Rape in South Africa*. Pretoria: Medical Research Council.

Menesini, E. and Nocentini, A. (2009) Cyberbullying definition and measurement: some critical considerations. *Zeitschrift für Psychologie*, 217 (4): 230–232.

Merton, R. (1957) *Social Theory and Social Structure*, New York: The Free Press.

Messerschmidt, J. (1993) *Masculinities and Crime: Critique and Reconceptualization of Theory*, Boston: Rowman and Littlefield.

Mienczacowski, J. (1997) Theatre of change. *Research in Drama Education*, 2: 159–217.

Millbank, J. (2009) De facto relationships, same-sex and surrogate parents: exploring the scope and effects of the 2008 federal relationship reforms. *Australian Journal of Family Law*, 23 (3): 160–193.

Mills, M. (1996) Homophobia kills: disruptive moments in the educational politics of legitimation. *British Journal of Sociology of Education*, 17 (3): 315–326.

Mills, M. (2001) *Challenging Violence in Schools: An Issue of Masculinities*, Buckingham, UK: Open University Press.

Mills, M. (2006) Issues of masculinity and violence in Australian schools. In F. Leach and C. Mitchell (Eds.) *Combating Gender Violence in and around Schools* (1st edition) (pp. 163–170). Stoke on Trent, UK: Trentham Books.

Mills, M. and Keddie, A. (2007) Teaching boys and gender justice. *International Journal of Inclusive Education*, 11 (3): 335–354.

Mills, M.D. (1999) Homophobia and anti-lesbianism in schools: challenges and possibilities for social justice. *Melbourne Studies in Education*, 40 (2): 105–126.

Milojevic, I., Luke, A., Luke, C., Mills, M., and Land, R. with Alexander, A., Budby, J. Ip, D., Louie, K., and Lingard, B. (2001) *Moving Forward: Students and Teachers against Racism*, Armadale: Eleanor Curtain.

Mitchell, C. and Reid-Walsh, J. (2002) *Researching Children's Popular Culture: The Cultural Spaces of Childhood*, London: Routledge.

Mlamleli, O., Napo, V., Mabelane, P., Free, V., Goodman, N., Larkin, J., Mitchell, C., Mkhize, H., Robinson, K., and Smith, A. (2001) *Opening Our Eyes: Addressing Gender-Based Violence in South African Schools*, Pretoria: Canada-South Africa Management Programme.

Mooney, K. (1998) 'Ducktails, flick-knives and pugnacity': subcultural and hegemonic masculinities in South Africa, 1948–1960. *Journal of South African Studies*, 24 (4): 753–774.

Morrell, R. (Ed.) (1996) *Political Economy and Identities in KwaZulu-Natal: Historical and Social Perspectives*, Durban: Indicator Press.

Morrell, R. (1998a) Gender and education: the place of masculinity in South African schools. *South African Journal of Education*, 18 (4): 218–225.

Morrell, R. (1998b) Of boys and men: masculinity and gender in southern African studies. *Journal of Southern African Studies*, 24 (4): 605–630.

Morrell, R. (2001) Corporal punishment in South African schools: a neglected explanation for its existence. *South African Journal of Education*, 21 (4): 292–299.

Morrell, R. (2002) A calm after the storm? Beyond schooling as violence. *Educational Review*, 54 (1): 37–46.

Morrell, R. (2007) On a knife's edge: masculinity in black working class schools in post-apartheid education. In B. Frank and K. Davison (Eds.) *Masculinity and Schooling: International Practices and Perspectives* (pp. 35–57). London, Ontario: Althouse Press.

Morrell, R., Epstein, D., Unterhalter, E., Bhana, D., and Moletsane, R. (2009) *Towards Gender Equality? South African Schools during the HIV/AIDS Epidemic*, Pietermaritzburg: University of KwaZulu-Natal Press.

Morrison, B. (2007) *Restoring Safeschool Communities: A Whole School Response to Bullying, Violence and Alienation*, Sydney: The Federation Press.

Mulroney, J. (2003) *Australian Prevention Programs for Young People*, Australian DV & FV Clearinghouse Topic Paper, 1–21.

Narushima, Y. (2011, 2nd July) Styled by mother – children taught to build online 'brand'. *Sydney Morning Herald*, retrieved 4 July 2011, from http://www.smh.com.au/national/styled-by-mother–children-taught-to-build-online-brand-20110701-1gv6j.html.

National Institute of Education (1977) *Violent Schools – Safe Schools: The Safe School Study Report to Congress*, Washington, DC: U.S. Department of Health, Education, and Welfare.

National Research Council and Institute of Medicine (2003) *Deadly Lessons: Understanding Lethal School Violence*. Moore, M.H., Petrie, C.V., Braga, A.A., McLaughlin, B. (Eds.). Division of Behavioral and Social Sciences and Education, Washington, DC: The National Academies Press.

Newman, K.S., Fox, C., Harding, D., Mehta, J., and Roth, W. (2004) *Rampage: The Social Roots of School Shootings*, New York: Basic Books.

Nichols, S.L. and Good, T.L. (2004) *America's Teenagers: Myths and Realities: Media Images, Schooling, and the Social Costs of Careless Indifference*, New Jersey: Lawrence Erlbaum Associates.

Niehaus, I. (2000) Towards a dubious liberation: masculinity, sexuality and power in South African Lowveld Schools, 1953–1999. *Journal of Southern African Studies*, 26 (3): 387–407.

Noguera, P. (1995) Preventing and producing violence: a critical analysis of responses to school violence. *Harvard Educational Review*, 65 (2): 189–212.

O'Donoghue, T. and Potts, A. (2007) Schools as dangerous places: preliminary considerations. In A. Potts and T. O'Donoghue (Eds.) *Schools as Dangerous Places: A Historical Perspective*. New York: Cambria Press.

Ohsako, T. (Ed.) (1997) *Violence at School: Global Issues and Interventions*, Paris: UNESCO.

Oksman, V. and Turtianinen, J. (2004) Mobile communication as a social stage: meanings of mobile communication in everyday life among teenagers in Finland. *New Media & Society*, 6 (3): 319–339.

Olweus, D. (1993) *Bullying in Schools: What We Know and What We Can Do*, Cambridge, MA: Blackwell.

Olweus, D. (2001) Peer harassment: a critical analysis and some important issues (Introduction). In J. Juvonen and S. Graham (Eds.) *Peer Harassment in School: The Plight and the Vulnerable and the Victimised* (pp. 3–20). New York: Guildford Press.

Opinion Matters (2010) *Wake Up to Rape Research Summary Report 2010*, Report commissioned by The Havens (Sexual Assault Referral Centres), UK.

Oram, A. (1988) Embittered, sexless or homosexual: attacks on spinster teachers 1918–1939. In A. Angerman et al. (Eds.) *Current Issues in Women's History* (pp. 183–202). London and New York: Routledge.

Osler, A. (2006) Excluded girls: interpersonal, institutional and structural violence in schooling. *Gender and Education*, 18 (6): 571–589.

Paechter, C. (2007) *Being Boys, Being Girls: Learning Masculinities and Femininities*, Maidenhead: Open University Press.

Palmary, I., Rauch, J., and Simpson, G. (2003) Violent crime in Johannesburg. In R. Tomlinson, R. Beauregard, L. Bremner, and X. Mangcu (Eds.) *Emerging Johannesburg: Perspectives on the Postapartheid City* (pp. 101–122). New York and London: Routledge.

Patchin, J. and Hinduja, S. (2006) Bullies move beyond the schoolyard: a preliminary look at cyberbullying. *Youth Violence and Juvenile Justice*, 4: 148–169.

Pegrum, M. (2009) *From Blogs to Bombs: The Future of Digital Technologies in Education*, Crawley, WA: UWA Publishing.

Petersen, J.L. and Hyde, J.S. (2009) A longitudinal investigation of peer sexual harassment victimization in adolescence. *Journal of Adolescence*, 32 (5): 1173–1188.

Pierce, S. (2001) Punishment and the political body: flogging and colonialism in Northern Nigeria. *Interventions*, 3: 206–221.

Pinnock, D. (1997) *Gangs, Rituals, and Rites of Passage*, Cape Town, SA: African Sun Press with the Institute of Criminology, University of Capetown.

Pollard, R. (2009, 9 November) Elite college students proud of 'pro-rape' Facebook page. *Sydney Morning Herald*, retrieved 30 September 2010, from http://www.smh.com.au/technology/elite-college-students-proud-of-prorape-facebook-page-20091108-i3js.html.

Ponsford, J. (2007) The future of adolescent female cyber-bullying: electronic media's effects on aggressive communication, Unpublished Thesis, Texas State University, retrieved 23 May 2011, from http://ecommons.txstate.edu/honorprog/64.

Poster, M. (1997) Cyberdemocracy: the Internet and the public sphere. In D. Holmes (Ed.) *Identity and Community in Cyberspace* (pp. 212–229). London: Sage.

Powell, A. (2007a) Sexual pressure and young people's negotiation of consent. *Aware*, 14: 8–16. Melbourne, Vic: Australian Centre for the Study of Sexual Assault, Australian Institute of Family Studies, retrieved 07 February 2012, from http://www.aifs.gov.au/acssa/pubs/newsletter/n14.html.

Powell, A. (2007b) Youth 'at risk'? Young people, sexual health and consent. *Youth Studies Australia*, 26 (4): 21–27.

Poynting, S. and Donaldson, M. (2005) Snakes and leaders: hegemonic masculinity in ruling-class boys' boarding schools. *Men and Masculinities*, 7 (4): 325–346.

Puro, J-P. (2002) Finland: a mobile culture. In J.E. Katz and M.A. Aakhus (Eds.) *Perpetual Contact: Mobile Communication, Private Talk, Public Performance* (pp. 19–29). Cambridge: Cambridge University Press.

Quadara, A. (2008) *Responding to Young People's Disclosure of Sexual Assault: A Resource for Schools* (ACSSA Wrap 6), Melbourne, Vic: Australian Centre for the Study of Sexual Assault, Australian Institute of Family Studies, retrieved 07 February 2012, from http://www.aifs.gov.au/acssa/pubs/wrap/w6.html.

Rao, A. and Pierce, S. (2001) Discipline and the other body: correction, corporeality, and colonial rule. *Interventions*, 3: 159–168.

Rasmussen, M. (2006) *Becoming Subjects: A Study of Sexualities and Secondary Schooling*, New York: Routledge.

Reay, D. (2002) Shaun's story: troubling discourses of white working class masculinities. *Gender and Education*, 14 (3): 221–234.

Renold, E. (2000) 'Coming out': gender (hetero)sexuality and the primary school. *Gender and Education*, 12 (3): 309–326.

Renold, E. (2002) 'Presumed Innocence': (hetero)sexual, homophobic and heterosexist harassment amongst primary school girls and boys. *Childhood*, 9 (4): 415–433.

Renold, E. (2005) *Girls, Boys and Junior Sexualities: Exploring Childrens' Gender and Sexual Relations in the Primary School*, London: Routledge Falmer.

Renold, E. (2006) 'They won't let us play unless you're going out with one of them': girls, boys and Butler's 'heterosexual matrix' in the primary years. *British Journal of Sociology of Education*, 27 (4): 489–509.

Ringrose, J. (2006) A new universal mean girl: examining the discursive construction and social regulation of a new feminine pathology. *Feminism & Psychology*, 16 (4): 405–424.

Ringrose, J. and Renold, E. (2010) Normative cruelties and gender deviants: the performative effects of bully discourses for girls and boys in school. *British Educational Research Journal*, 36 (4): 573–596.

Rist, R. (1970) Student social class and teacher expectations: The self-fulfilling prophecy in ghetto education. *Harvard Educational Review*, 40 (3): 411–451.

Robinson, K.H. (1992) Classroom discipline: power, resistance and gender. A look at teacher perspectives. *Gender and Education*, 4 (3): 273–287.

Robinson, K.H. (1996) *Sexual Harassment in Secondary Schools*, unpublished Ph.D. thesis, Department of Sociology, University of New South Wales, Australia.

Robinson, K.H. (2000) 'Great tits, miss!' The silencing of male students' sexual harassment of female teachers in secondary schools: a focus on gendered authority. *Discourse: Studies in the Cultural Politics of Education*, 21 (1): 75–90.

Robinson, K.H. (2002) Making the invisible visible: gay and lesbian issues in early childhood education. *Contemporary Issues in Early Childhood*, 3 (3): 415–434.

Robinson, K.H. (2005a) Doing anti-homophobia and anti-heterosexism in early childhood education. Moving beyond the immobilising impacts of 'risks', 'fears' and 'silences'. Can we afford not to? *Contemporary Issues in Early Childhood Education,* 6 (2): 175–188.

Robinson, K.H. (2005b) 'Queerying' gender: heteronormativity in early childhood education. *Australian Journal of Early Childhood,* 30 (2): 19–28.

Robinson, K.H. (2005c) Reinforcing hegemonic masculinities through sexual harassment: issues of identity, power and popularity in secondary schools. *Gender and Education,* 17 (1): 19–37.

Robinson, K.H. and Davies, C. (2007) Tomboys and sissy girls: young girls' negotiations of femininity and masculinity. *International Journal of Equity and Innovation in Early Childhood,* 5 (2): 17–31.

Robinson, K.H. and Davies, C. (2008a) Docile bodies and heteronormative moral subjects: constructing the child and sexual knowledge in the schools. *Sexuality and Culture,* 12 (4): 221–239.

Robinson, K. and Davies, C. (2008b), She's kickin' ass, that's what she's doing': deconstructing childhood innocence in media representations. *Australian Feminist Studies,* 23 (57): 343–358.

Robinson, K.H. and Davies, C. (2010) Tomboys and sissy girls: exploring girls' power, agency and female relationships in childhood through the memories of women. *Australian Journal of Early Childhood,* 35 (1): 24–31.

Robinson, K.H. and Jones Diaz, C. (2006) *Diversity and Difference in Early Childhood Education: Issues for Theory and Practice,* Maidenhead: Open University Press.

Robinson, K.H. and Ferfolja, T. (2001) 'What are we doing this for?' Dealing with lesbian and gay issues in teacher training. *British Journal of Sociology of Education,* 22 (1): 121–133.

Robinson, K.H. and Ferfolja, T. (2008) Playing it up, playing down, playing it safe: queerying teacher education. *Teaching and Teacher Education,* 24 (4): 846–858.

Rose, N. (1999) *Governing the Soul: The Shaping of the Private Self* (2nd edition), London and New York: Free Association Books.

Rosewater, A. (2003) *Promoting Prevention, Targeting Teens: An Emerging Agenda to Reduce Domestic Violence,* San Francisco, CA: Family Violence Prevention Fund.

Ross Epp, J. (1996) Schools, complicity, and sources of violence. In J. Ross Epp and A.M. Watkinson (Eds.) *Systemic Violence: How Schools Hurt Children* (pp. 1–23). London: The Falmer Press.

Ross Epp, J. and Watkinson, A.M. (1997) *Systemic Violence in Education: Promise Broken,* Albany: SUNY Press.

Saltmarsh, S. (2007) Cultural complicities: elitism, heteronormativity and violence in the education marketplace. *International Journal of Qualitative Studies in Education,* 20 (3): 335–354.

Saltmarsh, S. (2008) Disruptive events: elite education and the discursive production of violence. *Critical Studies in Education,* 49 (2): 113–125.

Saltmarsh, S. and Youdell, D. (2004) 'Special Sport' for misfits and losers: educational triage and the constitution of schooled subjectivities. *International Journal of Inclusive Education,* 8 (4): 353–373.

Sampson, E. E. (1989) The deconstruction of the self. In J. Shotter and K. J.Gergen (Eds.) *Texts of Identity* (pp. 1–19). London: Sage.

Schärf, W. and Vale, C. (1996) The Firm – organized crime comes of age during the transition to democracy. *Social Dynamics*, 22 (2): 30–36.

Schewe, P. (Ed.) (2004) *Preventing Violence in Relationships: Interventions across the Life Span*, Washington, DC: American Psychological Association.

Schrock, A. and Boyd, D.M. (2011) Problematic youth interaction online: Solicitation, harassment, and cyberbullying. In K. B. Wright and L.M. Webb (Eds.) *Computer-Mediated Communication in Personal Relationships* (pp. 368–398). New York: Peter Lang.

Seedat, M., Van Niekerk, A., Jewkes, R., Suffla, S., and Ratele, K. (2009) Violence and injuries in South Africa: prioritising an agenda for prevention. *The Lancet*, 374 (9694): 1011–1022.

Seekings, J. (1996) The 'Lost Generation': South Africa's 'Youth Problem' in the early-1990s. *Transformations*, 29: 103–125.

Seekings, J. and Nattrass, N. (2005) *Class, Race, and Inequality in South Africa*, New Haven, CT: Yale University Press.

Sefton-Green, J. and Buckingham, D. (1998) Digital visions: children's 'creative uses' of multimedia technologies. In J. Sefton-Green (Ed.) *Digital Diversions: Youth Culture in the Age of Multimedia*. London: UCL Press.

Segel, T. and Labe, D. (1990) Family violence: wife abuse. In W. Hoffman and B. McKendrick (Eds.) *People and Violence in South Africa* (pp. 251–287). Oxford: Oxford University Press.

Seidler, V.J. (2006) *Young Men and Masculinities: Global Cultures and Intimate Lives*, London: Zed Books.

Sewell, T. (1997) *Black Masculinity and Schooling: How Black Boys Survive Modern Schooling*, Stoke-on-Trent: Falmer Press.

Shariff, S. (2008) *Cyber-bullying: Issues and Solutions for the School, the Classroom and the Home*, New York: Routledge.

Shariff, S. and Gouin, R. (2006) Cyber-hierarchies: a new arsenal of weapons for gendered violence in schools. In F. Leach and C. Mitchell (Eds.) *Combating Gender Violence In and Around Schools* (pp. 33–41). Sterling, USA: Trentham Books.

Shaw, C. and McKay, H. (1942) *Juvenile Delinquency in Urban Areas*, Chicago: University of Chicago Press.

Shaw, M. (2002) *Crime and Policing in Post-Apartheid South Africa: Transformation under Fire*, Bloomington and Indianapolis: Indiana University Press.

Sheley, J., McGee, Z., and Wright, J. (1992) Gun-related violence in and around inner-city schools. *American Journal of Diseases of Children*, 146: 677–682.

Short, J. (1997) *Poverty, Ethnicity, and Violence Crime*, Boulder, CO: Westview Press.

Shroeder, W.R. (2000) Continental Ethics. In J. Laffollette (Ed.) *The Blackwell Guide to Ethical Theory*, Malden, MA: Blackwell.

Skelton, C. (2001) *Schooling the Boys: Masculinities and Primary Education*, Buckingham: Open University Press.

Smith, A., Agius, P., Mitchell, A., Barrett, C., Pitts, M. (2009) *Secondary Students and Sexual Health 2008*, Monograph Series No. 70, Melbourne: Australian Research Centre in Sex, Health & Society, La Trobe University.

Smith, P. (Ed.) (2003) *Violence in Schools: The Response in Europe*, New York and London: Routledge.

Smith, P. and Brain, P. (2000) Bullying in schools: lessons from two decades of research. *Aggressive Behaviour*, 26 (1): 1–9.

Smith, P., Morita, Y., Junger-Tas, J., Olweus, D., Catalano, R., and Slee, P. (1999) *The Nature of School Bullying: A Cross-National Perspective*, London and New York: Routledge.

Stainton Rogers, R. and Stainton Rogers, W. (1998) Word children. In K. Lesnik-Oberstein (Ed.) *Children in Culture: Approaches to Childhood* (pp. 178–203). New York: St. Martin's Press.

Steinberg, J. (2004) *Nongoloza's Children: Western Cape Prison Gangs during and after Apartheid*, Monograph written for the Centre for the Study of Violence and Reconciliation, Johannesburg, South Africa.

Stevenson, A. and Moses, A. (2011, 24 June) Websites trumpeting high school sexual slanders to the world. *Sydney Morning Herald*, retrieved 25 June 2011, from http://www.smh.com.au/technology/technology-news/websites-trumpeting-high-school-sexual-slanders-to-the-world-20110623-1ghoi.html.

Stoudt, B. (2006) 'You're Either In or You're Out': school violence, peer discipline, and the (re)production of hegemonic masculinity. *Men and Masculinities*, 8 (3): 273–287.

Strober, M. and Tyack, D. (1980) Why do women teach and men manage? *Signs: Journal of Women in Culture and Society*, 5: 494–503.

Student kills 8, and himself, at Finnish high school (2007) *New York Times*, retrieved 8 November 2007, from http://www.nytimes.com/2007/11/08/world/europe/08finland.htm.

Student Learning and Support Services Taskforce (2003) *National Safe Schools Framework*, Department of Education, Employment and Workplace Relations, pp. 1–15.

Sykes, H. and Goldstein, T. (2004) From performed to performed ethnography: translating life history research into anti-homophobia curriculum for a teacher education program. *Teaching Education*, 15 (1): 31–56.

Symes, C. (1998) Education for sale: a semiotic analysis of school prospectuses and other forms of educational marketing. *Australian Journal of Education*, 42 (2): 133–152.

Szalacha, L. (2003) Safer sexual diversity climates: lessons learned from an evaluation of Massachusetts Safe Schools Program for Gay and Lesbian Students. *American Journal of Education*, 110: 58–88.

Tapscott, D. (2009) *Grown Up Digital: How The Net Generation Is Changing Your World*, New York: McGraw-Hill

Titley, B. (2007) Magdalen asylums and moral regulations in Ireland. In A. Potts and T. O'Donoghue (Eds.) *Schools as Dangerous Places: A Historical Perspective*, New York: Cambria Press.

Tokunaga, R.S. (2010) Following you home from school: a critical review and synthesis of research on cyberbullying victimization. *Computers in Human Behavior*, 26, 277–287.

Tomkins, S. (1963) *Affect Imagery Consciousness: The Negative Affects*, New York: Springer.

Tomkins, S. (1995) Distress-Anguish. In E. Sedgwick and A. Frank (Eds.) *Shame and Its Sisters: A Silvan Tomkins Reader* (pp. 109–131). Durham : Duke University Press.

Town, S. (2002) Playing with fire: (Homo)sexuality and schooling in New Zealand. In K.H. Robinson, J. Irwin, and T. Ferfolja (Eds.) *From Here to Diversity: The Social Impact of Lesbian and Gay Issues in Education in Australia and New Zealand* (pp. 1–16). New York: The Haworth Press Inc.

Tutty, L., Bradshaw, C., Thurston, W.E., Tunstall, L., Dewar, M.E., Toy-Pries, D., et al. (2002) *School-Based Violence Prevention Programs: A Resource Manual to Prevent Violence against Girls and Young Women*, Calgary, AB: RESOLVE Alberta, retrieved 7 May 2008, from http://www.ucalgary.ca/resolve/violenceprevention/.

TV3 New Zealand (Producer) (2006, 28 October) Liam Ashley: Liam Ashley's Family Statement, *Campbell Live*. Podcast, retrieved 30 October 2006, from http://www.tv3.co.nz/News/tabid/67/articleID/12673/Default.aspx.

Twenty10, retrieved 18 September 2010 http://www.twenty10.org.au/about-twenty10.

United Nations (UN) (2006) *In-Depth Study on All Forms of Violence against Women: Report of the Secretary-General* A/61/122/Add.1, Geneva: United Nations General Assembly.

Vetten, L. (2000) Invisible girls and violent boys: gender and gangs in South Africa. *Development Update*, 3 (2): 40–53.

VicHealth (2007) *Preventing Violence before It Occurs: A Framework and Background Paper to Guide the Primary Prevention of Violence against Women in Victoria*, VicHealth, Victoria, Australia, retrieved 11 August 2008, from http://www.vichealth.vic.gov.au/preventingviolence.

Vogelman, L. (1990) Violent crime: rape. In W. Hoffman and B. McKendrick (Eds.) *People and Violence in South Africa* (pp. 96–134). Oxford: Oxford University Press.

Walker, J. (1988) *Louts and Legends*, Sydney: Allen & Unwin

Warwick, I., Chase, E., and Aggleton, P. (2004) *Homophobia, Sexual Orientation and Schools: A Review and Implications*, Thomas Coran Research Unit, Institute of Education, University of London.

Watkinson, A. and Ross Epp, J. (1997) *Systemic Violence in Education: Promise Broken*, Albany: State University of New York Press.

WayOut, retrieved 18 September 2010, from http://www.wayout.org.au/wayout-reports.html.

Weedon, C. (1987) *Feminist Practice and Poststructuralist Theory*, Cambridge, MA: Blackwell.

Weissberg, R.P. and O'Brien, M.U. (2004) What works in school-based social and emotional learning programs for positive youth development. *The ANNALS of the American Academy of Political and Social Science*, 591 (1): 86.

Wen-Chu Chen, E. (1997) Sexual harassment from the perspective of Asian-American women. In C.R. Ronai, B.A. Zsembik, and J.R. Feagin (Eds.) *Everyday Sexism in the Third Millennium*. New York: Routledge.

White Watson, S. (2007) Boys, masculinity and school violence: reaping what we sow. *Gender and Education*, 19 (6): 729–737.

Willis, P. (1977) *Learning to Labour: How Working Class Kids Get Working Class Jobs*, Westmead: Saxon House.

Willis, P. (2003) Foot soldiers of modernity: the dialectics of cultural consumption and the twenty- first century school. *Harvard Educational Review*, 73 (3): 390–415.

Wolfe, D.A., P.G. Jaffe, and C.V. Crooks (2006) *Adolescent Risk Behaviors: Why Teens Experiment and Strategies to Keep Them Safe*, New Haven: Yale University Press.

Wong-Lo, M. and Bullock, L. (2011) Digital aggression: cyberworld meets school bullies. *Preventing School Failure*, 55 (2): 64–70.

Wood, J. (2007) *Gendered Lives: Communication, Gender, and Culture* (7th Edition). New York: Thompson Wadsworth Publishing.

Wood, J.T. (1994) Saying it makes it so: the discursive construction of sexual harassment. In S.G. Bingham (Ed.) *Conceptualizing Sexual Harassment as Discursive Practice*. Westport, CT: Praeger.

Wood, K. and Jewkes, R. (2001) 'Dangerous' love: reflections on violence among Xhosa township youth. In R. Morrell (Ed.) *Changing Men in Southern Africa* (pp. 317–336). Pietermaritzburg/London: University of Natal Press/Zed Books.

Ybarra, M.L., Diener-West, M., and Leaf, P.J. (2007) Examining the overlap in internet harassment and school bullying: implications for school intervention. *Journal of Adolescent Health*, 41: 540–550.

Ybarra, M.L. and Mitchell, J.K. (2008) How risky are social networking sites? A comparison of places online where youth sexual solicitation and harassment occurs. *Pediatrics*, 121: e350–e350.

Yoneyama, S. and Naito, A. (2003) Problems with the paradigm: the school as a factor in understanding bullying (with special reference to Japan). *British Journal of Sociology of Education*, 24 (3): 315–330.

Youdell, D. (2006) *Impossible Bodies, Impossible Selves: Exclusions and Student Subjectivities*, Dordrecht, Netherlands: Springer.

Young, A. (1996) *Imagining Crime: Textual Outlaws and Criminal Conversations*, London: Sage.

Zalewski, M. (2000) *Feminism after Postmodernism: Theorising through Practice*, London: Routledge.

Index

Note: locators with letters 'f' and 'n' refer to figures and notes in the text.

moral panics, 22, 67, 140, 151, 152–3, 163
movies, *see* films, violence represented in
MTV, 142–3
mutuality and negotiation, 89, 136, 175–6, 178, 179
My Loose Thread (Cooper), 161–2, 163
MySpace, 7, 62, 63, 64, 156, 166n10

name calling/labelling, 21, 25, 35, 36, 40–2, 84, 101–3, 104, 106, 128n2, 131, 186
National Center for Educational Statistics, 152
National Council to Reduce Violence against Women and their Children, 169
National Plan of Action (2008), 169
National Safe Schools Framework, 143, 144
NBC news, 158
necklace murders, 47
neoliberalism, 14, 22, 33–4
'nested contexts', 39
New South Wales Department of Education and Training, 12
New Zealand Ombudsman's Report, 33, 34
Nine to Five (Higgins), 75
North Country (Caro), 75
Northern Kentucky Youth Correctional Center, 156
Northwestern University shootings, 152
NSW Rape Crisis Centre, 176
NZ Corrections Department, 33

offline bullying, 65, 66
online bullying/harassment, *see* cyberbullying
Opening Our Eyes: Addressing Gender-based Violence in South African Schools, 12
Oppositional Defiance Disorder, 25
the 'other', 17, 77, 83, 89, 100, 107, 114, 133, 135, 140, 144
'Out and Proud' (media report), 140–4

Paducah killings, 149, 156
Pakistan, lacking laws on sexual harassment, 6
Panopticon, 9–10, 64
parents
  child safety/security concerns, 10–12, 24, 35, 42, 48, 181, 183, 194
  and corporal punishment, 50
  encouraging violence/crime in children, 123, 138–9
  and lack of control/connection, 153, 161–2, 163
  same-sex and surrogate, 135
  and social learning theory, 42
  and tensions over identities, 150
  violence/crimes against, 33, 163, 165n2
patriarchal societies, 15, 49, 111, 113
peace education, 42
Pearl, Mississippi, shootings, 149, 155, 165n2
pedagogical approaches
  in classroom(s), 109–10, 132, 136, 140, 170–1, 177, 179–80
  in linguistic violence, 146–8, 191–2
  in Sex & Ethics programme, 179–80
  in school shooting rampages, 163–5
peer groups, 73, 77, 78, 84, 88–9, 152, 165, 188
personal branding, 63
poststructuralism, 56, 59, 72, 81, 132, 136, 154
poverty, violence due to, 41, 45, 52, 113, 114, 123–4, 161, 171
power relations, 71–93
  Foucauldian concept of, 2, 9–10, 64, 72–3, 137, 144, 173, 175
pressured/coerced/forced sex, 78, 176, 177, 179, 181, 182
pride, violence and, 126, 136, 141
primary schools, gender and sexuality in, 74, 97–9, 106, 133, 137–9
principals, and school violence
  against gangs, 45–6
  against homophobia, 141–2
  homophobic behaviour, 137–40, 145
  measures against rape, 48

school violence, masculinities and
privilege – *continued*
effective classroom strategies,
108–10; productive pedagogies
approach, 109–10; research
projects, 109
homophobic behaviours, 102–4;
displayed hatred, 102–3; 'just
joking' attitude, 104
notion of community, 95
in privileged high schools, 100–2
survival politics, 104–6;
alliance-forming, 105; avoiding
violence/support from
authorities, 105–6; the 'real
boy' fighting back, 106;
standing up/failing to stand up
for friends, 105
school violence theories, 9–10, 39–44
community context: social control
theory, social learning theory,
and social disorganisation
theory, 42–4
individual context: biological
theory and rational choice
theory, 39–40
school context: strain theory and
labelling theory, 40–2
Scouts, 171
'sea of pink', anti-bullying cause,
147–8
secondary schools
authority in, 89
boys' violence, 97, 99, 103, 106
student homophobic sentiments,
84, 133
violence prevention education, 169,
170
Second Life, 56
self-control, 27, 42
self-esteem, 42
self-fulfilling prophecy, 41
self-harm, 133, 144
see also suicides, resulting from
bullying/harassment
*Self-made Men: Identity and Embodiment
among Transsexual Men* (H. Rubin),
166n6
self-reflection, 178

self-ruling identities, 65
'self', sense of, 114, 136, 142, 146, 155
Sex & Ethics violence prevention
programme, 167, 176–82
sexism, 90
sexual consent, 18, 167, 169, 176, 177,
179
sexual harassment, issues of identity
and power, 71–4
Butler's notion of performativity,
73, 77
definitions, 75–6
effective policies and strategies,
92–3
by five- and six-year olds, 74
Foucault's definition of discourse,
72–3
girls' harassment from female peers,
75
GLBTQ students and teachers, 83–6;
homophobic brutality, case
example, 85–6; incidence of
suicide, 84; teacher's
intervention, case example,
84–5; violent sentiments/name
calling, 83–4
and intersections of identity, 86–8;
racial/ethnic stereotypes, 86–7
normalisation in heterosexual
relations, 78–83; Butler's
heterosexual matrix, 79; sexual
interest, feelings, responses and
negotiations, 79–82; teachers'
interventions, 82–3
performance of hegemonic
masculinity, 73–4, 76–8;
'authenticity', 77–8; cultural
bonding, 77–8; culture of
violence, 76–7
research in context, 74–6
as technology of power within
organisational structures,
88–91; abuse of women
teachers by male students,
88–9; dominant discourse of
Western authority, 89–91
shame, 54, 81, 88, 102, 126–7, 141
Share programme, 176
shebeens (informal bars), 44, 115

virtual violence, 56–68
vocational education, 171, 180
vulnerability, 17, 21, 23, 34, 98, 125,
    136, 152, 153, 163, 166n8, 186

war
    rape as technique of, 49, 50
    role in school violence, 49–50, 54,
        122
    The WayOut (Rural Victorian Youth
        and Sexual Diversity Project)
        report, 140
weapons, students bringing, 10–11,
    24, 123, 125, 155, 157, 161,
    165n2, 192–3
websites, harassment through, 7
white-collar crimes, 47
Women's Aid, 172
Women's Safety Survey (1995), 168
worker's compensation, 135
working-class schools, violence in, 94,
    97–8, 99–100, 102, 103, 107, 108,
    115, 120, 123

workplace mass killings, 152
World War Two, 122
Writing Themselves In Again, 144

youth aggression, *see* cyberbullying
'Youth Culture', alternative
    conceptual framework, 61–6
    creation of digital identities, 61
    cybersubjects/bodily elimination,
        65–6
    domestic/bedroom culture, 62–3
    Foucault's Panopticon, mechanism
        of surveillance, 64
    online participation relationships,
        64
    'personal branding', 63
YouTube, 56, 64, 156, 157, 157f, 158,
    159f, 166n9

Zero Day (Coccio), 161, 165
zero tolerance policies, 10–11, 40, 141
Zulu masculinity, 121–2, 126

Printed and bound in the United States of America